VICTORY IN THE POOL

VICTORY IN THE POOL

How a Maverick Coach Upended Society and Led a Group of Young Swimmers to Olympic Glory

BILL GEORGE

FOREWORD BY
DEBBIE MEYER, MIKE BURTON,
AND JEFF FLOAT

ROWMAN & LITTLEFIELD
Lanham • Boulder • New York • London

Published by Rowman & Littlefield
An imprint of The Rowman & Littlefield Publishing Group, Inc.
4501 Forbes Boulevard, Suite 200, Lanham, Maryland 20706
www.rowman.com

86-90 Paul Street, London EC2A 4NE, United Kingdom

British Library Cataloguing in Publication Information Available

Library of Congress Cataloging-in-Publication Data

Names: George, Bill, 1954– author.
Title: Victory in the pool : how a maverick coach upended society and led a
    group of young swimmers to Olympic glory / Bill George.
Description: Lanham, Maryland : Rowman & Littlefield, [2023] | Includes
    bibliographical references. | Summary: "This book tells the inspiring
    story of a swim club that accepted minority swimmers when others would
    not, a swim coach who could not swim, and his five young swimmers who
    became Olympic gold medalists"—Provided by publisher.
Identifiers: LCCN 2022044053 (print) | LCCN 2022044054 (ebook) |
    ISBN 9781538173718 (cloth) | ISBN 9781538173725 (epub)
Subjects: LCSH: Chavoor, Sherman, 1919–1992. | Swimming—United
    States—History—20th century. | Swimming coaches—United
    States—Biography. | Swimmers—United States—Biography. | Olympic
    athletes—United States—Biography.
Classification: LCC GV838.C49 G46 2023 (print) | LCC GV838.C49 (ebook) |
    DDC 797.2/1092 [B]—dc23/eng/20221013
LC record available at https://lccn.loc.gov/2022044053
LC ebook record available at https://lccn.loc.gov/2022044054

For my wonderful wife, Sue, with love and thanks
for her support and understanding

CONTENTS

ACKNOWLEDGMENTS

Many people assisted in providing invaluable information for this book. Former Arden Hills swimmer Brian Fong encouraged me to start the book and kept me on the rails as it progressed. Without him, this book would not have been written.

Stuart Cornew, a former U.S. financial executive in Mexico, provided invaluable insight into the importance of the 1968 Olympic Games to Mexico.

Sherm Chavoor's daughters, Sheron and Shelley, were generous with their time and filled in important gaps in the story.

Sacramento's sports superstar is Debbie Meyer. Her amazing accomplishments as a swimmer have almost been eclipsed by the goodwill she has engendered since she captured the world's attention in the 1968 Olympics. Her participation and encouragement were vital elements in bringing the book to print. Mike Burton, Jeff Float, Susan Pedersen, and Vicky King provided valuable insights and information that helped bring the book alive.

Jan Float's infectious enthusiasm is deeply appreciated, as is her keen eye for detail that helped shape the story.

FOREWORD

When I showed up at the Arden Hills Swim Club in Sacramento, California, I was a small twelve-year-old girl with a big dream of winning a swimming medal in the Olympics. I remember being awestruck at the number of laps the other kids were swimming, and my first instinct was to get out of the pool and never come back. But, thanks to a gruff, wisecracking, big-hearted coach named Sherm Chavoor, I learned to work harder than I ever imagined and found the desire to overcome obstacles to get to the Olympics. So when I won three gold medals at the 1968 games in Mexico City, I gave one to Sherm for the incredible care and love he showered on me all those years. I was just one of a whole host of Sacramento kids, including Mark Spitz, Mike Burton, Sue Pederson, Johnny Ferris, Vicky King, Jeff Float, and Dave Fairbank, many of whom won gold medals under Sherm's direction. This was accomplished during very troubling times in the Mexico City and Munich Olympics and a time of social upheaval in the United States and the world. This book tells the story of the swimmers and the times we lived through. It was the last gasp of amateurism, a time when there were few if any opportunities for women to participate in college athletics. Heck, we didn't even wear goggles! Our era was sure different than the world we live in today: more innocent, less cynical, and in some ways a golden age of sports. I know you will enjoy this story of hard work, heartbreak, and triumph, and about Sherm, the swimming coach who "didn't know how to swim" but did know how to coax greatness from people.

Debbie Meyer
Winner of three gold medals in the
1968 Olympic Games in Mexico City

There I was, thirteen years old, lying in the hospital, nearly broken in half after the bike I was riding was plowed over by a truck. After six weeks in traction, the doctors told me the injury meant I was finished with sports. The pain of that announcement hurt me almost as much as the accident. Fortunately there was one sport I could still compete in—swimming. I struggled at first, but under the guidance of Coach Sherm Chavoor I became a top distance swimmer and ended up with three Olympic gold medals. This book gives a vivid account of the dramatic Mexico City and Munich Olympics. Those games were cultural and athletic milestones and were plagued with protests and controversy and the 1972 terrorist attack. It's a complex and vivid story that reveals a slice of America during a turbulent time that changed the Olympic Games forever, and I know you will enjoy reading this fascinating account about the untold stories of the people that lived during those dramatic days.

Mike Burton
Winner of two gold medals in the
1968 Olympic Games in Mexico City
and one gold medal in the
1972 Olympic Games in Munich

Bill George has shared exactly what it was like to swim and compete under Sherm Chavoor's tough tutelage. Equal parts loved and scorned, caring and ruthless, book smart and streetwise, Sherm earned the respect and admiration of swimmers and coaches the world over. Upon our first introduction, when I was seven, he was curious as to my age group. In that brusque voice, he asked, "What's your birthday, Kid?" Slightly intimidated, "April 10," I muttered. "Well," Sherm quickly replied, "that's my birthday, too. How about that? Dive in and show me what you've got!" And the rest, as they say, is history. And this talented author tells it well!

Jeff Float
Winner of a gold medal in the
1984 Olympic Games in Los Angeles

1

A PLACE IN THE WORLD

Izikiel Correa[1] was born on April 10, 1919, near Hilo, Hawaii, the son of a worker in the sugar cane fields. When he was nine months old his father moved the family to Oakland, California, and took a job loading and unloading ships.[2] One of seven kids, the boy was often at odds with his tough, demanding father, who would brook no excuses and no failures. It seems no matter what he accomplished, it was never good enough for his father, who constantly yelled at him and demanded more. He found solace in his mother, Clotilda, who provided salve for the emotional wounds inflicted by his father. Perhaps he faced ethnic taunts and discrimination as a boy, and as an adult he often wrote about racial injustice.

He was destined to live in interesting, exciting, and troubled times. He came of age during the worst economic collapse in the history of the industrialized world, the Great Depression of the 1930s. An estimated three hundred thousand migrants, mostly from the Dust Bowl states, poured into California, causing wages to drop by 50 percent in the state's vast agricultural sector. "It was from hand to mouth surviving as food was concerned, but we survived," he remembered.[3] Like many Depression-era kids, he developed thrifty habits that lasted a lifetime. "I see a penny on the floor now and I pick it up," he said years later, when he was a millionaire. "You know why? For three pennies I could get a cup of coffee and two doughnuts when I was growing up. For five cents I could get a hamburger."[4] He was one of many children and adolescents who worked alongside their parents to help bring in money for the family, so he found work on the Oakland docks with his father.

That humble occupation was disrupted in May 1934, when he was fifteen. The longshoremen went on strike and were soon joined by machinists, tugboat crews, and sailors in what became one of the largest maritime work stoppages in history. Picket lines formed around Bay Area ports as police and

strikers clashed in a series of bloody brawls. As the strike wore on, the vio-
lence escalated when police fired tear gas and bullets into the strikers. Stri-
dent and often violent labor disputes continued for much of the decade.[5]
When the boy wasn't working or going to school, he was boxing, playing football or baseball, or running track, the popular boys' sports of the
era. He admired the sports heroes of the 1930s, among them the Hall of
Fame football coach Amos Alonzo Stagg, known for his tough discipline
as the head coach at the nearby University of the Pacific in Stockton.
He followed the exploits of the West Coast college teams and became a
UCLA fan, admiring a tough UCLA lineman who, in an era when players
played both offense and defense, earned a reputation for fierce tackling,
performance under pressure, and guts. That UCLA lineman was five years
older, and young Correa wanted to be just like him.

In 1939, the economy was improving and the twenty-year-old began
thinking about his future after high school. After the bleak Depression
years, young people could envision going to college, finding jobs, getting
married, and starting families. But as they were entering their twenties,
new threats crowded their vision of the future. The newspapers were full
of stories about wars raging in Europe and Asia, and many experts predicted the United States would enter the conflicts. Those born in 1919
turned twenty-one just in time to be subject to the first peacetime draft in
American history. The Depression had been part one of the cataclysmic
events that forged what later became called the Greatest Generation.
The war was a life-changing event that altered the world for millions of
people, many of whom, like Izikiel, entered the armed forces. Many
would find their true nature during wartime, and they emerged after
four long years of conflict as new people ready and eager to get on with
civilian life. That was especially true for the boy named Izikiel Correa.
He enlisted in the U.S. Army and became a cadet pilot in the Army Air
Force, and said he flew twenty-five missions as a pilot, bombing enemy
targets until, as he put it, there was "nothing left to bomb."[6] He was at
one point assigned to help train B-24 Liberator Bomber flight crews at
the remote Tonopah, Nevada, Army Air Base. The bombers were rushed
out of the aircraft factories into the hands of the trainers to get the aircraft
crews combat ready as soon as possible. While the posting may not sound as
glamorous as being a bomber pilot, the training was constant, dangerous, and
stressful, as evidenced by the events of August 19, 1944. Officers watched
as the four engines of a Liberator coughed, sputtered, and finally caught,
coming to life as the roar of the engines echoed off the nearby hills. The
young airmen flying the craft were trainees, getting experience at the

remote airfield located halfway between Reno and Las Vegas. Beloved by many, more Liberators were produced than any other bomber in America. But the rookie crew was also aware of rumors that the plane had problems. It was nicknamed the "Flying Boxcar," and it was tough to handle, especially in the base's 5,400-foot elevation. The ten-man crews struggled to learn the multiple tasks required to operate the bombers. Radiomen and navigators were also trained to defend the airships and learned to maintain, load, and fire its 50-caliber machine guns. An aircraft loaded with thousands of pounds of bombs, 2,900 gallons of gasoline, and eleven 50-caliber machine guns, every flight, from takeoff to landing, was one mishap away from annihilation.

The bulky bomber struggled into the air and was in immediate trouble, crashing and exploding two miles from the base. There were no survivors. Just an hour later another Liberator crashed, this time twenty miles from the airstrip, killing all crew members. But the training continued without pause. The Liberators and their crews were needed to fight the Japanese and the Germans, so the training flights took off one after another, all day, every day. Rumors spread through the army that the accidents happened because the base was jinxed. Army brass rejected the myth, and the training flights continued. By the end of the war, 140 men had died in the desert surrounding Tonopah. Plane wrecks and parts litter the bleak, dun-colored desert floor to this day.

As the war came to a close the training pace slowed, and Izikiel got a new assignment. "They asked if someone would help in the recreation department. I said I would help, and they threw me in swimming. I didn't know much about swimming at all. The sport immediately appealed to me because I could measure my athletes' progress on the stopwatch," he said.[7] At Tonopah he learned to teach, to give orders, to push young men under pressure to their limit, to get them to believe in themselves, to train and discipline them. He learned to handle long, hard work. He learned that, as General Douglas MacArthur said, there was no substitute for victory. These were traits he would often display in the future.

By the end of the war, Izikiel Correa, of Portuguese descent, no longer existed.[8] In November 1944 he legally changed his name to Sherman Chavoor and said he came from a "poor Dutch-French" family.[9] He picked the name of the gutsy UCLA football star he had admired and read about in the newspapers, and sometimes told people he was five years older than his actual age.

Confrontational, irascible, combative, gruff, tough, and demanding were adjectives commonly used to describe the new man named Sherm

Chavoor as he gained his reputation as one of the world's greatest Olympic swimming coaches. When he first met swimmers, he didn't focus on their strokes; instead, he looked for guts—the combination of courage and discipline that were the raw materials of greatness. He could judge if a kid had guts or not after a few minutes watching them swim. This and motivating swimmers were his greatest talents.

When rival coaches or sportswriters watched his team's practices, they were stunned at what they saw: the long, brutal workouts; the yelling and cajoling; the constant, relentless criticism that mocked his swimmers' efforts. His methods were on full display at early morning workouts at his club or in front of the world during the Olympics. There was, as the old saying goes, "no sugarcoating it." His critics saw him as a puffy, pot-bellied martinet, full of wisecracks and insults. He feared no one and took on everyone. He despised the racial bias in the sport, and immediately following World War II his first star was a Japanese American boy just returned from the internment camps. Later, his great star swimmer was Jewish. His career spanned the era when the International Olympic Committee (IOC) and the Amateur Athletic Union (AAU) had absolute power over amateur athletes. Their careers could be ended for wearing the wrong clothes or receiving small gifts. He bridled under their capricious authority and fought to change hypocrisy in amateur athletics.

To the outside world he appeared to be a slave driver, an obnoxious curmudgeon. But his swimmers knew better. Although they silently railed at him, they knew that under all the bluster, he cared for them. This combustible mix was the fuel that drove them to believe in themselves and accomplish things they never thought possible. His care and concern did not stop at the pool apron. Most of his swimmers were teenagers dealing with the doubts and fears of adolescence. They were among the first young athletes to compete under the glare of worldwide television coverage and international publicity that made them global household names. Chavoor was able to encourage, cajole, and nurture them through these periods of incredible stress. He was always available to them and guided them through their competitive lives and through their years after they left the pool. To his dying day, he said their success was due to guts.

~

Chavoor was honorably discharged from the army[10] and married in 1945. He settled in Sacramento with his wife, Joan, for what Chavoor thought would be a short stay until he returned to the Oakland area. He landed a job as a schoolteacher and then as principal of Ethel Phillips Elementary School. By early 1946, he was moonlighting for a few extra bucks as recreation director at the downtown Sacramento YMCA. The YMCA was a place where anyone, regardless of race, religion, or class, could come to exercise and make new friends. The Y was a good fit for Sacramento, which had had a diverse population since the days of the city's founding during the Gold Rush. Chinese, Japanese, Mexicans, and people from every nation in Europe had worked and lived in the city, and their descendants made Sacramento one of the most diverse cities in the United States. Excluded by law and custom from many golf courses and clubs, minorities joined the Y to shoot hoops, box, and learn to swim.

Among its members were Japanese Americans returning from internment camps. The order to evacuate all Japanese from the "entire" city of Sacramento had been issued by the 4th Army Command on Thursday, May 7, 1942. The large, thick headline in the *Sacramento Bee* read "All Japanese Must Get Out of Sacramento." They were allowed to take only the possessions they could carry. Homes and businesses had to be sold. Pets were not allowed and had to be left behind. They had nine days to resettle in a dusty camp of two hundred wood frame buildings in a cluster of oak trees just northeast of the city limits. Ten kitchens with army-style mess halls served five thousand people. One of the evacuees was ten-year-old Tak Iseri, who had no idea what was going on. All he knew was that his father's flower store was closed and his little buddies from "Japanese Alley" had vanished. During the next three years, little Tak and his family were sent to the internment camp in Tule Lake, near the California-Oregon border, and then to the Heart Mountain camp near Cody, Wyoming. There, he played basketball and football and learned to swim. When the internment ended, the family returned home to Sacramento, ready to resume life. Like many Japanese, Tak feared leaving the camp and worried that he would be beaten up. His father's prosperous florist shop was burned down. To support his family, Tak's dad took a job as a gardener on a large estate.

In 1946, Tak heard that the Sacramento YMCA was offering free swimming lessons, so he hopped on his bike and rode ten miles to the downtown Y and its indoor pool. Jumping into the water, he met swimmers that reflected the city's ethnic diversity. Black, white, and Asian kids frolicked in the water, having fun splashing each other. They paid little attention to the man with a whistle around his neck and a stopwatch in his hand. But that man was watching every move the kids made in the pool, and he quickly separated the kids who just wanted to horse around from those who liked to race. Chavoor was involved in many activities at the Y and coached boxing, refereed basketball games, and supervised swimming. He said he had been a Golden Gloves boxer in his youth and impressed the youngsters with his speed and agility in the ring. In whatever sport he was coaching, he stressed the importance of winning and told the kids they would have to dedicate themselves and work hard to achieve their goals. It seemed unlikely that Chavoor, who said he couldn't swim, would become a swim coach. In Sacramento, boxing, football, and baseball were popular activities, and there was little swimming tradition.

At first, Tak was wary of the coach with the military bearing, no-nonsense attitude, and booming voice. His instructions were served out in a constant barrage of criticism and instruction that one observer called "the dauntless mockery of the American G.I."[11] The words flew from his mouth so quickly they often ran together, and he jabbed his fingers in the air as he made a point. "Get in the pool before I hit you in the eye; get closer, I want to yell at you," he would command. "Are you working hard or are you goofing off? Come on, you gotta go faster, this isn't water ballet, see. Show some *guts* this time, will you? *Go fast*, will you? Go *faster!* Come on, hurry up! You can't beat anyone swimming like that! You looked around too much at the other swimmers," he would scold, or "you could have gone faster but you slowed up in the final ten yards, are you trying to get a suntan? You guys are driving me fruity."[12] While his voice was gruff, there was also a caring tone in it, and he frequently flashed a hint of a smile at the end of a tirade.

He wrote each swimmer's lap times down in a small notebook, keeping a precise log of how long it took them to swim the length of the 25-yard pool. When someone didn't show enough progress, he thrust the stopwatch in their face and barked, "The stopwatch never lies."[13] He taught his athletes how to master their minds as well as their strokes: "Conning and being a hell of a competitor are necessary. You have to be egotistical, cocky, and confident, and instill that confidence in the athlete."[14] Chavoor offered spare praise with stinging criticism, a method he would use on his famous swimmers in the future. No swimmer's performance seemed to be good enough for him. "Sherm's a tough guy; a lot of people didn't like him," Iseri remembered years later. "He pushed you and made you work out hard every day."[15] Some boys left the pool, but Iseri accepted the challenge and practiced two hours every day, six days a week. Like many who encountered Chavoor during his long coaching career, he learned that Chavoor not only worked him hard in the pool, he cared about the problems in his daily life. "My family didn't have much money at the time, and he helped me get jobs cleaning up around the Y or babysitting the younger kids so I could keep swimming," Iseri said. Similar stories would be told by many of Chavoor's swimmers throughout the years, and he referred to himself as a "Svengali" who would magically negotiate insurmountable obstacles. Young Tak felt like he had a big brother looking after him.

Tak was barely able to swim when he joined the Y, but Chavoor noticed the kid's strong leg kick and his determination. Chavoor wasn't concerned with how good a swimmer's stroke looked. He sought intense people who displayed "guts" and who practiced hard. While he may have been short on teaching swimming technique, Chavoor was a fanatic when it came to training. "Stopwatch Sherm," as the kids called him, relentlessly prodded the swimmers to swim more and more laps every day, pushing them with a mixture of praise and barbed humor. He developed an odd term for those he especially liked, calling them "nuts," a nickname he would eventually use on his great Olympic swimmers Mark Spitz and Debbie Meyer. His compliments could be rough but were always said with affection: One day, after a particularly long and hard practice, he told Iseri, "Say, Tak, you're a tough kid from a tough family; I bet your uncle bombed Pearl Harbor." For a kid like Tak, uprooted and moved four times in as many years and never knowing what the next day would bring, Chavoor's confidence in him was as important as any swimming lesson. "His cheerleading and motivating never ceased," Iseri said. "He made me believe I could do anything, that I could become as good as any swimmer. Most importantly, he made me believe I was accepted and equal to the other kids. He was my hero."[16] He instilled that same dose of confidence in others. Ted Miyagawa, another Japanese American kid, was a thirteen-year-old orphan hanging around the Y when he met Chavoor and started swimming. "He would never back off, you felt like you couldn't lose or you would let him down," Miyagawa said. "He was a great guy who has done a lot of good for a lot of kids."[17]

Chavoor did not have much money, but he devoted the few resources he had to the kids. He packed his athletes into his 1940 Ford and ferried them to athletic competitions throughout the region. One year he stuffed the boys into the old car and drove 390 miles to Los Angeles to enter his team in a basketball tournament, coaching his "nuts" to the tournament championship.

The boys grew together, putting the animosity and tensions stirred by war in the past. A newspaper photo taken at the Sacramento swimming championships shows Tak, Miyagawa, African American Allen Wimberly, and a white kid named Lowell Johnson in the pool, smiling broadly, under the headline "Winners All."[18] In an era of thoughtless racism, when ethnic taunts were sometimes hurled at athletic adversaries, Chavoor did not tolerate any racist comments by fans or opponents. He confronted anyone who made an ugly comment and threatened to pull his boys out of an event if the behavior didn't stop. When Wimberly was refused service at a restaurant in Merced, California, Chavoor walked out with the team.

Chavoor noticed his swimmers' times were rapidly improving, becoming as fast as the swimmers in local swim meets. The Y's pool was used mainly for recreational swimmers, and he could reserve only a few hours every day for his team's practices. Once he decided the boys were good enough to compete, Chavoor pushed and cajoled Y officials, managing to get extra minutes in the water, and he cut down rest time during the workouts. The hard work paid off, and Tak and his teammates were soon taking home medals and ribbons at local competitions. Tak became the team leader and was so fast his victories and record-breaking race times led to speculation that great things were in his future. In 1948, Tak won the breaststroke competition in the prestigious Pacific Amateur Association championships. "A Future Champ?" the *San Francisco Examiner* headline asked above a picture of Tak in the pool. "The fifteen-year-old Japanese American boy won the 100-yard breaststroke in a time that gave meet officials a thrill."[19]

Tak and his teammate John Stebbins were dominating Northern California in the breaststroke. Overlooking the difference in the boys' ethnicity, the *Sacramento Bee* dubbed them "the breaststroke twins."[20] San Francisco swim coach Charlie Sava, who had coached national champions at his Crystal Plunge Swim Club, said both boys could make the 1952 Olympic team. Sacramento took notice. In a headline below an illustrated montage of Tak in action, the *Sacramento Bee* proudly proclaimed, "15-year-old local swimming star looms as certain Olympic performer of future."[21] Tak wasn't sure he was fast enough for the Olympics, but he began to dream that he would someday go to college and swim for the University of California Golden Bears in nearby Berkeley.

Led by the Breaststroke Twins, Chavoor's YMCA team won seventeen of eighteen dual meets. The young coach took his teams to three straight Pacific Southwest YMCA titles and five state championships. Tak won the 100-yard breaststroke competition at the prestigious Far Western meet, and Stebbins won the national junior college breaststroke title. By 1949, they were nationally ranked and ready to compete with the best swimmers in the world at the AAU championships at the Los Angeles Swimming Stadium. Chavoor took the boys to the meet, and although

Tak did not qualify for the finals, Stebbins finished fourth in the 200-meter butterfly. Stebbins became an All-American and star of the College of the Pacific team that upset Pacific Conference powerhouses California and Stanford.

Returning from Los Angeles after the national championship, Chavoor continued to excel as a swim coach. While continuing to teach middle school and still coaching at the YMCA, he took on yet another part-time job and led the Cal Aggies (today the University of California, Davis) to the conference championship. Two of his YMCA swimmers, Allen Wimberly and Lowell Johnson, were ranked first and second nationally in the juniors' 50-yard breaststroke by the AAU. Johnson continued to swim at Stanford, but it was Wimberly, an African American, who seemed to offer the greater upside. In 1951, he won the breaststroke championships at the Junior Olympics in San Francisco. An outstanding athlete, Wimberly led his high school basketball conference in scoring and was a star quarterback. Chavoor's hopes for Wimberly's swimming career were dashed when Wimberly decided to pursue those sports over swimming. The lack of participation in swimming by minority athletes would trouble Chavoor for the rest of his life.

Tak's dream of attending Berkeley began to slip away, not due to his swimming performance, but because of his grades. He did not qualify for admittance and was contemplating quitting swimming and attending junior college to get his grades up. Most coaches would have shrugged and wished the kid well, but Chavoor found a spot on the Davis swim team, and two years later, his grades repaired, he transferred to Berkeley. There he mastered the butterfly, a new swim stroke that was just becoming popular in competitive swimming. Using his strong kick, Tak became the Pacific Coast Conference champion in the 100-yard butterfly. In his senior season, just nine years after leaving the internment camp, he was elected cocaptain of the swim team, which he later called the "highest honor of my life."[22]

In the few years since Chavoor started coaching, he had established an unprecedented record of success for Sacramento swimming, and his team was a force in Northern California. This was also when he began seeding the mythology that would help him gain notoriety in the future. When his Cal Aggie team won the conference championship, his swimmers followed tradition and threw the fully clothed coach into the pool. Chavoor later dramatically claimed he nearly drowned that day and had to be pulled from the pool gasping for his life and had water pumped from his lungs. It was a story he often repeated, and years later, when his swimmers became international celebrities, it gave reporters the lede to their stories about him. He was the famed Olympic swim coach who "couldn't swim a stroke."[23] It was one of many media techniques Chavoor developed that would keep his and his swimmers' names in the news. The truth, however, was a shade different. When *Sacramento Bee* sports editor Marco Smolich pressed him about his legend, Chavoor "sheepishly" explained, "Actually I never was much of a swimmer. Maybe I was fair, nothing better. When I began coaching, I'd swim with the youngsters. Pretty soon they were showing me up. So I decided to keep out of the water and escape embarrassment."[24]

Even with that story in print, Chavoor kept telling the press he couldn't swim. The tale stuck and earned him publicity his entire career.

Could Tak have fulfilled earlier predictions and become an Olympic champion? Chavoor thought so, but Tak felt that at just 5-foot-7 with small hands, he was too small. His studies as a pharmacy major ate into his training time, and he was looking forward to starting a family. One day on the seventy-five-mile bus trip home from Berkeley to Sacramento for a holiday, he met a quiet, cute girl. He got to know her on those trips and eventually married her. He earned his pharmacy degree and worked long hours filling prescriptions while raising three boys: accomplishments, he said, he would never have achieved without Chavoor.

The postwar world Sherm Chavoor and Tak Iseri returned to in California was new and full of excitement, opportunity, and challenge. After the Depression and the war, people were ready to leave years of poverty and scarcity behind and start to enjoy life. Chavoor and Tak became rarities—longtime Californians—in a sea of newcomers descended from New York, Ohio, Iowa, Indiana, and other frozen places. Many of them had caught a glimpse of the Golden State while they were stationed on military bases, or else they worked manufacturing aircraft, ships, and weapons. The sun and surf proved to be a seductive lure, and the state's population boomed.

Eager to get on with life, couples married quickly, intent on starting families. In the late 1940s a woman got pregnant every seven seconds. Every year between 1946 and 1964, an average 4.24 million babies were born in the United States, and California's population grew faster than that of any other state. The men found secure jobs in the booming postwar economy, earning enough money that many moms could stay home to raise the kids.

All those new people needed homes, schools, and grocery stores. They wanted big yards and nice parks. To meet that demand the government created the Veterans Emergency Housing Program, which was a prime reason that 2.5 million new homes were constructed, mostly on land bordering cities. The migration out of the cities had been going on for decades before the war. In 1920, only about 9 percent of Americans lived in the suburbs, but by 1960, that number jumped to 30 percent of the population.

Americans began to reshape the country, and California birthed a whole new culture of casual outdoor living. Drive-ins (Harry and Esther Snyder founded In-N-Out Burger in 1948, the same year Mac and Richard McDonald opened their first restaurant); outdoor theatres; lush, lighted landscaping; elaborate backyard barbeques; and the centerpiece of the backyard, the in-ground swimming pool, bloomed in fast-growing suburbs up and down the state. Once the purview of the privileged—the swimming pools of the Roaring Twenties cost between $100,000 and $200,000 to build in today's money—pools became more accessible when changes in construction techniques, especially the development of gunite, dramatically lowered the cost of pool construction in the 1950s.

Innovations in financing also played a role, as banks offered financing for home improvements. While some thought swimming pools were a foolish luxury, many people jumped at the opportunity to buy a pool for the kids to splash around in during California's long summers. Advertisements explained how it was all so affordable: "The most common loan is for $2,500 extending over a three-year period. With interest, the monthly payments on this schedule total about $80.00." In 1956, the *Los Angeles Times*, sitting in the middle of rising suburban prosperity, provided a ringing endorsement: "A swimming pool project is no longer the major undertaking it once was. Everything, including the financing, has been well worked out in order that a family can have an enjoyable and sound investment."[25]

"The veterans and their wives grabbed for the good things as if there was no tomorrow,"[26] one social critic acidly noted, perhaps forgetting that the concept of tomorrow was an abstract one for men who had been in hand-to-hand combat in the jungles of the Pacific and the beaches in Normandy just a few years earlier. The young parents of the postwar boom had grown up ill housed, ill clad, and ill nourished during the Great Depression, then experienced rationing during World War II. Now, most seemed to be striving toward the goal of prosperity and unity. People were pleased. In California even politics seemed free of dissension. In 1946, Earl Warren received the nomination for governor from the Republican, Democratic, and Progressive parties, winning more than 90 percent of the vote in November 1946.

2

AN ANTIQUATED MESS

The postwar era saw the widespread use of antibiotics and thera-
peutic medicines that improved health and eliminated many feared
child-killer diseases. But one virus continued circulating, spreading fear
and panic. The mere rumor that polio was present was enough for com-
munities to close down gathering places. Tragically, the virus most often
struck children: sometimes killing them, often infecting their spinal cords
and leaving them unable to move their arms and legs. The sight of tiny
kids wearing braces and hobbling on crutches broke the nation's heart and
spurred a frantic search for a cure. In Marin County, California, just north
of the Golden Gate, young mothers showed up at the local swimming pool,
tenderly lowering their children into the water and the arms of Red Cross
volunteer and swimming instructor Beth Kaufman. In her early fifties, she
recruited teenage girls to massage the children's stricken limbs in the water.
The method was called hydrotherapy, and slowly, steadily, day-by-day,
many of the kids showed improvement, and some became strong enough
to swim. As their limbs grew stronger, the kids began swimming longer and
longer distances, then began racing each other. Almost miraculously, they
went from near paralysis to being strong swimmers. Kaufman noticed that
there were few opportunities for young swimmers to compete in organized
meets where winners and times would be recorded.[1]

She tried to organize some meets but ran into a system that excluded
most young swimmers. During the twentieth century, the Amateur
Athletic Union ruled American swimming, and the autocratic association
had a stranglehold on deciding who advanced to the national championships and the Olympic teams. Talented young swimmers who aspired to
the Olympics had to overcome a system rigged against them by "a few
monopolists and opportunists," according to AAU swim director Carl

13

Bauer. Bauer was the rare unpretentious AAU official, a youth coach since the 1920s who was outspoken, hardheaded, and willing to fight for change. "Only a few aquatic stars and champions were developed to their fullest," Bauer argued. "Many potential stars did not get a chance to gain national recognition due to the selectivity of the monopolists. Specialty coaches and managers handled the guidance of our nation's foremost swimmers and divers."[2] To compete on a national level, child swimmers had to swim against senior-level swimmers who were years older than they were. Kaufman and Bauer joined together in the quest to create a national program to serve the thousands of kids flooding into swimming. What they had in mind was bold, unprecedented, and enormous, influencing almost every swimmer and swim team in the country. The concept became known as "age group swimming," with competitions held under the AAU's banner of Junior Olympics. The plan was to create a system that established racing categories by age. The first classification was age 10 and under, followed by ages 11–12, 13–14, and 15–16. After age 16, competitors entered the Senior Division. Swim meets were organized by parents who banded together to rent a pool, schedule the meet, record the times, and send those times to the AAU. This way, swimmers from around the nation could be ranked by their times, not by favoritism. The fastest swimmers were invited to regional and national competitions and ultimately to the Olympic trials.

Despite Bauer's years of lobbying, the men's AAU committee refused to authorize the program and shelved it. But in 1951, the AAU's women's committee, facing an unrelenting fusillade from Beth Kaufman, allowed age group competition as a pilot program in the AAU's Pacific Region. In a bit of marketing genius, the program was called the Junior Olympics. Now kids and parents saw themselves as part of the Olympic movement, and winners were crowned Junior Olympic Champions.

The program exploded in popularity. Kaufman, always aggressive in promoting swimming, kept busy enlisting parents, finding pools for events, and walking into newspaper offices to plead with editors to write stories about upcoming swimming meets. She stuffed kids in cars and drove hundreds of miles to regional and national competitions. On multi-day trips, she would stop along the way, searching for swimming pools in parks and motels so her girls could get in an hour of swimming to maintain their conditioning. Parents became the race timers, the stroke and turn judges, and the record keepers.[3] As the program grew in popularity, regional meets attracted hundreds of people, and interest grew from local business leaders who liked to see their towns, restaurants, and hotels filled with tired, hungry swimmers and their families on the weekends. Meets went on all day Saturday and Sunday, week after week, all over California. Swimmers and their families would decamp poolside with lawn chairs, coolers full of food, towels, and blankets. Newspapers began to fill up their sports pages with rows of agate type listing the top finishers. The excitement continued to build, and meets were added as the seasons stretched past the summer into the fall.

The Junior Olympics quickly spread from the Pacific Coast to the rest of the United States. Teenage swimmers began to dominate the senior competition, and in 1956, just five years after the program started, fourteen-year-old age grouper Sylvia Ruuska of Berkeley, California, won silver and bronze at the Olympic Games in Melbourne.[4] Age groupers won most of the medals won by U.S. swimmers at the 1960 Rome Olympics, and in the 1964 Tokyo Olympics, the United States won twenty-nine of fifty-four swimming medals, including thirteen of eighteen gold medals. One writer called it a "waterslide." For the next fifty years, the United States, powered by half a million age group swimmers, established a dynasty in Olympic swimming, and from 1960 to 1976, the United States won approximately 60 percent of all Olympic swimming medals, making the U.S. swim team one of the most successful teams in history in any sport. The program was especially popular with young girls and their parents, who had few other organized athletic outlets at the time. Age group swimming became so cherished by the sport's leaders that when the "power grabbing" National Collegiate Athletic Association (NCAA) tried to set up a rival program in the late 1960s, parents and coaches took quick action to stop it. One unidentified coach told the *New York Times* that "the AAU is doing such a magnificent job that it would be suicidal to the sport to interfere by setting up a parallel organization that wouldn't do a tenth as well."[5] The mighty NCAA backed off.

Kaufman was a relentless promoter, marching into newspaper offices excitedly waving swimming results at reporters.[6] Her efforts helped create the biggest Olympic youth sports program in history, rivaling even Little League baseball. Swimming participation multiplied ten times in five years, attracting thousands of athletes who would otherwise have gone into baseball, basketball, or football and never given swimming a second thought.

3

A CLUB TO FIT HIS VISION

In just five years after leaving the army, Chavoor had built an enviable record of success at the Sacramento YMCA, and he now set his eyes on even greater challenges. Chavoor's achievements attracted attention, and soon new opportunities were presented. Chavoor left the YMCA and began coaching at the Sacramento Elks Club in early 1951. The Elks had a private swimming pool, and Chavoor was able to get much more pool time than he could at the Y. But the coach of champions Tak Iseri, an Asian, and Allen Wimberly, an African American, left when he learned minorities were not allowed to participate in the Elks' sports programs. So in 1953, Chavoor joined a group of investors and established a swim and tennis club. With a glittering new pool, solid financial backing, and luxury amenities, it seemed Chavoor had everything he needed to create a genuinely great swim team.[1]

But he lasted barely half a year, leaving in March 1955. He left, he later wrote, when he discovered "the board of directors . . . had set up a screening committee to keep out Jews and [what they called] other undesirables."[2] Besides, the owners did not want to pay to heat the pool in the winter, making it impossible to train swimmers year-round. The time had come for Sherm Chavoor to leave the antiquated facilities, racial and ethnic prejudices, and elitism of the swimming world behind. He decided to create his own world, a world where an athlete's race, religion, or economic background didn't matter. His club would be a contravention of the method used by most swim clubs, which tried to please as many people as possible. "It was unusual at the time, and perhaps even now, as most swim and tennis clubs do not develop Olympic-caliber swimmers because of the inherent conflict between adult patrons and age group swimmers," said Ralph Mohr, a longtime California swim coach.[3] In Chavoor's new club, members knew the youth swim team had priority in the pool. Having spent his postwar years teaching and coaching, Chavoor was not wealthy when he decided to build his facility in the early 1950s. So he asked everybody he knew for loans and raised enough money to buy ten acres of raw land for $25,000. The property was on the corner of Fair Oaks Boulevard and Mission Avenue, on the edge of Sacramento, bordering the growing suburb of Carmichael. Chavoor had picked the perfect spot for a club that catered to young families. After the war, the area was transformed from pastures and fields to houses and schools to accommodate the armies of families moving in. Built out between 1950 and 1965, it was full of young kids.

The property he chose had small, gentle hillocks studded with magnificent century-old Valley Oaks that would provide pleasant shade. He placed the pool at the bottom of a swale with the slopes forming seating, creating a natural amphitheater. Shortly after purchasing the land, Chavoor and his wife, Joan, wandered through the site, sitting under the oaks in the warm Sacramento evenings.[4] The main road through the area is Arden Way, and Joan is credited with originating the club's name, Arden Hills Swimming and Tennis Club. With the land use permit issued in December 1954, Chavoor went door-to-door in the neighborhoods near his proposed building site to sell memberships. It took him three months to sell all his five hundred memberships at $100 each. Dues were $10.80 a month. Whether by good planning or circumstance, Chavoor could not have picked a better economic time to build his club, as new housing tracts were being constructed at a record rate.

The facility included four tennis courts, a 25-yard swimming pool (a second pool would be installed in 1962), a putting green, and a large hall for luncheons, dances, and meetings. The 10,000-square-foot clubhouse featured a wall of wood and glass overlooking the main pool. It also contained a small office where Chavoor would sit, overlooking his growing kingdom. "Arden Hills was a wonderful place for a swim meet with grassy viewing areas, trees for shade, and a no-hassle attitude for visitors," remembered Mohr.[5]

When Chavoor opened his club in 1954, Sacramento's population stood at around three hundred thousand. California's sleepy capital was seen as a boring government town surrounded by farm fields, a stop on the road between San Francisco and Lake Tahoe. In the sports world, Sacramento was a nonentity. The city had one professional team, a usually poorly performing Pacific Coast League baseball team called the Solons. The team managed to provide one of the town's few sporting highlights to Sacramento when it won five games in a row over the Los Angeles Angels to win its only championship in 1942. The pennant-clinching victory came when the team's star, a local boy named Tony Freitas, pitched a four-hitter in the Solon's 5–1 championship-clinching victory. Unfortunately, Sacramento did not produce many world-famous athletes. One of its few champions was Tamio "Tommy" Kono, who, like Tak Iseri, lived in an internment camp during the war. There he became a weightlifter and would go on to win gold medals at the 1952 and 1956 Olympics.

Nicknames for the quiet government town included "Sacratomato," referring to the tomato fields and processing plants that employed many people in town. Another nickname was "River City," for the American and Sacramento rivers that flowed past it. Other Californians called it a cow town, a backwater, Hicksville.

Arden Hills Swim and Tennis Club was a success, both financially and athletically from its first days. The tennis and swimming programs quickly filled up, and soon the clubhouse hosted luncheons, dinners, and banquets. Chavoor enlisted the major local news radio station, KFBK, and the *Sacramento Bee* to sponsor his youth sporting competitions. He also brought a crew of five outstanding swimmers—kids he had started training when they were eight and nine years old—from the YMCA to the club. If the swimmer was good enough, Chavoor found odd jobs for the kid and his family to offset the membership fees. But the heart of the swim team would be kids from the local neighborhoods. Entire families signed up, and the pool was soon teeming with kicking and splashing siblings.

While it was an excellent facility, the amenities for kid swimmers were a bit bare. Sacramento's weather features blistering hot summers and foggy, dreary winters where the temperatures often drop into the low 40s and high 30s. A phenomenon called the Tule fog—so named for the thick mists that spring up from the reed-choked vernal pools and marshes in the area—envelops man and beast. Add 80-degree pool water and lights shining up from the bottom of the pool, and the Arden Hills complex in cool weather looked like a scene from the Scottish moors.

Practice usually began with swimmers getting on a kickboard and kicking for 1,000 yards to build leg strength. They would then grab an inner tube, wrap it around their ankles, and, using only their arms, "pull" for 1,000 yards; this was followed by a 1,000-yard swim. The coaches devised novel ways to keep things interesting for kids who had their heads stuck underwater for hours. They would swim 200 yards ten times, followed by ten 200-yard pulls and ten 200-yard swims. They would alternate long and short races, with thousands of yards swum every day. The swimmers lined up a few feet apart and swam a circle pattern, up one side of the lane and back down on the opposite side. During every workout, they were trying to catch the swimmer ahead of them, chasing their feet, lap after lap after lap, while trying not to get caught by the swimmer behind, in an intense, continuous competition. This occasionally led to verbal exchanges, most often if one swimmer kept touching another swimmer's feet during the races instead of passing the kids ahead of them. When it got colder, so much mist came off the pool that swimmers couldn't see the pool's far end or the coach. Every practice day was an intense competition. The faster swimmers were plucked from the pack and elevated to the elite "Sherm's team." There, the training and hours in the pool intensified as he developed dozens of kids for competition against swim teams from clubs around Northern California.

Chavoor never missed a chance to publicize his kid swimmers. His fourteen-year-old star Brian Hogan held records in the 100- and 200-yard individual medleys, and Chavoor saw a bright future for his young star. "Frankly, if Hogan maintains his enthusiasm and hard work, I don't see how he can miss being among the best swimmers in the United States within a year or two. He has what it takes," Chavoor told the *Sacramento Bee* sports editor confidently.[6] In September 1955, Chavoor landed the Junior Olympic short course championships, drawing some five hundred boys and girls from around the nation to compete in the event. Five of Chavoor's swimmers won Junior Olympic national championships, and Chavoor arranged a photo in the paper of him awarding emblems to the boys. He trained his kids so hard and for so long that Arden Hills won fifteen of sixteen meets, beating colleges like Cal Poly, San Jose State, and UCLA. The Berkeley varsity team would not even get in the pool with them. "A big, major school like that, they figured they had nothing to gain and everything to lose," Chavoor said, flashing a big grin.[7]

The tag end of the 1950s was an age of innocence in sports. Newspapers covered a seemingly endless number of local sports stories, everything from women's softball leagues, men's hardball leagues, hunting, and fishing. Pictures of outdoorsmen displaying salmon, trout, and bass hooked in the local rivers and streams were splashed on the sports pages, along with happy deer and duck hunters. Country club golf and tennis champions were featured, and table tennis and bowling tournaments championships got spreads in the paper. The events drew large crowds in the era before the television pro sports explosion of the 1960s. With so many events to write about, reporters and headline writers strained to come up with new words to describe the participants and their activities. Female athletes were referred to as being from the "distaff" side. Tennis players were "netters," basketball players were "cagers," track athletes were "harriers," and football players were "gridders" who played on the "gridiron." Swimmers were "paddlers" who paddled in a "tank" and, depending on their gender, were "aqua maids," "naiads," or "mermen." The sports section was filled with page after page of agate type listing not just the top finishers in events but everyone who competed, and every athlete in town must have had their name in the paper at least once.

Chavoor knew that the secret to developing strong swimmers was family support. Even Mark Spitz "would have had about as much chance as a tomato in a ketchup factory without his family," he said.[8] In the early years, perhaps the most accomplished swimmers were the children of the Ferris family—in birth order Patricia (Pat), Carolyn, Joan, and John. Joan showed her talent at an early age, with Chavoor calling her "top-flight" in the press when she was just eleven years old. When Arden Hills hosted the AAU Junior Olympic Short Course Championships, the *Sacramento Bee* ran an illustration on the top of the sports page featuring large individual sketches of the four Ferris kids. "The Four Pose a Threat to Any Challenger—They're all Good," the cartoonist wrote. It pictured an official at the registration desk asking, "Where do these young scallywags get all the energy?"[9] The Ferris family proved they had energy and talent. News items and headlines of the mid-1950s to the mid-1960s proclaimed stories like "Ferris Family Is Big" and "Ferris Family Stars in Meet." In August 1961, Carolyn set a U.S. women's record in the 220-yard freestyle, and at the end of the 1961 season, Carolyn and Joan held many national AAU records.[10] In 1964, Joan ranked fourth nationally in the 200-meter individual medley and qualified for the Olympic trials held on September 26 in New York's Astoria Pool. It was a sign that Arden Hills was stepping up to the top tier of U.S. swimming. Unfortunately, swimming against the top U.S. swimmers, Ferris missed qualifying for the Olympic team.

The girl who finished first in the medley was seventeen-year-old Donna de Varona, who had been on the 1960 Olympic team. She represented the Santa Clara Swim Club, about 120 miles from Sacramento but miles ahead in developing world-class swimmers. Santa Clara was run by George Haines, who had years of experience in the water. Haines began competitive swimming as a teenager, and at age eighteen, he joined the Coast Guard and taught marines and sailors survival swimming. After the war, he attended San Jose State University, where he was a champion swimmer. He landed a teaching job at nearby Santa Clara High School and founded the swim club there. In 1960, Santa Clara placed six swimmers on the Olympic team, and Haines received worldwide attention for the team's success. But its domination was just starting. Led by Don Schollander, who left his home in Oregon at age fifteen to train under Haines, and de Varona, Santa Clara won an astounding thirteen gold medals in the 1964 Tokyo Olympic Games.

Back in Sacramento, Chavoor, undaunted by Santa Clara's gold rush, kept asking questions and learning more about swimming and the limits of human endurance. And he identified the kids in his pool who would challenge Haines, Santa Clara, and the world for Olympic glory.

4

SHOW ME WHAT YOU CAN DO

One of the world's greatest swimmers began competitive swimming due to a horrific traffic accident. On September 13, 1960, thirteen-year-old Mike Burton was perched on the handlebars of his friend's bike, riding home after playing basketball. The boys were crossing a two-lane highway when they collided with a furniture truck. The pair was tossed into the air, and Burton came down on the road, bleeding badly. He was rushed to the emergency room and into surgery. The patellar tendon holding his kneecap to his shin was sliced in half, and the force of the impact almost tore his right hip from its socket. The doctors operated for eight hours, trying to put him back together. After the surgery, he was encased in a cast that extended from his crotch to his toes. He was confined to a hospital bed, flat on his back, unable to move, in traction for six weeks. He healed slowly, and he could not extend his right leg more than 45 degrees for the rest of his life, walking with a limp. But the harshest pain came when the doctors told him he was finished with sports: no more baseball, basketball, or football, all the "real games" boys played.

When he was released from the hospital, he tried playing basketball again. When he tried to pivot, his hip wouldn't respond. His sprint dissolved into a gallop. He was angry and devastated and rued his fate, wondering what would replace athletics in his life. He didn't live in the lovely neighborhood near Arden Hills. His family lived in the rough North Highlands area on the north side of town. His dad drove a truck, and his mom worked full time. In his first year of high school, he began running with a tough crowd. "A lot of the guys were involved in breaking, stealing, and stuff," Burton remembered. He was a self-described tough guy, clothed in the bad-boy togs of the day. He wore a leather jacket. His hair was slicked back on both sides to create a feathery ridge on the back of the head—the infamous ducktail haircut of the early 1960s, the hallmark of kids the cops and teachers called "juvenile delinquents." A wrong turn here, a trip down the wrong street there, and Mike Burton could have ended up in jail.[1] But fate was beginning to turn in his favor. His father enrolled him and his younger brother in a small swim and tennis club. When he was fourteen, his dad entered him in a swim meet in Redding, three hours north of Sacramento. Despite his limp, he swam well enough to catch the attention of some of the Arden Hills parents watching the meet. Impressed, they put him in touch with Chavoor.

They arrived at the Arden Hills parking lot in his father's truck and pulled in next to the deluxe Caddies, Studebakers, Avantis, and Lincolns that were the luxury cars of the day. Hobbling through the gate, Burton passed the club's young scions and headed toward the glittering swimming pool, feeling the stares of the towel-clad swimmers. Chavoor, whistle around his neck, stood waiting poolside. Neither coach nor swimmer had any idea of what to expect. Not wasting time on introductions, Chavoor told him to "get loose and show me what you can do."[2] Burton nervously hopped into the pool. His stroke looked more like a whirling windmill than the graceful motion of a competitive swimmer. His damaged leg and small feet provided little propulsion. Burton swam the length of the pool and back, then repeated it, pounding the water furiously with every ounce of strength he could muster. After two laps, exhausted, he nearly sank to the bottom of the pool. The slender rich kids looked on in disdain as Chavoor ended the session. Breathing hard, Burton looked up at the coach on the deck. Not hesitating, Chavoor barked, "Be here for Monday afternoon workout." The kid was elated but baffled. How could Chavoor make such a quick decision? "You've got the right pull underwater," the coach said, then walked away. Chavoor noted his new swimmer's arm strength and competitiveness in a few minutes. But, more importantly, he glimpsed that rare quality he called "guts."[3]

When he returned for his first workouts, Burton was trounced badly by the boys. After that, he would have to swim against and beat the girls to get a spot on the team. "He wasn't about to be embarrassed by any rich kids, so he made up his mind that he was going to be better than them," Chavoor remembered. Burton needed every advantage he could muster. In addition to the commute to Arden Hills, he was not on a solid high school swim team. So Chavoor asked Burton's dad if he could move the family closer to the club and enroll him in a school with a good team. His father rented half a duplex and moved the family. Chavoor made the transition easier when he offered Burton the opportunity to "work his ass off raking leaves to pay his fees and expenses."[4] But the hip country club kids and their parents still looked down on the newcomer from across town. In the pool, he didn't respond to the demeaning stares; he focused on the black line on the bottom of the pool as he swam lap after lap. At the end of a long day, exhausted and sore, he came out of the pool far behind the leaders. He kept plowing on, his raw, flailing stroke pulling his limp leg through the water. Finally, he began to close the gap on the top swimmers. Then he began to beat them. Burton set a strategy that led to rapid improvement. In practice, he would pick out a top swimmer and shadow them: "I started to work against a strong kid until I could beat them, and then I'd move on to the next person." He continued until he'd bested nearly every kid in the pool. Chavoor insisted his swimmers perform the breaststroke, butterfly, backstroke, and freestyle, and Burton relished the challenge of mastering them all. "I enjoyed working, and I enjoyed the work that Sherm gave me. I was able to improve at a much faster rate than most other kids."[5]

Chavoor marveled at Burton's pain tolerance: "Here was a boy who had learned to suffer and conquer pain and was willing to do everything I told him to do without complaining or resentment. No one I knew ever worked out that hard. He actually seemed to enjoy punishing himself."[6] His legend began when Chavoor put the team through a brutal two-hour practice, a series of butterflies totaling about five thousand yards. Chavoor loved to impose the butterfly stroke, which many think is the most painful stroke, on his swimmers. When the final yards were completed, the exhausted kids began to climb out of the water. Suddenly Chavoor yelled, "Hold on!" A collective shudder went through the team. They knew "hold on" meant more work was coming. "Okay," Chavoor said, "we're going to swim a fast sixty-six." That meant sixty-six laps, almost a mile. A wail of complaint rose from the water. Undeterred, Burton decided to swim as fast as possible to finish the workout and go home. Exhausted after the long practice, the other swimmers were dogging it a bit, struggling to get through the ordeal. Burton sprinted past everyone and began lapping the field, finishing first by several laps. He had already showered and dressed by the time the other swimmers finished. His dad was waiting for practice to end when Burton spotted him. "Dad, we have to get something to eat," Burton said. They pulled up at Lou's Burgers, a drive-in known for hamburgers so large they filled an entire plate. Burton wolfed down the burger with French fries, onion rings, and a large chocolate milkshake. When they got home, he went into his bedroom, laid down, and passed out. "I've never been that tired in my life, neither before nor after that Saturday," Burton later said. "But I knew from that point on that there was nothing Sherm could give me that I couldn't handle."[7] A bond that would last a lifetime was forged.

Soon Burton was working out three and a half hours a day, seven days a week. His specialty became distance swimming, especially the arduous 1,650-yard (1,500-meter) event, the brutal mile swim. At age sixteen, he first drew national attention when he finished ninth against the best swimmers in the United States in the 1963 Far Western AAU meet. "After the meet, the swimming coaches at the Universities of Southern California, Oregon, and Washington came over to me and were asking all kinds of questions about Mike," Chavoor said. Burton told the *Sacramento Bee* he'd like to swim in the Olympics, but it would take a lot of hard work. Chavoor agreed. "If Mike progresses in the next few years like he's done this year, he'll be great," Chavoor said.[8] No one thought he'd be contending for a spot on the U.S. Olympic team that would compete in Tokyo. But his hard work paid off, and in 1964, he earned a spot in the Olympic trials, finishing fifth in the 1,500 meters; however, only the top three finishers made the cut. "I should have made the team," he said. "I was very close, and I knew that I was going to make the 1968 team."[9] Chavoor agreed and told Burton that if he'd had another month to train, he would have been an Olympian.

5

GET A GOOD LOOK
AT EACH OTHER

Legend has it that Mark Spitz was an instant swimming star. But Spitz may not have been the best ten-year-old swimmer in the Arden Hills pool.

Spitz was born in Modesto, California, on February 10, 1950, the eldest child of Lenore and Arnold Spitz. Lenore was a mild-mannered, nurturing woman who could defuse household conflicts instantly. But Arnold had the opposite temperament. As a child, he lived on a chicken ranch in the Central Valley town of Turlock, California, where he lost his father at an early age and was abused by his mother. One of the few Jews in the area, he felt the lash of anti-Semitism. He was further hardened by his experiences as a gunner on a B-29 bomber in the Pacific during World War II. Like many veterans, Arnold elected to go to work after the service and did not get a college degree. After starting his career as an appliance salesman, he got a job in the scrap metal industry, rising to the executive ranks. As a young man, many felt Arnold was overbearing, but his wife defended him as "a no-BS kind of guy who was a great husband but a better father."[1] Aware of the prejudice against Jews, Arnold saw his role as being his family's provider and aggressive protector. He demonstrated time and again that he would make any sacrifice for his family.

When Mark was two years old, his father landed a new job, and the family moved to Honolulu, Hawaii, where Mark swam at Waikiki Beach every day. He immediately took to swimming, and his father taught him the basic crawlstroke while his mother looked on in amazement. "You should have seen that little boy dash into the ocean," she said. "He'd run like he was trying to commit suicide."[2] His mother remembered that he'd throw a tantrum when they had to leave the beach.

When Mark's father landed a new job in 1959, the Spitz family—Arnold, Lenore, Mark, and his two younger sisters, Heidi and Nancy—moved to Sacramento and bought a house in South Land Park, a pleasant middle-class neighborhood just a few miles south of downtown. The flat-roofed modernistic homes featured an "aesthetic that merged indoor and outdoor living."[3] The homes featured a few basic floor plans with three or four bedrooms, two baths, a recreation room, and a two-car garage, perfect for growing families. Lenore remembered that the neighborhood featured "lots of normal middle-class families."[4] But the neighborhood lacked a primary ingredient of 1950s America: a Little League program. So instead of grabbing a glove and a bat, Mark was enrolled in the Sacramento YMCA. By the time Spitz arrived in 1959, Chavoor had left the Y and started his swim club. Mark showed up without any interest in swimming and participated in various activities. But the Y's swimming instructor noticed the eight-year-old splashing around in the pool a bit more gracefully than the other kids.

The coach was Paul Herron, the first American to swim across the English Channel in both directions.[5] A Stanford man, he made the 1940 Olympic swim team, only to see the games canceled because of World War II. What would have happened had Herron not noticed the eight-year-old among the mass of kids in the water? Would a less trained eye have seen him? Perhaps he would have become Mark Spitz, star pitcher, rather than Mark Spitz, Olympic champion. But thanks to Herron, Spitz began swimming. From then on, he was blessed with a succession of outstanding coaches who would harness his talent and help make him one of the greatest swimmers in history and a household name.

Those early days in the Y's pool were easy, undemanding romps. Herron only worked the kids out two or three times a week for a leisurely forty-five minutes or so. In his first YMCA race, Mark had the best time in his heat and was awarded a purple ribbon for his accomplishment. But his race was just one of a series of timed heats. Race officials gathered the times of the heat winners, and the fastest overall swimmer took home the 1st place blue ribbon, the second-fastest won the red ribbon, and the third-fastest was rewarded with a white ribbon. Mark was not one of the top three. Suddenly the realization that he had not won the race sunk in, and the purple ribbon lost its meaning. Angry, he went home and told his mother, "I hate purple, I hate red, and I hate white! From now on, I'm only winning blue ribbons."[6]

Those colors and what they represented bored into his psyche and stayed with him throughout his life. He preferred blue in everything, even his clothes and shoes. Years later, his preference for blue would play into a famous incident at the 1972 Olympics. Wanting those blue ribbons, Mark continued swimming in YMCA meets. "He was only eight-and-one-half, but he was beating everybody," Arnold Spitz proclaimed with a bit of exaggeration. "It was then that I chose swimming for him as his major sport." The senior Spitz claimed it was he who had recognized his son's natural swimming talent and "his extremely long stroke," and started him on the path to be a competitive swimmer.[7] From the start of his swimming career, Spitz possessed many innate lethal swimming skills and was soon easily defeating the kids at the Y. It was time for Arnold Spitz to find sterner tests for his son, and that meant leaving the Y and its casual approach to competitive swimming. Arnold learned that if Mark wanted to advance as a swimmer, he would have to enter the new world of age group swimming run by the AAU. Arnold did not know much about the AAU, but he learned from the parents of other swimmers and entered Mark in a novice swim meet in the tony Bay Area suburb of Walnut Creek, about seventy miles from Sacramento. Such meets drew the most competitive swimmers who were strongly supported by parents willing to do what it took to launch their kids on an athletic career. It was a noisy, lively, animated place as kids and their parents showed up to register for the races. Arnold, somewhat fazed by the new surroundings and wondering why most of the swimmers had sleeping bags, almost failed to get Mark signed up in time for his first heat. Closely observing the scene with the eye of a newcomer, Arnold realized his son needed to fit in with the other kids, who were snuggling in sleeping bags waiting for their heats. Arnold raced to the nearest sporting goods store and bought a sleeping bag. He returned in time to proudly watch his son win his first race that day. There was no purple ribbon for Mark, just the coveted blue ribbon he'd lusted for since his first race.

On February 14, 1960, Spitz received a mention in the *Sacramento Bee*. Under the headline "Capital Swimmer Equals Record," the paper reported, "Mark Spitz, 9, of Sacramento, equaled the national record of 14.6 seconds for the 25-yard butterfly in his age group yesterday in the fifth annual YMCA swimming meet."[8]

But Spitz kept coming up against stronger swimmers from Arden Hills: John Ferris and Mike Butler,[9] two of the best youth swimmers in California, who "clobbered" him. Soon, Arnold and Chavoor were talking about the Spitz family joining Arden Hills. Arnold asked, "If my boy comes here, will he be just another swimmer and get lost in the shuffle?" Chavoor replied that he would give Mark a fair shot at Ferris and Butler and thought he could compete with them. Chavoor had seen something special in the dark-eyed boy and recognized Mark's ability to "surge in the last fifteen or twenty yards" of a race. Chavoor called it "a natural, inborn talent to extend himself beyond all physical endurance," a trait he would witness many times in the future.[10]

But there was a deeper, darker discussion. American Jews were rare in the elite, privileged amateur swimming world, and the elder Spitz was worried about how his children would be treated at Arden Hills. Chavoor confided that thirty-five Jewish families and many Asian swimmers belonged to the club. This was undoubtedly a convincing thing to say to the father of a Jewish swimming prodigy. Another issue remained: Arnold Spitz claimed his family could not afford the monthly dues. In his first dealings with Mark and his family, Chavoor showed that he recognized Spitz's talent and was willing to make accommodations so Spitz could swim for Arden Hills. While it was true that Chavoor paid swimmers to help clean up at the club to help them afford the dues, not many were given a discount. He offered to reduce the Spitz family's dues, a gesture that helped relieve Arnold's anxieties about his son joining the elite club. Mark Spitz was soon competing for Arden Hills.

Entering Chavoor's compound for the first time for a 6 a.m. workout, Spitz was awed, impressed, and scared, like a Little Leaguer walking onto a Major League Baseball field. Sacramento can dip into the low and mid-30s in winter, and it was on such a wintry early morning that Spitz first saw the Arden Hills complex. A dense ten-foot-thick wall of fog hovered over the pool, generated by the collision of the 80-degree pool water with the cool surface temperature. At first glance, Spitz feared Chavoor, who presided over the misty scene "with his potbelly and stopwatch."[11] Here Spitz would be competing with the boys who had waxed him in the AAU meets and who swam thousands of yards a day, while Spitz had swum a fraction of that. Spitz had heard of Chavoor's reputation as an unblinking, demanding coach who would brook no nonsense while imposing unheard-of demands on his young swimmers. The young swimmer had not yet experienced the pain, exhaustion, and sheer boredom of swimming long hours every day. Chavoor's early impression of Spitz was that he was introverted, shy, and afraid of him and his father.

The initial workout exhausted but did not discourage Spitz, and he kept plowing through the water day after day. His swimming distance gradually rose, from the hundreds of yards a day he was used to at the YMCA to thousands of yards a day, from a few workouts a week to practices six days a week. Chavoor was a master of arranging every detail in his swimmers' lives. In the first workouts, Chavoor was savvy enough to place him a few lanes away from Ferris and Butler, still the stronger swimmers. Chavoor did not want to risk the novice getting discouraged by being in the lane next to the more experienced swimmers and becoming demoralized as they sprinted past him.

Spitz progressed quickly, and Chavoor moved him next to the faster boys. Spitz displayed a "defiant look" that at least outwardly conveyed a certain savage competitiveness and confidence, and in just a few weeks, Spitz was able to stay close to Ferris and Butler during workouts. Intense competition developed as each practice lap turned into a mini-Olympics. Soon harsh feelings grew among the three young competitors, highlighted by an occasional shoving incident. Chavoor recognized that if the roughhousing got out of hand, it could become an insidious problem for the boys. Chavoor pulled the swimmers out of the pool one day after a hotly contested swim. He noticed that the boys were stealing peeks at each other in their races to see who was ahead. That brief head flick can cost a swimmer hundredths of a second, sometimes the difference between finishing first or second in a race. Chavoor knew he had to break them of that habit if they were to become world-class swimmers. He ordered the shivering boys out of the water and told them to stand on the pool deck.

"Now stay there for twenty minutes and study each other until you know what each of you looks like."[12] Soon the other kids noticed the strange ritual and started giggling. The boys felt the hot sting of embarrassment crawling up their necks.

Chavoor had taken the opportunity to correct a technical mistake and leveraged it to form a bond between the boys. He would employ similar strategies countless times to make his swimmers faster while developing their character. The tension eased, and the boys began twittering, giggling at their absurd position. "Almost from that moment on, I had the nucleus of a great team which continued through the 1960s and 1970s," Chavoor said.[13]

Despite his fast improvement, Spitz lagged behind Ferris and Butler, partly because he missed practice one day a week. Chavoor felt he had to develop his swimmers to their maximum potential, even if he had to confront the Almighty to do it. The Spitz family were reliable members of the B'nai Israel Temple, the oldest Jewish temple in Sacramento, dating back to 1849 and the Gold Rush. Arnold even volunteered to set up decorations for an event by the temple's Israel Sisterhood.[14] So it must have come as some surprise when Chavoor summoned him into his office one day to discuss religious matters. Specifically, Chavoor was concerned that Mark was losing ground by missing Tuesday workouts to attend Hebrew school. "He'[d] never beat Johnny Ferris" if he kept studying Hebrew instead of swimming every day, Chavoor warned.[15] Arnold went to lobby the Rabbi and returned to tell Chavoor he had worked out a deal. Mark would be able to skip Tuesday instruction in exchange for attending religious services on the weekends when it did not interfere with Mark's practice time. Arnold said he'd convinced the rabbi to change the schedule when he told him "even God likes a winner."[16]

That summer of 1960, Ferris, Butler, and Spitz formed the heart of two medley and freestyle relay teams that went undefeated. "Yesterday, John Ferris, Mike Butler, Jonathan Baker and Mark Spitz set a Junior Olympic record of 1:04.5 in the 100-yard medley relay," the *Sacramento Bee* reported on June 6, 1960. The day before, Spitz, Butler, Ferris, and Mark Shelley set the age group record in the 100-yard free relay. In individual races, John Ferris was consistently winning and garnering headlines. Ferris set the record in the 50-yard free at an AAU meet in Alameda, with Spitz finishing fifth. In June, Ferris set another national record in the 50-yard free, while Spitz set a national record in the 50-yard butterfly. By the end of the season, the Arden Hills boys helped establish the club as a force in AAU junior swimming. Chavoor's juniors captured twenty-four national age group first-place finishes and set six Junior Olympic records, more than any other club in Northern California. Ferris, a half-year older than Spitz, set five individual records, while Spitz set three and Butler two. "Swimming experts see quite a future ahead for Arden Hills' crack relay team," the *Sacramento Bee* reported, not disclosing that the "swimming expert" was probably Chavoor.[17] Chavoor thought that John Ferris, not Spitz, was the best on the team.[18]

By this time, the boys' initial dislike had faded and turned into friendship. The boys would stay overnight at each other's houses and talk about swimming. "It was a big party then," Spitz remembered years later. "Man, you were in competition. That was the living end. It was something to be playing a little touch football on the lawn and tell your friends what you did at workout that day. When you're small, you don't know anything."[19] It was the summer of the 1960 Rome Olympics, and the United States led the world with fifteen swimming medals, including nine gold, with Australia right behind with five gold and thirteen total medals. It was the first summer an Olympiad was shown on U.S. television, if only for a few minutes each night, and the boys watched and wondered if they could be champions like the great Australian Murray Rose or American Mike Troy, the 200-meter butterfly champion.

As Spitz's win total improved, he and his father began drawing notice at the pool. Mark's cousin, Sherman Spitz (later best man at Mark's wedding), said Arnold had an "obsession" with Mark's swimming. Father and son were intensely competitive and loudly egged each other on at meets, often to the annoyance of parents and rival swimmers. When Mark won a race, Arnold would loudly ask him how many remaining races he would win. Of course, the young swimmer said he would take home all the blue ribbons. Arnold Spitz was quoted as saying, "Mark, how many lanes in a pool? How many win?"[20] The answers were eight lanes and one winner. For Arnold, swimming wasn't important, only winning was, and he was never shy about proclaiming it loudly. A childhood teammate remembers the pair feeding off each other at swim meets, loudly and obnoxiously celebrating Mark's wins. Many thought Arnold was trying to live his life through his son.

Arnold demanded perfection from Mark and rode him hard in everything he did. When Arnold felt Mark's bar mitzvah thank-you notes weren't personalized enough, he threw them out and made his son write them again. Mark got so upset he said, "I hope I get big and strong because one day I want to pin down that SOB and never let him up."[21] As Mark rose to become one of the greatest swimmers in the world, Arnold's handling of his son would be the subject of many news stories critical of his perceived over-the-top involvement in his son's life. He was unapologetic: "If I pushed Mark, it was part of his development—and you know why I pushed him? Because he was so great, that's why. I can't believe any parent would say, 'Honey, if you're tired, you don't have to go to workout.' A child who has his parents behind him can govern his time and know there is a time to work and a time to play. If the parent isn't behind the child, there can be nothing outstanding."[22] Chavoor soon understood that much of Mark's success came from his relationship with his father.

While father and son appeared to be supremely confident, the truth was that Mark felt the pressure as he approached and prepared for swim meets. Chavoor noticed a disturbing trend: Mark would miss workouts, stay out of the pool, and say he had stomachaches or headaches. Chavoor realized the ailments were the result of mental, not physical, strain. Chavoor would back off the harsh training and pull Mark aside, knowing his young swimmer had to be coddled and fussed over a bit. He was able to help Mark get over his anxiety and back in the water. Chavoor could read his young swimmer's mood like no one else, and he knew how to snap him awake and ready him for a race. It was a technique he mentally filed away, ready to use when the stage turned from local swim meets to intense global competition years later.

In mid-1961, Mark Spitz left Arden Hills, and Chavoor knew he was losing a great swimmer. In later years, some journalists wrote that Arnold left Sacramento so his son could join the Santa Clara Swim Club. But the record is clear: Spitz left Arden Hills because his dad was transferred to Oakland, some eighty miles and lots of Bay Area traffic away from Arden Hills. Chavoor was philosophical about losing a potential all-time great. He recognized that swimmers were the "children of the affluent," and their parents often held executive-level jobs that required families to relocate as they climbed the corporate ladder. "Every year, I lose some [swimmers], and I gain some."[23]

In the few years they were together, Spitz and Chavoor had developed a relationship that would last a lifetime. Just as importantly, Arnold and Chavoor forged a strong bond that none of Mark's other illustrious coaches could match. That bond would later bring Mark back to Arden Hills for a shot at his greatest triumphs and get Mark through the most significant crises in his swimming career. But for the time being, Chavoor would have to build his team into a champion without Spitz.

6

THE BEST RIVALRY GOING

While Debbie Meyer would become famous, Chavoor's first super-star was a shy girl named Susan Pedersen, one of the greatest age group swimmers of her era. Sue grew up in Sacramento, the youngest of three children, in a 1,337-square-foot, three-bedroom, two-bath home on a pleasant, leafy street. Sue was so full of energy that by age three, doctors told her parents to get her into a sport that could absorb her spirit and in-tensity or she would drive them crazy. Tall for her age, she was dominating recreational races by age five. Her talent was evident, and when she was nine, her parents determined she would benefit from the Arden Hills pro-gram and Chavoor's coaching. Like other newcomers to Chavoor's system, she soon learned she had entered a new world of long, relentless workouts. Chavoor pointed to Mike Burton, who spent hour after hour pounding through the pool, as an example of the required work ethic and commit-ment. Burton's workouts were so intense—he told Sue he approached every practice like an Olympic race—that it awed and inspired her. Soon Sue was swimming more than ten hours a week, bobbing in the water, struggling to stay near the older, stronger Burton. But swimming was a joy for her, and she embraced a life that revolved around swimming, eating, and school. After a few weeks in Chavoor's pool, she realized "swimming was for real," and soon she was closing in on the older swimmers.[1]

By age ten, she was a sensation. As a five-foot-five, 135-pound fifth-grader, she possessed unnatural strength and endurance, combined with a strong and fierce competitive spirit. In March 1964, she set five national age group records; in June, she crushed the 10-and-under 200-yard indi-vidual medley record. But her singular achievement was becoming the first ten-year-old, boy or girl, to break a minute in the 100-yard freestyle.[2]

Her accomplishments drew so much attention and became so well known in Sacramento that newspapers referred to her by her first name in headlines. Halfway through the year, the *Sacramento Bee* headlined, "Only 10, But Susan Is Swim Star Already." Coaches began comparing her favorably to Donna de Varona and Chris Von Saltza, Olympic stars of the day. She swam so fast in the 1,650 that she could have qualified for the Senior Division, but the rules wouldn't allow it. Chavoor had coached her for only a year and said she would have developed even faster, but "her biggest problem was not knowing how to work hard."[3]

All the success was tinder for speculation she would soon be an Olympian herself. The *Sacramento Bee* prominently positioned a large photo of Pedersen with the caption, "Olympics in '68?" In the picture, she poses as if she is ready to plunge into the pool. Her arms are swept behind her, a sure, confident smile on her face, her eyes gazing four years into the future. Chavoor said if she kept developing normally, she was a "cinch" to make the 1968 Olympic team and be one of the world's great swimmers. "Of course, you never know until it happens," he concluded.[4]

Chavoor described Sue as muscular, towering, tall, majestic-looking—a full-blown woman at age eleven—but still a sweet, lovable little girl with loads of talent. The *Bee* called her the girl next door. Maturing early, she was beautiful and already getting the attention of boys, and Chavoor told her to stop wearing blue eye shadow to help keep them away. As 1965 began, Pedersen was the golden girl of the pool, getting stronger and faster every day. Moving from the ten-year-old to the eleven-and-twelve-year-old age group, she still towered over most girls and many boys her age. Her mom told her not to let the attention give her a big head, warning her that someone would sneak up on her and beat her if she got overconfident.

While her future looked bright, she faced the toughest competition in the world from swimmers clustered in California. To be an Olympian, she would have to contend with rivals like Santa Clara's Pokey Watson, already an Olympic veteran, who was three years older and three seconds faster in the 100-yard free. In addition, new competitors were constantly emerging.[5] Age group swimming was pumping out faster and faster swimmers at younger and younger ages as it spread from California throughout the country.[6] But her main rival, it would turn out, would soon land in her home team pool.

Tomato fields surround Sacramento, and one of the crop's most significant gifts was Debbie Meyer. She would never have arrived at Arden Hills if the Campbell Soup Company, famous for its tomato soup, had not transferred her father from New Jersey to Sacramento in late December 1964. Debbie was the daughter of Leonard, known as "Bud," and Betty

Meyer, quintessential members of the Greatest Generation. Bud, a Marine Corps aviator, had flown missions over the Pacific during World War II and served in the army in Korea, winning two Bronze Stars. Debbie credited her renowned work ethic to her dad's influence on her.[7] A serious man who also joked around with young people, he was always finding novel ways to inspire his daughter to greatness.[8]

Debbie was the second child and grew up following her older brother around, "wanting to do what he did," and she took to athletics readily. "I was always a tomboy," she said, "and I loved playing sports. When I was eight, I played Little League, and I remember getting through three games before someone found out I was a girl, and I got kicked off. There weren't many options for girls to play sports at that time." So she played baseball, football, and ice hockey with her brothers. She tried ice skating, "but when it came to doing shows with foo-foo outfits, I was out; that just wasn't me."[9] She learned to swim in the Chesapeake Bay during the summers, and her parents joined a seasonal swim club, where she loved to race but averaged only about two thousand yards a week in the pool, a total that would not cut it in Sacramento.

Like most twelve-year-olds would be, she was anxious about moving across the continent, and she cried the entire plane trip west from Philadelphia. Her father had gone ahead of the rest of the family. "When Daddy met us at the airport, I had this idea that he was going to dump us all in the ocean," she remembered.[10] She arrived at Arden Hills as the new girl in town, with no friends and anxious to fit in. The family settled into a 2,600-square-foot, four-bedroom, two-bathroom house just minutes from the club. One day her mom showed up at Chavoor's pool with Debbie, a five-foot, 100-pound twelve-year-old still wrapped in baby fat. He ordered her to swim five hundred yards. After just four laps, she pulled herself out of the pool, exhausted. "Here, we do fourteen thousand yards a day," Chavoor told the stunned girl.[11] Debbie went home and told her mom the workouts were too tough, and she wanted to quit, stay home, and watch TV. A feeling of failure swept over her that day as she contemplated her future. "I didn't think I'd be anything," she remembered.[12] Her mom would have none of that and told her she would not be allowed to sit around and do nothing, so she would have to discover new activities or return to swimming. Reluctantly, Debbie headed back to the pool and kept trying. Every morning she woke up in the darkness to make it to practice on time. There were dozens of talented girl swimmers in the pool, and she fell woefully behind the pack in practice. But Debbie dug in and swam harder every day. Her parents encouraged but never pushed her.

They always told her if she didn't want to swim, she could quit. But the competitive fire that raged within her could not be extinguished. Debbie decided to emulate Sue Pedersen—at eleven years old, a year younger than Debbie but much bigger, stronger, and more experienced. Debbie shadowed her and the other Arden Hills girls in daily workouts, slowly and doggedly closing the gap. After a few months, she finally did an entire practice without stopping and increased her distance from a few hundred yards a day to five thousand yards or more a day.

Chavoor took notice of the cute, cuddly kid with sparkling eyes and an easy, confident manner. She was plainspoken with a good sense of humor and used words like "uckie," "icky," and "phooey" in conversations with reporters. One day, Chavoor noticed a rather odd necklace draped around Debbie's neck. It was a stopwatch on a chain, unusual jewelry for a twelve-year-old. It was a gift from her father, who noticed how excited she had been watching the 1964 Tokyo Olympic swimming competition on television. Chavoor asked to look at it. On the back of the stopwatch was inscribed "Mexico City, 1968." Obviously, the new addition to the Arden Hills pool did not lack optimism—or confidence.[13]

She eagerly wanted to be entered in the big Junior Olympics meet at Arden Hills on June 6, 1965. Including the qualifying events held at multiple locations weeks earlier, the meet had attracted some ten thousand entries, with many Olympic hopefuls competing. Debbie dreamed of swimming with Sue on the relay team. "In my usual unpleasant way, I snarled at her," Chavoor said. "You can't even think about making the relay team until you break thirty seconds in the 50-yard freestyle," he barked. Still, "just for the hell of it," Chavoor decided to give her a shot in the 50-yard free against some of the toughest competition in the region.[14] Chavoor promised that if she swam the 50 in under 30 seconds, she could join Sue in the relay race that day. In a meet that would feature Santa Clara's Claudia Kolb, a silver medalist at the Tokyo Olympics, and Pokey Watson, a member of that same Olympic team, no one expected much from the new kid in the pool. All the swimmers hoped to take home gold medals, seeing the Junior Olympics as stepping-stones to the actual Olympics. Debbie's parents squeezed into the bleachers packed with excited fans who were accustomed to the home team winning races and setting records just about every time out. Few noticed the new girl entering the pool. Watching her, Chavoor was sure she would lose badly and possibly lose enthusiasm. The crack of the starter's gun drew a roar from the crowd as the swimmers splashed into the water. Stopwatch in hand, Chavoor watched in amazement as Debbie stayed even with the two leaders as they neared the first turn. The trio pounded down the final 25 yards, a blur of rotating arms, flailing legs, and splashing water as they touched the wall within an instant of each other. "Debbie's in the winner's circle," someone shouted, but no one could tell for sure who won. They would have to rely on the timers' eyesight and judgment to see who touched out first. The officials quickly huddled and declared that Debbie had indeed finished first, but in a tie. Chavoor looked down and checked his stopwatch. He did a double-take; Debbie had bested the 30-second mark easily, finishing in 27.8. Chavoor gulped. He always wanted to beat Santa Clara and his rival coach George Haines. Now, in the midst of a hotly contested meet, Chavoor had to live up to his promise to allow the inexperienced Debbie to swim in the relays with Sue.

Arden Hills and Santa Clara, Mark Spitz's new team, were neck-and-neck for first place. Mike Burton helped the home team's cause by beating Spitz in the 200 free. Burton and John Ferris led Arden Hills to victory again, beating Spitz and Santa Clara in the 200-yard free relay as the home crowd roared in appreciation. Even Arden Hills' ten-year-olds chipped in, winning the 200-yard relay medley. Sue was her usual dominating self, winning her three events. Arden Hills fans were surprised when they saw Chavoor put Debbie on the third leg of the 200-yard freestyle relay team, especially in such a close meet. Once again, Debbie would have to face the confident Santa Clara girls, who were strutting about like champions. It was another close race, with Arden Hills holding a tight lead as they entered the third leg. It was Debbie's turn to swim, and she needed to keep the race close if her team was to have a chance to win. Debbie swam as fast as she could, but she could not hold the lead. Touching the wall, Debbie looked up as Sue sailed majestically over her, diving into the water with barely a splash and engaging her long powerful arms as she gobbled up the last fifty yards. She sprinted past the Santa Clara girl in the last few seconds, her five-foot-seven frame powering her and the team to victory. Arden Hills won the relay, and Debbie had her first Junior Olympic victory[15]—the first of many wins to come.

The *Sacramento Bee* assigned Don Bloom to cover many Arden Hills events. A tall, engaging man with a friendly personality, Bloom had been a college hurdler at San Jose State University and deeply loved track and field. He covered many major sports events and was the Oakland Raiders beat reporter during the team's glory days in the upstart and exciting American Football League. Great sports reporters look for details that add "color" to their stories and bring the athletes alive in their readers' minds. Bloom heard that Debbie liked peanut butter and asked her mom if it was true. "Debbie's been eating peanut butter and jelly sandwiches since she was six," her mother confirmed. "Every day—lunch and then afternoon snack. She loves them!" Bloom gave her the nickname "Peanut" and worked it into many of his stories, and the "Peanut Butter Kid" was born.[16] Debbie's peanut butter story would become an essential detail in her media narrative, setting her apart in the eyes of the world from the other great swimmers of her era. Chavoor didn't care what she ate. He knew with Debbie and Sue he had something special in the pool, "the best possible rivalry—two youngsters who were close enough in ability to press each other on to greater effort."[17]

7

SWIMMING FOR THE ENEMY

When Mark Spitz left Chavoor and Arden Hills, he embarked on a long, wandering journey that would take him in search of a new swimming home and involve many twists of fate. Chavoor recommended that he join the Aqua Bears at the Berkeley City Club, advice he and his father took. His new coach was the esteemed Laurabelle Bookstover, who had helped train three Olympians, but during this critical time in his developmental swimming years, Spitz made little progress. In June 1964, competing in the fourteen-year-old age class, his old Arden Hills teammate John Ferris beat him in the 100 fly and 200 free.[1]

Feeling that Mark was not getting proper training, his father drove him 160 miles to Sacramento to train with Chavoor at Arden Hills every weekend. Realizing this commute was unsustainable, Chavoor found Spitz another new coach: Hungarian immigrant and Olympic water polo hero Ervin Zador, head of the Pleasant Hill Swim Club. "Mark liked swimming for Zador, but Arnold and Zador did not get along," noted Spitz biographer Richard J. Foster, without further explanation. Once again, Arnold Spitz was concerned that his son was not progressing and blamed Zador. Once again, father and son were looking for a new coach.[2]

Arnold consulted Chavoor again and moved Mark to the Santa Clara Swim Club to swim under George Haines. Mark Spitz gave Chavoor credit for "displaying the unselfish, swimmer-focused attitude" in calling his archrival Haines and asking him if he would bring Mark into his program.[3] After a brief conversation, Haines said he was happy to coach the phenomenal young swimmer. "That was the turning point in my life," Spitz said. "That was the point where I really went into swimming for a business, where I decided that I wanted to be good, to be somebody."[4] Arnold moved the family to Santa Clara, and soon Mark was uneasy teammates with the greatest swimmers in the world.

The Santa Clara Swim Club was famous. *Life*, one of the most popular publications in the country, produced an eleven-page spread full of color photos about Haines and his team. A tall, handsome man with bright blue eyes and a commanding "California cool" air about him, Haines projected a much different image than the gruff and rumpled appearance Chavoor displayed. The 1960 women's Olympic coach and the 1964 men's coach, Haines had a cocksure attitude that never allowed him to take a back seat to anyone. At a coaching clinic in Birmingham, Alabama, Haines thought the swimming coaches were talking about Paul "Bear" Bryant, the legendary University of Alabama football coach, with too much reverence. Walking up to the classroom chalkboard, he wrote, "Bear Bryant is not God." After the chuckling subsided, Haines scribbled, "I am."[5]

Haines told his young swimmers he had magical abilities to turn them into champions and told them he could walk on water. The kids knew he was joking, but such was the confidence he projected that his swimmers wondered if perhaps he had a trick method of mastering the waves. Haines used many tactics to keep his swimmers motivated during the hours upon hours of training they had to endure. He would skim kickboards across the pool or flip canvas camp chairs high into the air and land them upright on the pool deck, much to his swimmers' amusement. But he also had a harder edge. In the view of many, the Baby Boom generation was not as disciplined as previous generations. Long hair, social protests, drug use, and even clothing were seen as part of a "generation gap" that separated those who had grown up during the Depression and then served in World War II from those born after the war. In spending a week at Santa Clara, *Life* noted that "Haines is able, by a delicate mix of love and fear, to maintain a controlled discipline that is astonishingly old-fashioned in today's permissive world of sports."[6] Drug use was not tolerated, and boys needed to keep their hair short. He ran his squad relentlessly, "in a kind of demonic fury," driving the kids to exhaustion. Once practice was over, that was it, and Haines did not make himself emotionally available to his swimmers, maintaining, "I've always kept the kids at a certain distance."[7]

Compared to Haines, Chavoor was a drill sergeant. "He's a warm person out of the water, a cold guy when you're in it," one Santa Clara swimmer said about Chavoor. "For him, you swim until you drop."[8]

When Spitz arrived at Santa Clara, Haines made a decision that would affect Spitz's career. He converted Spitz from a distance freestyler to the butterfly. "I looked around and saw where we—the U.S., not Santa Clara—needed help for the 1968 Olympics and figured the fly would be our weakest spot."[9] Spitz enjoyed the more manageable pace at Santa Clara. But he would soon experience problems he never faced at Arden Hills.

At Arden Hills, Sue Pedersen continued to dominate the AAU age group swimming and was ready to enter the national spotlight in senior competition. The five-foot-seven, 145-pound seventh grader from St. Ignatius School faced experienced rivals on March 15, 1966, at the Los Angeles Midwinter Invitational, where she was going against the best swimmers in the nation. Settling into the starting blocks before the 500-yard free, twelve-year-old Pedersen looked down the line and nervously surveyed the competition. There she saw Pokey Watson, four years older and winner of a gold medal at the 1964 games; Sharon Finneran, twenty-one years old and a world record holder in three events and a silver medalist in Tokyo; and Patty Carreto, the fifteen-year-old distance world record holder. The women were cagey veterans compared to Pedersen. Taking a few deep breaths, she felt her nerves settle as she struggled to focus her mind on the swim before her, not her opponents' reputations. She hardly needed to worry and showed no signs of inexperience or nerves as she quickly worked her way into the lead and won convincingly. Chavoor was satisfied but hardly exultant, telling the media Pedersen had a lot to learn about how to pace herself during races if she wanted to beat the top competitors consistently. "Yes, I'd say she's beginning to mature as a swimmer," was the highest praise the gruff Chavoor would offer. But he didn't dispute the newspapers' assessment that she could be one of the biggest U.S. stars at the 1968 Games.[10]

Debbie Meyer continued to practice and work hard. Like Pedersen, she idolized Mike Burton, and she "would get in the lane right next to him so I could race him."[11] Soon she began to catch up and beat him once in a while. The workouts were so intense that Meyer broke world records in practice. "She was very tough, just a very hard worker," Burton said. "Every practice, I was just trying my damnedest to stay ahead of her."[12] Her work paid off, and in a surprise upset, she beat Pedersen in the Far Western Senior meet, a victory that gave her confidence and belief that she could be a championship swimmer.

In June 1966, sixteen-year-old Mark Spitz returned to Arden Hills with his Santa Clara Swim Club team to compete in the Junior Olympic Short Course Championships. Although Spitz had been gone a few years, he and Chavoor had stayed in touch and maintained their relationship. Spitz recalled "savoring" his chats with Chavoor after practices and enjoying Chavoor's visits to his home when he swam at Arden Hills. Unfortunately, it was a relationship Spitz was not developing with his new coach, George Haines, who did not socialize with swimmers or their parents after practices.[13] Spitz felt out of place in Santa Clara and began a troubled relationship with Olympic champion Don Schollander, a college student at Yale who had little in common with the cocky new high school swimmer.

But Spitz's father claimed there were other problems in Santa Clara. Arnold Spitz said his son had been elbowed, scratched, and spit on because he was Jewish. Arnold had grown up and started his career during the "height of anti-Semitism in America. He worked hard to shield his children from prejudice. But he also jumped to accusations of bigotry at the mere trace of a snub, keenly aware of the perceived, subtle and overt discrimination against his people."[14] Santa Clara swimmers did not recall any incidents. "I don't think a lot of the kids even knew he was Jewish," Schollander said.[15] While Chavoor doubted Haines would condone such behavior, he thought the Santa Clara coach was too removed from his athletes to know what was happening in the pool. "I don't blame George [Haines] at all," Chavoor wrote. "I think at that point he wasn't aware of what was going on; if he did know, he discounted it."[16] Mark's sister Nancy, who also swam at Santa Clara, didn't remember any discrimination but said the only Jews at Santa Clara High School were the three Spitz kids.

Spitz acknowledged that he was brash and arrogant at the time, focused on winning races, not forging relationships. He thought he was capable of beating anyone and had little respect for the older swimmers and their accomplishments. He let his feelings be known, saying that Schollander, winner of four gold medals at the Tokyo Olympics, "really wasn't my role model or hero. . . . [I]t may seem cold, but he was my objective. I wanted to surpass everything he had done in the pool." Spitz shadowed Schollander in the pool to copy his smooth strokes, one time even diving to the bottom to look up as Schollander swam above him. This irritated Schollander, who would move over several lanes to escape Spitz's prying eyes, only to see Spitz show up next to him a few minutes later. "I got a secret charge knowing that I had the capacity to exasperate him," Spitz said.[17] Others felt Spitz was conceited, cocky, and a hotdog, always showing off. Yet the competition in the pool, combined with Haines's coaching, turned Spitz into a champion. While he excelled at every stroke, he was powerful in the butterfly. He compiled a list of stunning achievements, qualifying for the AAU national championships at age fifteen and winning his first AAU title in the 100 fly.

On a June day in 1966, Spitz returned to Arden Hills for the Junior Olympics. The bleachers were packed as people wedged themselves into the grandstand to watch the big meet. Sixteen-year-old Spitz was facing off with John Ferris, his old rival from his days as a ten-year-old. Ferris continued to excel and racked up Junior Olympic and high school championships almost as rapidly as Spitz. Fans and coaches marveled at Ferris's compact and streamlined stroke and how he started races. Ferris was one of the first to use the starting dive, "diving into a hole in the water," as he described it, taking a steeper, deeper angle than other swimmers of his time. Many coaches in that era did not worry about how big a splash the swimmers made entering the water, but that action caused surface tension and drag that slowed the swimmers. Instead, Ferris would dive out over the water as far as he could and then drop his hands and head to punch a hole in the surface. The rest of his body would follow into the hole, making just a tiny splash, forcing a strong "dolphin kick" that propelled his body like a rocket through the water. Ferris would shoot underwater as long as he could, avoiding the tension at the surface, while most swimmers struggled with the resistance on top of the water. Ferris later attended Stanford University, where his coach, Jim Gaughran, said his revolutionary dive had "all the velocity and grace of a frisky killer whale. There isn't a swimmer in the world who doesn't use John's innovation."[18]

Both swimmers prided themselves in the fly, and the pair were scheduled to face each other three times during the two-day meet. They would go head-to-head to determine which one was the best. Using his big diving start, Ferris jumped out to the lead in their first event, the 50-yard fly. He held it easily for the first 25 yards, but Spitz's finishing kick propelled him to a narrow victory, much to the home crowd's disappointment. The 100-fly was next, and Ferris took off to an even bigger lead as the crowd, literally jumping with excitement, urged on the home-pool favorite. Like a predator stalking its prey, Spitz once again caught Ferris in the last 20 yards, winning in an AAU junior record time. Once again the crowd groaned in disappointment as Spitz took the top rung on the platform and draped in gold. The last test was the 200-yard individual medley, where swimmers must use the freestyle, butterfly, breaststroke, and backstroke in the race. This time Ferris employed some pre-race strategy. In the preliminary heat, Ferris finished fourth and Spitz second, which was just what Ferris wanted: In the final, there would be someone between him and his rival, making it harder for Spitz to keep track of Ferris during the race.

The medley began with the butterfly, and for the third straight time, Ferris jumped ahead at the 25-yard mark and kept his lead for 50 yards. Ferris maintained the lead with his steady backstroke and increased his lead on the third leg, hammering the turns and using his superior underwater technique to stay ahead of Spitz. The final leg was the freestyle, and Ferris was well aware that Spitz was one of the strongest freestyle swimmers in the world. With Spitz's unique, freakish ability to close out a race in the final yards, no lead over him was safe. Exhausted and gasping for air, Ferris pulled with everything he had as the crowd "went bananas,"[19] pushing their hero to victory in a new national record time, with Spitz an instant behind. The crowd roared as their home-pool hero defeated his great rival. As the rest of the field glided to the finish, Ferris's excited brother, clad in cutoff blue jeans, jumped into the water to celebrate his younger brother's win an instant before the last swimmer finished. Ferris and Spitz shook hands, and, beaming, Ferris emerged from the pool, ready to receive his gold medal. But suddenly, race officials held up their hands in caution. The ceremony was delayed as the crowd and the swimmers milled around in confusion, waiting for an explanation for the delay. Finally, referee Ed Olson of San Francisco, the AAU Pacific Association president, announced that Ferris was disqualified because of the premature celebration by his brother, even though it did not affect the race. Spitz walked over and mounted the medal stand. But he stopped on the second level, leaving the champion's position unoccupied. Shaking his head "no" when an official tried to drape the gold medal around his neck, Mark Spitz, the kid people called a show-off and a hot dog, would not accept the gold medal, impressing observers with his good sportsmanship. Ferris and his family were disappointed by the disqualification. But the rivalry between Ferris and Spitz would continue to grow in the next few years, with reward and disappointment for both swimmers on the grandest stage. As he became the world's most famous swimmer, hundreds of profile stories would be written about Mark Spitz, describing him as an arrogant, self-centered jerk, his act of sportsmanship that day largely forgotten.[20]

Despite its growing success, Arden Hills was not recognized as a national swimming power or considered in the same tier as Philadelphia's Vesper Boat Club or the Santa Clara Swim Club. So that August, there was little attention when Mike Burton, Debbie Meyer, and Sue Pedersen qualified for the Outdoor National AAU Championships in Lincoln, Nebraska. Much of the pre-meet chatter focused on the 1,500-meter race, with Spitz challenging Steve Krause from Washington State, who had recently become the first swimmer to break the 17-minute mark. But unheralded Mike Burton created a sensation. Burton took out at a ferocious pace. He was ahead of everyone by at least five body lengths at the halfway point. Even Chavoor was amazed at what he was witnessing. Five thousand people began screaming, yelling, and slapping each other on the back in disbelief as they watched the unheralded swimmer pressing on, clearly threatening to set a new world record. Burton was sprinting the entire way, unheard of in the grueling mile race. Surely Burton would begin to cringe in agony, pain surging through his body as the laps mounted. First, his shoulders would feel the piercing pain, then his arms would begin to numb and his pace would drop. Finally, his back would tighten and begin to sink slower in the water. Or so they thought. But Burton continued his blazing pace as fans and officials kept asking, "Who is that guy?"[21] Burton sprinted up and down the pool, lap after lap, going faster, not slower. Burton won in 16:41.6, breaking the old record by an astonishing 17 seconds and obliterating the field.[22] Witnessing Burton's ability to shrug off the pain, his power, and his will to win, Spitz decided he was better built for the sprint races. "You know, Mike, I really don't want to swim this distance in the future," he told Burton after the race.[23]

In the 1,500-meter race against world record holder Patty Carreto, Meyer and Pedersen got off quickly and set a blistering pace, swimming side-by-side, just inches apart. They were still leading as they entered the last 200 meters when Meyer popped into the lead by a head or so. But the veteran Carreto began to close in and powered through the last 25 meters, winning in a new world record time with Meyer a close second and Sue finishing third. In writing the story of the race, *Sacramento Bee* reporter Don Bloom gave partial credit for Meyer's performance to her peanut-butter-and-jelly diet, a tale circulated in the national press. Arden Hills' performance thrust Chavoor and his team into the top tier of U.S. and international swimming. Chavoor was on cloud nine after the meet, hailed as an expert on distance swimming. It wasn't long before coaches and swimmers from around the world traveled to Sacramento to try to learn his secrets.

By the end of 1966, Sue Pedersen had done almost everything imaginable for a Junior Olympic swimmer. She held more than fifty age group records and took second place at the AAU Nationals. But because of Debbie Meyer's strong showing in the nationals and her rapidly improving times in practice, Chavoor began to think that she, not Pedersen, might be the star of the next Olympics. Pedersen's mom felt Chavoor was favoring Meyer. Chavoor resented the insinuation. Never one to coddle his swimmers' parents, the coach deflected any responsibility for the change in status of his female stars: "Suddenly, her daughter, the Queen, was getting beaten. How come? When their kid wins, it's heredity; when their kid loses, it's the coach."[24] For Chavoor, dealing with Mrs. Pedersen became a constant "haggle."[25] Things almost came to blows, with the bigger Mrs. Pedersen throwing a scare into the smaller Chavoor in a poolside confrontation. In contrast, Meyer's parents adopted a hands-off approach with Chavoor's coaching. Meyer grew closer to her coach and began to consider him to be her second father. For Chavoor, it was time for a change in Arden Hills' royal family. "So two years before the 1968 Olympics, a new Queen was crowned at Arden Hills," he wrote. And that queen was Debbie Meyer.[26]

Chavoor's hard work and accomplishments were recognized when he was named head coach of the women's swimming team for the Pan American Games, which would be held in the summer of 1967 in Winnipeg, Manitoba. The announcement drew national media coverage, but along with the attention came its nasty cousin, scrutiny. The *Bee* reported that Chavoor said he was a 1937 graduate of UCLA, "where he played football and was on the boxing team." If Chavoor had graduated in 1937, he would have been just eighteen, the age of most university freshmen. Yet the records showed that a Sherm Chavoor graduated from UCLA and not only played football, but also was an All-Pacific Coast selection in 1935 and had been named UCLA's most valuable player as a linebacker and center. He was described as a man "who played a fierce game and was known for his courage and sportsmanship." Those are astounding accomplishments for a sixteen-year-old, the age Chavoor would have been in 1935.

As a teenager, Chavoor idolized a UCLA football star named Sherman Chavoor, born in 1914, five years earlier than the "Sacramento Sherm." As the swimming Chavoor's fame spread, a letter appeared in the offices of the *Los Angeles Times*. It read, "I am Sherman Chavoor, and I played football at UCLA in the 1930s, but I am not a swim coach of any kind. I wrote because some friends were kidding me, they asked me where I found the time as a high school principal to moonlight on the job. Anyway, I thought I'd write and keep the record straight."[27] At the time, the letter writer was a high school principal in the Burbank Unified School District, some 375 miles south of Arden Hills.

The Sacramento Sherm had some explaining to do. But confronted with the issue, Chavoor did not admit that his real last name was Correa and doubled down on his claim that he attended UCLA. "I don't know anything about the Burbank principal, but I played football for UCLA, too," Chavoor maintained. "I never claimed I was a great player, but I did back up the line for the [UCLA] Bruins." UCLA was contacted for comment: "The swim coach has sort of adopted this school, and we think very highly of him," said assistant athletic director Bob Fisher. "He is an awfully nice guy and a fantastic swim coach. To my knowledge, he did not attend UCLA." So ended the mystery of the two Sherms.[28] Despite UCLA's statement, Chavoor never stopped claiming he'd been a college football player. In his book, published in 1973, Chavoor wrote that he'd worked his way through several colleges, both undergraduate and graduate, and said he had a master's degree in psychology. He also said he graduated from Berkeley with a major in psychology.

By 1960, the Arden Hills Tennis and Swim Club was so popular that ads for homes for sale in the area used their proximity to the club as a selling point. The club's six hundred memberships were sold out, and when people resigned from the club, the opening was soon snapped up. While Chavoor made sure his youth swimming teams had plenty of time to practice, he also had a vibrant adult program that filled the pool during weekdays and a robust tennis program with youth stars. The club's swim meets drew more entries every year. Each event featured as many as ten heats with eight kids per heat, a total of eighty swimmers in each event. Hundreds of kids and their parents, some from other states, jammed into Arden Hills during the big meets. At the center of it all were Chavoor and his wife, Joan, hovering over the check-in table, making sure swimmers were in the right race at the right time, and handling the thousand and one last-minute issues and confusion that nervous coaches, kids, and parents presented. In addition, he recruited an army of volunteers to serve as race officials, announcers, timers, marshals, referees, and stroke and turn judges to staff every race.

Smeared with suntan lotion and clothed in white, sitting under big floppy hats to protect them from the searing Sacramento sun during frequent 100-degree days, the swimmers' parents sat poolside for the dozens of races that consumed the weekends. As the program's reputation grew, AAU officials dropped by along with swimmers and coaches from around the country and even foreign nations. Always the promoter, Chavoor constantly fed the local media details about the visitors and news about his meets and the swimmers participating in them, even if they were stars from other clubs. He was on his way to becoming the only millionaire swimming coach in America. But few would begrudge him his wealth. Most swim coaches worked for clubs, schools, or municipal recreation departments. After coaching for the day, they went home and relaxed. Chavoor rose before dawn almost every day, seven days a week, to train the swim teams. On many weekends he led his team hundreds or thousands of miles away to compete in regional and national meets. Taking a gaggle of teenage swimmers on the road, putting them up in motels, then putting up with their hijinks when they weren't in the pool is enough to stress anyone to the breaking point. Fortunately, some parents showed up at the meets on the road and helped handle the kids. But the parents of championship long-distance swimmer Mike Burton couldn't afford to travel. When Burton found himself short of money for meals, Chavoor picked up the tab. If a kid lost a close race or broke up with their boyfriend, Chavoor was there to console and comfort them in his gruff, no-nonsense fashion. No matter how hard he worked or how often he was distracted, he usually ensured his swimmers' every need was met, in and out of the water. He never stopped working. Weekdays found him supervising the adult programs from his office, which was close enough to the pool that he had a bird's-eye view of what was happening. He administered the nagging details of a small business, from billing members to paying the bills, sometimes griping about the cost of providing hot water for the showers. His day finally ended as the sun was setting after evening workouts. After the long days, mostly spent outdoors, Chavoor hopped into his Mercedes Benz two-seater sports car with the license plates that read "SHERM" for the short drive home. No one would blame him if he mixed a martini for himself when he got home to relieve the stress of the day. But Chavoor didn't drink alcohol, preferring carbonated Fanta fruit drinks. When he went to bed, especially during the big meets, he fell asleep thinking about his swimmers and their strokes, moods, and motivations.[29]

Like most swim clubs, Arden Hills had few African American members, although it had several Asian and Jewish swimmers. The lack of minority swimmers bothered Chavoor, from his days as a YMCA coach until the day he died. Chavoor decried the fact that club swimming was an expensive sport that mostly kept lower-income kids out of the sport. His own star swimmer, Mike Burton, the son of a truck driver, would never have developed as an Olympic swimmer without the financial help Chavoor provided. In that era, only 25 percent of the high schools had swim teams, and few of those had girls' teams. Very few champion swimmers developed outside the mainly all-white suburban country clubs. "But the cost factor is only part of the reason for the shocking fact there are no Blacks in big-time U.S. swimming," Chavoor said. "It's a disgraceful aspect of American sports that constantly grates on me, and I'm determined to do something about it."[30]

Like he usually did when he encountered a problem, Chavoor surveyed the situation and sought out opinions. His primary source of information was his close friend Stan Wright, the track coach at Sacramento State. In 1966, Wright became the first Black head coach of a U.S. national track team when he coached the U.S. team in dual meets against Poland and the Soviet Union. Chavoor asked Wright to "find me five Black kids I could attempt to develop into champions at Arden Hills." Wright told him it would be a daunting task. For many years, he said, mythology held that Blacks had a different body structure and were not as buoyant as other races. Wright said it was nonsense but that he had read graduate degree papers supporting the "theory" and said even many young Black athletes believed it was true. Another theory explaining the lack of Black swimmers was the absence of Black swimming heroes. Worse were the country club covenants that banned minorities from belonging. Wright said that swimming had to do what tennis had done—allow Black swimmers to compete in national championships whether they belonged to a club or not.[31] Chavoor thought the sport needed a Black swimmer the equivalent to Major League Baseball's Jackie Robinson, a great athlete who could break the swimming color barrier. But Robinson had been coached and encouraged to play baseball as a kid. There were few opportunities for minorities to get the coaching, training, and pool time necessary to become champions. In 1975, Chavoor successfully recruited a pair of promising young Black swimmers to Arden Hills, ten-year-olds Danny Scales and Jerry Jones. In a feature story in the *Bee*, Chavoor said, "Jerry is a neophyte because he hasn't been swimming long, but Danny looks good. He reminds me of Mark Spitz with his wiry build. He's as good as Mark was at age ten." Danny agreed: "I want to break Spitz's record of seven Olympic gold medals, my dad wants me to be the first Black swimmer in the Olympics in about 1984. I think I can do it." His friend Jerry was even more optimistic: "I want to be better than he [Spitz] was. I'm going to try to break all of his world records."[32]

Chavoor's temper, rough language, and gruff demeanor landed him in an argument with a man at his club in 1983. Dexter Del Mar and his girlfriend were in the Arden Hills facility when Chavoor approached them and asked Del Mar what he was doing. Heated words were exchanged, and Chavoor evicted Del Mar, cursing him several times and using a racial epithet. Del Mar contacted the California Fair Employment Practices Commission, which initiated a hearing. Chavoor expressed regret for the racial slur, said he was not a racist, and "before it was fashionable, I did everything I could to fight racism." The affair was settled when Chavoor agreed to pay $20,000 and issue a letter of apology to Del Mar.[33]

8

PAIN AND AGONY

To become champions, swimmers must work hard in the water for hours daily. Great swimmers get acquainted with pain in practice and have to fight through it in competition. "Hurt, pain, agony," were the words inscribed on the banner above the pool at Indiana University, the credo of the great swim coach James "Doc" Counsilman.[1] He told his swimmers that if they wanted to be national or Olympic champions, they would have to swim every day until they were in pain. "The punishment is unbelievable," Mike Burton said. "You simply have to accept the fact you are hurting yourself all the time. The pain becomes the symbol of maximum effort, and you work against it instead of the clock. I used to judge my progress by the amount of pain I was suffering."[2] The pain begins as swimmers reach the end of their endurance. The only way to increase endurance is to battle through the agony and keep pushing. At exhaustion, the stomach muscles begin to weaken, the muscles start to vibrate, and then arrows of heat radiate along the muscles. Arms turn leaden, and pressure forms on the swimmer's back, like a giant pushing them down. As the swimmer's momentum wanes, they begin to sink in the pool, pushing through deeper, heavier water. "As you swim, the pain starts in the legs," Debbie Meyer said. "First, they feel numb and itch from the lack of oxygen. Then the numbness turns into a searing ache. It spreads up from the legs, into the midsection, and then into the lungs. Every breath becomes torture. Then the pain moves into the arms and you almost wish they'd drop off."[3] When Meyer slacked, even for an instant, Chavoor would be on her, demanding she pick up the pace. She often wanted to jump out of the pool and choke Chavoor for pushing her through her workouts. But, like all great swimmers, she learned to embrace the pain and push past it.[4]

Great swimmers deal with the pain and boredom of having their heads underwater almost every day for years. While their teenage friends are enjoying high school, having fun going to the movies and concerts and occasionally smoking a joint, swimmers live a regimented life ten months a year. They begin their day by grabbing a quick breakfast and rushing to the pool before 7 a.m. for a two-hour workout. Then they attend school all day before heading back to the pool for another two-hour workout. Finally, there is time for dinner, homework, and maybe a TV show before they blessedly fall asleep.

What type of person does this? Chavoor struggled to understand why swimmers undergo such torture. He would not allow his daughters to swim, switching them to horseback riding and tennis. He couldn't see his children suffer the punishment he'd have dish out to make them champions.[5]

Chavoor knew he had to instill fear of himself in his swimmers, a fear so intense it overcame the pain and abuse his swimmers suffered. "It made me wince," Chavoor said. "I'm not proud of the fact. But without it, you can't make a potential superstar stay in the pool and suffer" enough to be a champion.[6] There were a thousand swimmers in the sea, Chavoor would say, but only a few could suffer enough to become champions.

A television reporter once asked Chavoor what made him a successful coach. "Well," he said, pausing, "of course, you have to have the material. It's a necessity."[7] Despite the loss of Mark Spitz, the Arden Hills pool was brimming with "material." By the end of 1966, Debbie Meyer and Sue Pedersen were being favorably compared to Olympic swimmers of the past, with the idea growing that they would be top contenders for the 1968 Olympic team. Mike Burton had accepted a scholarship to swim for UCLA but returned to Arden Hills to train and compete in the big summer meets. Chavoor's pool had more Olympic-caliber talent than many colleges and most other nations.

To ensure this talent resulted in Olympic gold medals, Chavoor perfected a harsh training program he had been developing for years. He was intrigued by the issue of human endurance. The questions he wondered about were: How much punishment can the human body take? How many miles can a person run? How long can an athlete train before it ceases to help the athlete and begins to hinder their performance? Most importantly, how many hours and yards can a person swim? These questions have puzzled athletes and trainers for a century. In the early days of the twentieth century, the prevailing theory was that light workouts were preferred. Football and baseball players limited weight training for fear of becoming muscle-bound and losing their agility and speed. Johnny Weissmuller was one of the early American swimming stars. He parlayed his five gold medals in the 1924 and 1928 Olympic Games into a movie career that featured him starring as Tarzan. His workout sessions consisted of less than a thousand yards daily, which would have been a warm-up for most of the Arden Hills Swimmers.

Chavoor loved athletes who had courage, endurance, and guts. The famed coaches of the era were renowned for the toughness they instilled in their players. College football coaches like Bear Bryant, Woody Hayes, Bo Schembechler, and especially Amos Alonzo Stagg, the legendary football coach at the University of the Pacific in Stockton who Chavoor especially admired, left an enduring impact on Chavoor's coaching philosophy. These rugged, authoritarian coaches brooked no nonsense and had their athletes drill and practice until they dropped. As Chavoor studied swimming, he became convinced that the key to swimming success was to focus not on refining stroke mechanics but on how many yards a swimmer swam each day. He built a coaching philosophy he described as "overdistancing"—or, in simple terms, torture.

Chavoor said he spent twenty-five years evolving his overdistancing method. In the late 1930s, Chavoor heard the Germans were developing runners using new training techniques. German long-distance runners ran twelve miles a day when other world runners were content to work out for just one or two hours. Track coaches of the era were concerned that too much running would result in their runners' muscles tightening, leading to muscle pulls. But many worried that the Germans were progressing rapidly and would break the "unbreakable" four-minute mile barrier and dominate the 1940 Tokyo Olympics. World War II derailed the German athletic program, and the track experiment was abandoned and fell into obscurity. But Chavoor kept the overdistancing concept in the back of his mind until the war ended and kept a close watch on athletic research around the world. In 1954, the year Arden Hills opened, Roger Bannister broke the magic four-minute mile barrier. Bannister wrote extensively on his feat. He was a physician and developed great insight into human physiology and the human body. He believed humans could absorb much more physical punishment than many athletic coaches commonly thought, and he startled competitors when he started training fifteen miles a day.[8]

Chavoor studied Bannister's writings on endurance, convinced that athletes could improve quickly with more extended and arduous workouts. He witnessed this firsthand at the 1949 AAU national swimming championships in Los Angeles. His lesson came from a surprising source: swimmers from Japan. Japan had been a swimming powerhouse before the war, winning twelve medals and beating the Americans in the 1932 Games in Los Angeles. Japan was banned from the 1948 Olympic Games, but the Japanese participated in the AAU national championships in Los Angeles a year later. Tak

Iseri and John Stebbins, two of Chavoor's YMCA swimmers, qualified for the event, and Stebbins finished fourth in the 200-meter breaststroke.[9] A crowd of seven thousand, about half of whom were Nisei, showed up for the meet. The Japanese, led by Hironoshin Furuhashi, "The Flying Fish of Fujiyama," swept the 400-, 800-, and 1,500-meter events in world record times.[10] People wondered how the Japanese could dominate after being barred from competition for almost a decade. Coach Masaji Kiyokawa said his swimmers were simply putting in much more time in the pool than the rest of the world's swimmers, often working out for four hours a day, while most U.S. swimmers were working out for less than an hour a day.[11] It was a defining moment for Chavoor, a crucial piece of the evidence he was assembling to construct a radical new instructional regime that would help propel several of his swimmers to Olympic glory. But it would take him many years and much more thought, experimentation, and work to fine-tune his system.[12]

Chavoor began developing his swimmers on his overdistancing program. He had eight-year-olds swimming 1,650 yards a day, despite swimming no more than fifty yards in competition. Some parents were worried that overdistancing could cause lung damage. To counter those concerns, Chavoor recruited Dr. John Baker, who had three sons swimming in the Arden Hills program. Baker assured parents that Chavoor's taxing regime would not result in their hardworking children's lungs exploding in the pool or their arms falling off. Soon, Chavoor's swimmers dominated competition in the greater Sacramento region. Working with his distance swimming star Mike Burton, Chavoor developed one more breakthrough. People marveled when he ripped off a series of ten 100-yard swims in a row, with a short rest in between. Then, Chavoor started to cut down the rest time, or interval, between sprints. "I gradually cut down his rest intervals to a minute, then forty-five seconds, then thirty seconds—and finally ten seconds or less," Chavoor said. Eventually, Burton's breaks were just three seconds, barely long enough to stick his head out of the water for a few deep gulps of air. Chavoor drove all his swimmers up to eight thousand meters a day; it was, he said, the "constant pressure method." There was nothing mysterious, no hidden secrets, Chavoor explained: "I simply take body conditioning beyond all the limits of endurance that were previously thought possible for human beings."[13]

Coaches can scream and yell and search for a thousand ways to motivate athletes. But many know the key to developing a great team is to have one athlete who sets the tone and example for everyone else.

Burton's work and intensity served as an inspiration for the rest of the swimmers. "Mike was awesome. His workload was crazy, and I was intimidated just trying to stay in the water with him. I wondered why he worked so hard, what drove him? He never stopped. But he was the model, and we dug in and followed him," Pedersen said.[14] Burton was a few years older than Meyer and Pedersen and became their big brother and protector in addition to being an example.

The amount of work the Arden Hills swimmers endured simply staggered coaches who heard about it. A favorite Chavoor drill involved the 800-yard medley. Each swimmer swam two hundred yards each of the backstroke, the freestyle, the breaststroke, and finally the most punishing stroke of all: the butterfly. After ten seconds of rest, they repeated the drill, over and over, until the swimmers' muscles shrieked in pain and protest. Many didn't believe kids could be pushed that far and made pilgrimages to the Arden Hills pool to witness the suffering firsthand. Seeing it was believing, and the pilgrims became converts to overdistancing. As coaches imposed longer and longer workout programs for their athletes, they created a tongue-in-cheek mantra: "Asphyxiating fatigue precedes all others and does not harm the organism." In other words, as one coach put it, "a coach can work a child to exhaustion with a clear conscience; and it is worth noting that swimming is the only sport in which this is true."[15] Mike Burton had no fancy names or theories about what he was doing. "I was trying to go faster and harder," he simply said.[16]

9

IT FELT REAL EASY

While Arden Hills was becoming a swimming powerhouse, the swimmers' former teammate, Mark Spitz, was quickly developing into one of America's greatest swimmers at the Santa Clara Swim Club. In 1965, he got his first taste of international competition at the Maccabiah Games in Tel Aviv, Israel, winning four gold medals, and was named the most outstanding athlete.[1] He would later say that his success in Israel gave him an important shot of confidence as he first began to feel the pressure of intense competition.

On June 25, 1967, Spitz, just seventeen, set his first world record in the 400-meter freestyle at the San Leandro relays. The race was the first time Spitz competed in a meet against Don Schollander, who, three years after his dazzling success in the Tokyo Olympics, was viewed by many as the top swimmer in the world. Spitz opened strong and established an early lead, expanding it after two laps and widening it to almost three body lengths ahead of the field, finishing easily and eclipsing Schollander's world record by half a second. The accomplishment was highlighted in a brief Associated Press story that quoted him saying, "It felt real easy."[2] It was the first of seven world records Spitz would set that summer, and the press began anointing him the world's next great swimmer. As Spitz continued to set world records that summer, Santa Clara coach George Haines told the press that one day Spitz would be the greatest swimmer in the world, a statement Schollander did not appreciate. Schollander had recently returned to California after his spring term at Yale, where the college swimming season was short, and his reduced training schedule meant he was not in top shape. Schollander began to worry about the possibility that he was no longer the best swimmer in the world and wondered if Haines still believed in him. He was twenty-one, and people were already calling him the old man of swimming. He said he "worried about having a competitor as good as Mark Spitz. Already people were talking about whether Spitz would win more gold medals than I had won in 1964—and the 1968 Olympics were still more than a year away."[3]

The events of 1967 would go a long way toward determining which athletes would represent the United States in the Olympic games in Mexico City the following year. The Arden Hills swimmers would be tested repeatedly in regional and national AAU events that season. Then, if they made the U.S. team, they faced international competition at the Pan American Games in Winnipeg, Manitoba. The feeling was if the American team did well in Canada, Chavoor would be in a prime position to be named an Olympic coach.

The year 1967 gave birth to a new creature on the North American continent: the long-haired, sometimes bearded hippie. Enjoying marijuana, engaging in free sex, dressing in headbands and multicolored loose-fitting clothes, and often going shoeless, their mantra of "if it feels good, do it" ran counter to everything Chavoor taught and his "nuts" practiced.[4] One of the big moments of the movement came in San Francisco, just an hour and a half from Sacramento, during the legendary "Summer of Love." Pop culture icon Timothy Leary spoke at the Human Be-In, a gathering of thirty thousand young people in Golden Gate Park, and urged them to "turn on, tune in, and drop out. Drop out of high school, drop out of college, drop out of graduate school."[5] He left swimming off his list of things to drop out from. But the swimmers were mainly conservative, and Leary's message failed to penetrate their world. Chavoor's swimmers weren't tuning out of anything; they were diving into swimming harder than ever. For them, the summer of 1967 would be one of long days, hard work, discipline, and unprecedented success.

Mike Burton began the year winning races for UCLA. In March, the five-foot-nine Burton beat Greg Buckingham (who was six-foot-four) of Stanford in the 1,650-yard NCAA swimming championships, setting the U.S. and NCAA records. Once school was out, Burton headed back to rejoin the team at Arden Hills. Then the boys headed to Dallas for the Men's AAU Indoor Swimming Championships in April. Again, Burton was the star of the meet, winning the 1,650-yard and the 500-yard freestyle races in record time.

In early 1967, Debbie Meyer began repeatedly setting records in the distance races. She started her run in January in a meet in the old YMCA pool in Sacramento, taking 22 seconds off the American record in the 1,650-yard freestyle. Chavoor's confidence in her was growing every day. He concluded that no swimmer in history could compare to Meyer at her age. Don Bloom of the *Sacramento Bee* made a bold speculation: "Next year, you might be reading about a fifteen-year-old [She would actually turn sixteen just before the games.—*Ed.*] Olympic Games gold medalist being nominated for the Sullivan Award. Debbie Meyer is that great."[6] Meyer broke records in February and then again in March at the Southern California Invitational Championships.

The girls' stunning performances the next month at the National AAU Women's Indoor Swimming Championships in Ohio left the press wondering what Chavoor was feeding them to fuel such excellence. Making no mention of peanut butter, Meyer declared she was fueled by "wheat germ, iron and vitamin C, taken two times a day." Facing the best swimmers in the nation in the 1,650-yard freestyle, Meyer followed Chavoor's standard advice and went out fast, lapping Sharon Finnerman, the twenty-one-year-old world record holder, at the halfway mark. She shattered the U.S. record by an astounding 32.8 seconds, knowing she had set a world record because she was "dead tired on the last six laps."[7] Sue Pedersen set a U.S. record for the 400-yard individual medley and cried tears of joy in the pool. Chavoor confidently told a reporter that Pedersen was headed for the Olympic games.[8] Excitement grew in Sacramento, but the only way fans could watch the event on television was a week later when *ABC's Wide World of Sports* broadcast some recorded highlights of the action.[9]

The performances were so scintillating they moved the *Sacramento Bee*'s editorial board to issue a paean about Sacramento's kid swimmers:

> They could refer to Sacramento as the City of Champions—swimming, that is—thanks to Debbie Meyer, Susan Pedersen and Mike Burton. Sacramento is immensely proud of these young champions. There is no question that Debbie, Susan and Mike, all products of the Arden Hills Swim Club and tutored by Coach Sherman Chavoor, will fare well in the summer Pan-American games in Canada and chances are all three may make the 1968 Olympic Games in Mexico City. Wherever they go they take Sacramento's name with them. They do honor to the city, their club and their families.[10]

The *Bee*'s rosy forecast no doubt cheered readers and left them with hearts full of hope and pride. But it somehow left off mentioning John Ferris, who was determined to knock Spitz off as the top butterflyer in the world. He shocked everyone when he shattered Spitz's world record in the 200-meter fly at the World University Games in Tokyo, only to see Spitz reclaim the record a month later in West Berlin. Ferris's efforts had marked him as a strong contender to earn a spot on the Olympic team.[11]

Chavoor and his swimmers next faced competitors from the Americas in the Pan American Games. The U.S. team was vastly superior to its neighbors, although Mexico and Canada had several top swimmers. Arriving in Winnipeg that July, the U.S. swimmers were faced with heaping amounts of food. Tables groaned under piles of chops, roasts, steak, seafood, potatoes, and vegetables. Many swimmers sampled it all. They finished it off with mountains of fruit and ice cream as Canada displayed its agricultural bounty for the world to see and the athletes to eat. The major scandal of the event, causing the Canadians some embarrassment, occurred when a souvenir seeker swiped the flags of sixty nations off the stadium's rim before the opening ceremony. Prince Philip, the dashing forty-six-year-old Duke of Edinburgh, officially opened the games, releasing twenty-five hundred pigeons into the sky as cannons roared and a five-hundred-voice choir sprang into action. Next, the greatest pilots in the Canadian Air Force amazed the twenty-four hundred athletes with a daredevil aerial show. The athletes who craned their necks skyward to watch the performance had to react quickly and cover up to deal with the bombardment from startled pigeons.[12]

The Arden Hills swimmers competed in a new $2.7 million pool that they soon found to their liking, as Meyer took home gold in the 400- and 800-meter freestyle events, with Pedersen finishing second in the 800 meters.[13] Santa Clara's seventeen-year-old Claudia Kolb was the female star of the games, winning three gold medals and a silver medal and establishing herself as one of the world's top swimmers. She had to set a world record in the 400 individual medley to hold off thirteen-year-old Pedersen, who finished second in both the 200- and 400-meter medleys, finishing the meet with three silver medals. Meyer and Pedersen had sparkled in their first international competitions and served notice that they were strong contenders for Olympic Gold.

Mike Burton, the unanimously elected team captain, maintained his domination in the 1,500-meter free, leaving the field far behind in a convincing victory. At the same time, Mark Spitz continued his summer of dominance, winning five gold medals at the Pan American Games and garnering flattering headlines. The rivalry between Spitz and Schollander that had started that spring went public, and the seeds of discord were sown when an Associated Press reporter named Will Grimsley wrote that Spitz was aiming to outdo Schollander's record of four Olympic gold medals. "Sure, I'd like to duplicate Don's four gold medals in the Olympics and go him one better if I could, and if the schedule permits, I could go for six," Spitz was quoted as saying. The reporter further quoted Spitz as saying that

Schollander was "hanging on" and that the rivalry between the two had split the U.S. men's team: "Either you're a pro-Spitz or a pro-Schollander man."[14] Spitz and his father both said Mark never made those comments, but the damage was done.

The story created ill will that would linger with many of the older swimmers who ultimately ended up competing in Mexico City and did not like to see Schollander, a hero to many of them, trashed by a high school kid. Moreover, Spitz's reported comments about how many Olympic gold medals he could win became, in the minds of some rivals and the media, a bold, arrogant prediction. For the next year, news stories said Spitz had "predicted" winning five, six, or even seven Olympic gold medals. The stories bothered Schollander, whose concerns about being surpassed by Spitz grew more prominent in his mind.[15]

The predictions and growing expectations also put tremendous pressure on Spitz. Publicly, he remained so confident of victory that many thought he was arrogant. But he began to worry about the predictions that he would win so many medals, and with Coach Haines's distant demeanor, the teenager believed there was no one he could talk to about his insecurities.[16]

Meyer turned fifteen in August, and the girls headed east to the National Women's AAU swimming championships in Philadelphia. It was a homecoming for Meyer, who had lived her early childhood in the suburb of Haddonfield, New Jersey, a short drive from the championships. She thrilled old friends and the cousins, aunts, and uncles who came to see her set another world record, shattering the 1,500-meter mark by 20.7 seconds and becoming the first female swimmer to break the 18-minute mark, finishing at 17:50.2. That two-tenths of a second rankled her, since she had aimed at breaking the record in 17:50 even. "I'll get it next time," she quipped, flashing a big smile. She had a friendly way of expressing herself that endeared her to people, in contrast to the impression Spitz left with reporters. Meyer's statement "sounded cocky, but it wasn't," Associated Press reporter Ralph Bernstein noted. The *Philadelphia Inquirer* gushed about the hometown girl: "Debbie Meyer is a child of her times—atomic times. She seemingly runs on atomic power, smoothly and swiftly through the water, blowing world records mushroom high."[17] Pedersen finished second, and both girls' performances at the nationals earned them a trip to Europe that fall, where they would join a U.S. team in a series of low-key exhibitions. A few days after the nationals, Chavoor was named head coach of the U.S. Olympic women's swimming team, which he called "his biggest honor in sports." A brief biography said Chavoor was a "pleasant-faced man who coaches swimming as a hobby," had played football at UCLA, and had flown twenty-five missions as a bomber pilot.[18]

In December, the accolades streamed in for Meyer. As many observers expected, *Swimming World* magazine named her female World Swimmer of the Year (an honor that would be repeated the next two years). But people were stunned when the official Soviet Union news agency TASS named her the "World's Outstanding Sportswoman of 1967." Citing a poll of thirteen news agencies worldwide, TASS picked Meyer over a bevy of outstanding athletes, including Billie Jean King, who had won Wimbledon and the U.S. Open that year. During the Cold War rivalry between the Soviet Union and the United States, TASS was likelier to throw brickbats than compliments at U.S. athletes. The Olympics served as a proxy war between the Western nations and Communist Europe as a test of which society was better. Chavoor was less than statesmanlike when he quipped, "This is the first time the Russians have ever been right." Commenting from her sick bed, where she was fighting the flu, Meyer managed a cheery "that's great" when she heard the news.[19] The *Christian Science Monitor*, then a popular and influential national newspaper, found a hopeful message in the Soviet award:

> It is pleasant to read that Tass, which has long been a main vehicle of Communist attack upon the United States, has struck this generous blow for sportsmanship and better international understanding. Debbie is irresistible in any ideology. But Tass's gesture should not be underestimated. It is another step on the long, bumpy, winding, often uneven road of better Soviet relationships with the non-Communist world. In the past, most Russian effort had gone into boosting the image of Soviet athletes. This is welcomed and hopefully will be reciprocated by the American press when great Soviet athletes are concerned.[20]

While better relations with the Soviet Union were welcome, many people were concerned about events in the United States that seemed to be tearing the country apart. The relative peace and calm of the mid-1960s turned into a violent nightmare. In 1968, the assassinations of Dr. Martin Luther King Jr. and Senator Robert F. Kennedy shocked the nation. In the aftermath of King's assassination, the country was engulfed in chaos as a wave of urban riots erupted in more than 120 cities.[21]

But for Arden Hills' swimmers, 1968 was the year they had dreamed of for most of their lives. This was the year they left behind the club swimming pools and regional swim meets and were thrust onto the bright global stage in Mexico City, where years of dedication and self-denial would be recognized and rewarded. The point of all the hard work, expense, self-sacrifice, and dedication by the swimmers and their families was to make it to the Olympics. Gone were the friendly Junior Olympics and low-pressure dual meets. The ribbons, records, and titles they had already won were just so much bric-a-brac.

Of course, with fame came a certain strange call to civic duty. Thus, one of the year's first Olympic-related events was a benefit luncheon at Arden Hills featuring Meyer and Pedersen parading the latest clothing styles while John Ferris and Mike Burton served as escorts. The luncheon was optimistically called "Olé Olympics," as many club members looked forward to watching their swimmers compete in Mexico City.[22]

At the start of the year, it was clear that Arden Hills had several swimmers with legitimate chances of winning Olympic gold medals. Seventeen-year-old Mark Shelley was making great strides in the 1,500 meters. Sue Pedersen, a fourteen-year-old freshman at Rio American High School, was strong in the freestyle and individual medley. Mike Burton was a twenty-one-year-old undergraduate at UCLA and the favorite in the 400- and 1,500-meter races. Debbie Meyer was a fifteen-year-old junior at Rio Americano; already her winning personality and record-smashing exploits had made her so famous that accomplished swimmers from around the world, male and female, were flocking to Arden Hills to train in hopes the magic would rub off on them. John Ferris had set the world record in the 200-meter butterfly. A twenty-year-old sophomore at Stanford, Ferris had spent much of his life in the shadow of Mark Spitz, whom he had competed with since he was nine. Their battle to be the top butterflyer in the world would be waged across the nation and would not be settled until they faced off in the Olympic pool in October.

Even though Spitz had left Arden Hills and joined the Santa Clara Swim Club, he and his father had stayed in close contact with Chavoor. As problems developed between Spitz and Haines, Spitz and his father came to increasingly rely on Chavoor's counsel. The relationship became further complicated when Chavoor was named head coach of the women's Olympic team and Haines the coach of the men's team. It seemed a recipe for baked-in conflict in Mexico City.[23]

Managing the swimmers' schedules required detailed planning. The essential meets of the season provided a road map to the Olympics, each meet presenting a different set of challenges. The road to Mexico City was lined with a gauntlet of stiff tests that would challenge the mental and physical mettle of the competitors. Putting the athletes through the fire of competition was the characteristically American way of picking a team.

Many other nations selected their top hopefuls and sequestered them in training for a year, avoiding the travel and rigor of competition. The U.S. swimmers would fight it out head-to-head for an exhausting nine months before they finally settled matters in the Olympic trials.

Chavoor's concern for every mental and physical detail of his athletes was a crucial factor in his swimmers' success. In the enormous pressure of the year, his close observation of the relationship between their personal lives and their performance in the pool became a unique advantage. When he sensed his swimmers were having emotional problems, Chavoor swung into action, tapping his vast network of contacts to find solutions. The pressure of the Olympics would elevate issues to gigantic proportions, every roadblock becoming a massive wall of fear the swimmers struggled to overcome. He managed his swimmers' rivalries and relationships with their parents and with U.S., Mexican, and Olympic officials while leading them across the country and into Mexico. Meals had to be planned, hotel rooms booked near practice pools, and training time secured. Chavoor had little regard for U.S. Olympic Committee volunteers and fought with them over the quality of the team's lodgings, the water temperature in the pools, and even the seat assignments on their flights. Chavoor would need to use all his resources and his bag of psychological tricks to navigate through the year and turn them into Olympic champions.

Competitive swimming at the highest level involves a tiny group of people in intense competition for gold medals. At the start of the year, Chavoor assembled his swimmers and preached total discipline. He told them that one drink, one cigarette, or a few skipped practices could cost a swimmer a gold medal. For a year, the swimmers would spend hours each day swimming with their heads underwater, existing in a world of physical pain and psychological tedium. Chavoor called the swimming pool the "50-meter jungle." In that hostile environment, they would confront one another in Darwinian combat, with winners and losers separated by tenths and hundredths of a second.

Psychological tactics would be used to the fullest. Swimmers would try to psych themselves up while trying to psych competitors out. They mentally beat on their rivals, trying to shatter their opponents' self-confidence. Don Schollander said that once the top swimmers in the world enter the pool, "they are so nearly equal in ability that mere ability is no longer the deciding factor. A race is won on psychology and very often by psyching out a competitor long before the race." He believed winning was twenty percent physical and eighty percent psychological.[24] Chavoor was an avid participant in the psych-ops charade. As competitors lined up poolside before a race, he would loudly announce how great his swimmers had been training and then make an outrageous and false claim about how fast they were going. Chavoor said this caused their competitors to lose hope and go into the water defeated and aiming at finishing second. Chavoor recalled when Meyer and Pedersen sat on either side of a rival and stared her down for fifteen minutes before a race.[25] Vicky King, a world-class swimmer who moved from St. Louis to train at Arden Hills, described Meyer's method as they waited for a race to start: "Debbie Meyer, my most formidable opponent and teammate, leaned against a post during the national anthem. She was trying to psych me out, and I knew it. The idea of her leaning against a post while I was standing was supposed to make me feel tired. It worked. It reminded me of how tired I really was."[26]

Every emotion was disguised, a carefully rehearsed masquerade. Injuries were covered up so that opponents did not learn of them and use them as a weapon. If they found out someone was hurt, they said, "Too bad you pulled a muscle in your leg, and there's no way you'll be able to kick as hard as you usually do." Swimmers tried never to allow opponents to see them flinch or appear to doubt themselves. They practiced appearing to look unconcerned, uncaring, and inattentive, like the whole thing was in the bag and all they had to do was show up to win. Meyer sometimes casually arrived moments before a race, and if she didn't have time to get wet, she would deliberately false start, taking a stern glare from the starter and the other kids on the blocks. She would yawn and act bored. She would announce that she didn't need to warm up, never disclosing that she had gotten her practice laps in at another pool. Then she would crush them in the race, knocking their confidence back even more. Her rivals knew that the appearance she presented to the world as the perfect kid, cute and cuddly, was a mirage. They knew her for what she was in the water: a competitive killer.

10

THE GAUNTLET

For the Arden Hills women, 1968 began with a low-key January meet in the Sacramento YMCA pool. Anyone with the fifty-cent admission fee could watch these top swimmers as they breezed to five gold medals in an easy, relaxed manner. But soon, the competition ratcheted up, and Sue Pedersen and Debbie Meyer were swapping wins and records. In February, Pedersen beat her "sensational" teammate Meyer in the Northern California AAU Invitational in San Francisco, setting the American record in the 500-yard freestyle. Pedersen also won the 100-yard free at the meet, while Meyer broke the American record in the 1,650-yard freestyle. Rival Claudia Kolb of Santa Clara, approaching her swimming prime, bested her U.S. record in the 200-yard individual medley.

But Chavoor thought Meyer was not performing up to her potential. "She was not improving in her best events, the 500 and 1,650," and her time in the 100-yard free fell by an inexplicable three full seconds.[1] Chavoor investigated and learned that the reason for her declining performance was Meyer's concerns about new gender tests the International Olympic Committee was imposing on female athletes: "She went through an agonizing experience for a sensitive young girl of sixteen. For a while at Arden Hills, early in 1968, she thought she was a man." Chavoor noted that "on the surface, Debbie had developed early as a woman, and she had a big bust at fourteen."[2] But as she approached her sixteenth birthday, she had not menstruated. Assurances that some girls naturally began menstruating later than others did not assuage her. Her imagination receded into fear, and she was sure she would be judged to be male. Years later, Meyer remembered it as "a very funny" story: "I was nervous about passing the gender test because I hadn't started menstruating. I got worried I wouldn't pass the test because I didn't know what it involved. To put me at ease, [Chavoor] said,

69

'Debbie, I'll get you tested now [in the spring of 1968, half a year ahead of the Games].'"[3] "She was in a terrible mental state," Chavoor said, "and it was affecting her performance." In his mode as "fixer," Chavoor talked with Meyer's father, and they decided to seek out a genetic specialist and have a genetic test conducted. Chavoor apparently did not want Meyer to know he had arranged the test—or know that she was being tested at all. When the test came back showing "she's all woman," Chavoor said he had to handle the situation delicately and not embarrass her. "I went out to the pool and played it dumb. I said, 'Hey, Debbie, some doctor called and said your chromosomes are all right. What's that all about?'" Meyer never acknowledged the question but "turned red and swam like hell."[4]

Meyer was back in form in April 1968 as the indoor season drew to a close at the Women's Short Course Championships in Pittsburgh. Meyer won three championships in three events, all in U.S. record time. And she still wasn't satisfied. She had held the record in the 1,650-yard freestyle for a year and obliterated it by almost 34 seconds. But she was disappointed that she missed finishing under the magic seventeen-minute mark by 4.4 seconds. "I'm sort of disappointed, but I'm sure if I work real hard, I'll break 17," she told awestruck reporters.[5] Earlier in the meet, she won the 200- and 500-yard freestyle races and was drawing accolades like "amazing" and "stunning." She was obliterating the competition. She explained the keys to her success: not wasting time on boys, logging twelve thousand yards a day in the pool, and devoting her life to her sport. Chavoor figured she would make the Olympic team unless she broke a leg or came down with pneumonia. Vicky King of Arden Hills finished second in the 1,650 and was getting better as the year progressed. Sue Pedersen was still in grade school but battled older, stronger opponents to finish second in the individual medley events and the 100-yard free.[6]

July was a critical month with two major events: the Santa Clara International Invitational Swimming and Diving Meet and the Los Angeles Invitational. The Santa Clara meet drew many worldwide Olympic contenders who wanted to measure up against the U.S. swimmers before they met them in the Olympics. The Los Angeles Invitational was held later in the month, the final tune-up leading to the Olympic trials in late August. Each meet would be a delicate balancing act for the swimmers, who wanted to build speed and strength but not peak too early for the trials.

The Mexican swim team chose Santa Clara as the spot to put the world on notice that they would be a serious Olympic threat. Guillermo Echevarría was a veteran distance swimmer who had competed in the 1964 Olympic Games. He was favored by many to contend for gold in the

1,500 meters. Swimming experts thought he had a considerable advantage in the race since he lived and trained in Mexico City's altitude of seventy-two hundred feet. The effect of the high elevation played on the minds of athletes and coaches around the world, since no international event had ever been held at such heights. Many wondered what effect the altitude would have on the athletes, especially those competing in distance events. Mike Burton was clearly the world's best distance swimmer. Chavoor was concerned that Burton was developing an obsession about how the altitude would affect his swimming. In May, he temporarily induced Burton to drop out of UCLA and sent him to train at the mile-high U.S. Air Force Academy to experience the impact altitude would have on his body. While Chavoor knew there were physiological changes between performances at sea level and seven thousand feet, he felt the psychological impact on Burton was just as important. But Chavoor had added to Burton's insecurity. Chavoor was so proud of his coaching techniques that he often shared them freely with instructors throughout the world. During the 1967 Pan American Games in Winnipeg, Chavoor provided Echevarría's coach, Ron Johnson, with tips on swimming the 1,500, a move he later regretted. Johnson was a successful American coach who was Mexico's head coach for the 1968 and 1972 Olympic Games. He was very familiar with Burton's strengths and weaknesses,[7] and he used the tips from Chavoor to dramatically boost Echevarría's performances, which had significantly improved when he showed up in Santa Clara to challenge Burton in the 1,500.

Early in the race, the two slowly pulled ahead of the other swimmers as it became a two-man race. At first, Echevarría conserved his energy and just wanted to keep up with Burton. But at the 800-meter mark, the Mexican surged ahead. He finished with a fourteen-lap kick, leaving Burton "fading badly in his wake," to win in convincing fashion. Echevarría also placed second by a half-stroke to Spitz in the 400-meter freestyle. His teammate Felipe Muñoz also impressed, winning the 200-meter breaststroke. As the press raised the alarm that U.S. swimming would be seriously challenged in Mexico City, Olympic coach George Haines saw the Mexicans' victories as an ominous portent. "I don't think there's any question that Echevarría is the favorite in the 400 and 1,500, and it'll be next to impossible to beat him in Mexico. It was a real shot in the arm for him to beat Burton at sea level," Haines said.[8] Schollander went even further in his praise for Echevarría, asserting that the Mexican's victory proved a point. "Now we know he's good, but we know too he'll be even better at Mexico City's altitude. I'm predicting right now he'll beat Mike Burton in the 1500," he proclaimed to the press.[9]

As Burton's anxiety soared, Chavoor's concern deepened. Perhaps discounting his role in boosting Echevarría's physical improvement, Chavoor said that Burton would lose if his "altitude phobia" continued. Mexico had never medaled in swimming, and the country was infected with a high dose of Olympic fever. A gold medal in swimming was Mexico's dream, and that dream looked like it was on the brink of reality. Now Echevarría had to deal with the pressure of his nation's expectations. He knew Burton would not rest a day in his quest for gold medals, and in the 109 days before they met in the 1,500-meter Olympic final, Mike Burton would spend as much time as he could churning away in the high-altitude U.S. Air Force swimming pool in Colorado Springs. There was no doubt he would be ready for Echevarría and Mexico City's altitude.

The Santa Clara International was also the site of one of the more bizarre events in the annals of U.S. swimming. Once again facing Claudia Kolb, who had not lost to anyone since Sue Pedersen had beaten her two years earlier, Pedersen set a world record in the 200-meter individual medley. In doing so, she accomplished a miracle, setting the world record—and finishing second in the race. The timers showed the results; Pedersen finished in 2:25.0, Kolb at 2:25.1, a tenth of a second behind. But the place judge, relying on his eyes, ruled that Kolb had touched out first, even though the stopwatches all showed Pedersen had finished faster. As fate would have it, a chap named Willam Lippman, chairman of the U.S. Olympic Committee's men's swimming team, happened to be at the meet. As the crowd buzzed, wondering at what they had just witnessed, Lippman grabbed the rule book and helpfully explained that "under international rules, when the second finisher [Pedersen] has a faster time than the first [Kolb], then the time must be adjusted and given to the first-place finisher [Kolb]." The three human timers had three different times. But a timing machine called "the mechanical clock" had Pedersen at 2:25.1, a dead heat with Kolb. When it was all settled, Kolb was declared the winner by an eyelash. Pedersen had no time to ponder events or be disappointed, as she was immediately thrust onto the pool deck to swim the first leg of the 800-meter free relay. Undismayed, she set another world record in the 200-meter freestyle, pacing the Arden Hills girls to victory and the world record in the relay. The press had a field day. "Miss Pedersen had one world record taken away from her, and almost before she knew it, she got another one," the *Oakland Tribune* reported, calling it "a hectic half hour."[10] Asked if she was angry about losing the record, the always calm Pedersen told the reporters she was "more tired than upset." One official succinctly explained the conundrum while unconsciously commenting on the farce: "We're trying to eliminate the human element," he said, "but you can't as long as you deal with people." Pedersen added a win in the 100-meter free in one-minute flat and predicted she would lower that mark to 0.58 at the Olympics, a time most experts thought would be rewarded with a gold medal.[11]

The Santa Clara Swim Club did not enter the Los Angeles Invitational that year, but Arden Hills was there in full force. Meyer, battling bursitis in her left arm, broke world records in the 800- and 1,500-meter freestyle. Unfortunately, media attention in a busy Olympic year was distracted, and her incredible feats were missed by many. Still, *Swimming World* put her epic achievement into the context it deserved: "Debbie Meyer displayed one of the greatest athletic achievements ever by a woman when she demolished the world marks for the 800- and 1,500-meter freestyle. Her time for the 1500 (17:31.2) was so fast that few men in the world would have been able to stay with her," the magazine proclaimed.[12]

As August began, Chavoor and his crew headed to the humid plains of Lincoln, Nebraska, and the AAU Long Course National Championships at the Woods Park Pool. Nebraska officials had waged a successful lobbying campaign to land the championships, overcoming the objections of AAU officer Jack Kelly, a former Olympian and brother of the beautiful Grace Kelly, princess of Monaco, one of the most famous actresses of all time. Jack Kelly, a Philadelphian, claimed few fans would travel to Nebraska, that "Godforsaken country," to watch the national championships.[13]

Chavoor took seventeen Arden Hills swimmers to Lincoln. In addition to the kids he had trained for years, there were two veteran swimmers who spent the summer at Arden Hills under Chavoor's demanding gaze, looking for every advantage in their battles to win gold. They were former Olympians John Nelson, a twenty-year-old Yale University student who had won a silver medal in the 1500-meter event in the Tokyo Olympics, and Erika Bricker, a nineteen-year-old from the San Joaquin Valley who had competed at Tokyo on a 400-meter freestyle relay team.

Most intriguing of all was Vicky King, a promising fourteen-year-old distance swimmer from St. Louis. She had first tried to get on the Santa Clara team but was rejected by George Haines, who thought that at four-foot-ten and ninety pounds, she was too small to be a world-class swimmer. She then tried Chavoor, and he sensed her ultracompetitive persona and saw that she possessed the attribute he most valued in his swimmers: guts. He liked her so much that he invited her to live with his family. Like most swimmers new to Arden Hills, Vicky was agog at the number of laps the team was swimming. She thought she was in good shape when she showed up and was dismayed by how far behind she was. But like Debbie Meyer and Mike Burton before her, she dug in and improved rapidly. She soon earned that most valued Chavoor sobriquet: "nut." Despite her small stature, she established herself as a contender in distance events.[14]

With numerous world record contenders for national championships, the national media seemed to suddenly understand that U.S. swimming was enjoying a banner year that would most likely result in a bonanza of Olympic gold medals. As a result, media contingents, including *ABC's Wide World of Sports*, the marquee television sports program of the era, descended on Lincoln to bring viewers "the thrill of victory and the agony of defeat" at the national championships.

As the athletes arrived, summer thunderstorms rocked the humid plains in an unnerving spectacle for the Californians, who had seldom seen such violent weather. Sue Pedersen got a jolt shortly after she arrived when a lightning bolt hit the rental car she was riding in and left a dent in the door. Chavoor found the venue uninviting. He didn't like the thunder and lightning; the city pool was unheated, the water "freezing"; and the swimmer's lips turned blue as they shivered through postrace media interviews.[15]

The electrical storms were a portent of a meet that featured exciting races, a dramatic and historic changing of the guard in men's swimming, and a brash prediction that would affect the men's Olympic swimming teams for the next two Olympiads. The Arden Hills swimmers faced their individual ghosts. Burton was challenged by Echevarría once again in the 1,500 meters. Pedersen had to contend with Claudia Kolb, now recognized as the greatest women's swimmer in the world. Ferris was still intent on beating Spitz, a considerable task considering Spitz was peaking and seemingly on the brink of world domination and threatening to depose Schollander as the top U.S. swimmer. Meyer seemed unchallenged and confident, a sure shot for national championships, world records, and a berth on the Olympic team.

Meyer and Pedersen went head-to-head in the 400-meter freestyle, as they had so many times before. "Debbie stood cool at the back of the starting block, her close-cropped hair falling softly over her forehead and her hands at parade rest behind her back," *Sports Illustrated* observed.[16] In a psych-out role reversal, "Sue arrived late. She was off talking with some friends somewhere and had to be collected for the race by one of the officials," the magazine reported. Actually, Pedersen wasn't trying to psych anyone out; she was getting a back massage from one of the coaches as she limbered up for the race.[17] It was their usual close race, with Meyer pulling ahead on the last lap, setting a world record time, with Pedersen just a stroke behind her. Meyer went on to win the 1,500 meters, setting a world 800-meter mark along the way. Few noticed that new Arden Hills star Vicky King finished in second place, joining Meyer as the only women at that time to finish under eighteen minutes. Facing a tremendous challenge, Pedersen beat world record holder Claudia Kolb in the 400-meter medley, and Claudia, "a competitor of acknowledged great heart," beat Pedersen by a long hand touch in the 200-meter individual medley. The press noticed Pedersen's emerging challenge: "[Kolb] has generally been considered the best all-round swimmer in the world, but it is a crown that Sue is now laying claim to, jewel by jewel." Pedersen would keep accumulating those jewels as she approached the Olympic Games.[18] Chavoor's women completed an outstanding meet when Meyer and Pedersen joined Vicky King and Linda Williams to claim the national championship in the 800-meter freestyle relay and setting the world record.[19]

Much of the pre-meet buildup centered around the men's 1,500-meter freestyle rematch, where Burton once again encountered Echevarría. While Burton and Echevarría focused on each other, fifteen-year-old John Kinsella of Hinsdale, Illinois, was mounting a more-than-serious challenge to the favorites. As usual, Burton went out as fast as he could, hoping to leave Echevarría in his wake. And for most of the race, it seemed Burton would win in comfortable fashion. But the determined Mexican steadily closed the gap, and he and Burton were engaged in a side-by-side duel as they approached the last lap. Young Kinsella was content just to stay close to the leaders, but as he turned into the final 50 meters, Kinsella was startled to see that he was close enough to win. He was strong and surging and felt he had enough strength left for a closing kick to win the championship. Burton, focusing on Echevarría, was jolted when he noticed that Kinsella, in far-away lane eight, was surging toward the finish. "Never in anyone's memory had such a long race been so close," the *Lincoln Journal-Star* reported as Kinsella slipped past Echevarría and drew even with Burton in the final few meters.

The fans stood as one and roared like they were cheering a goal line stand at a Nebraska Cornhuskers football game, straining to see the finish obscured by the spray from flashing arms, splashing water, and churning wakes. Past pain, his body numb, straining with every muscle in his body, and exhausted after pulling through a mile of cold water, Burton made a last, desperate arm thrust toward the wall. The timers strained to look through the spray and clicked stopwatches. Burton looked up at the clock, thinking he had finished first, but he couldn't be sure. Would the same thing happen to him that had happened to Pedersen in Santa Clara, where she had set a world record yet lost the race? The Nebraskans buzzed with excitement as the officials caucused to determine the U.S. national champion. Suddenly the officials broke their huddle and pointed to the swimmers.

Mike Burton thrust his right arm in the air with his fingers three inches apart, signifying the length of his victory over young Kinsella. Chavoor enthused that it was "the greatest race I've ever seen. Mike and John Kinsella of Illinois were only inches apart at the finish. That's incredible for 1,500 meters."[20] Echevarría, exhausted in the last twenty meters, had fallen behind but still finished a close third.[21] Burton won, but many thought Echevarría's performance proved he was still the favorite to win in the Olympics. After all, the Mexican star had almost won while swimming at sea level, in cold water, on American soil and in American water, with American fans rooting their countrymen on. When he was back at his accustomed altitude in Mexico City, with Mexico's fans behind him, pushing him on with wild cheering, certainly he would beat Burton and the U.S. swimmers and bring gold to Mexico. All of Mexico believed in him and began counting the medal as their own. But as Echevarría drifted in the water while his tense muscles relaxed after the stress of the race, his coach, Ron Johnson, began wondering if they had pursued the right strategy by competing in the U.S. national championship.

The Mexican team had received a big psychological boost from the Santa Clara meet. They could have spent their time honing their advantage by training at altitude in their home pool, not getting worn down traveling and competing. As soon as he could, Johnson got the Mexican team back to the altitude at Mexico City. John Ferris suffered a disheartening loss when Spitz beat him in the event at the nationals. Spitz was established as one of the great butterfly swimmers in the world, but he faced a crucial challenge in the 200-meter free. His Santa Clara teammate and nemesis Don Schollander was standing in his way. Now Spitz, the eighteen-year-old "glamour boy" and rising star, was challenging the twenty-two-year-old legend on the national stage.

In a newspaper photo taken before their race, Spitz and Schollander are standing next to each other in the pool, smiling broadly while looking up at their coach, George Haines, perched on the pool deck. It's the very image of comradeship and tranquility that belied the tension that the trio had dealt with the past two years.[22] Reporters were writing that Spitz was poised to replace Schollander as the new king of world swimming. Adding to the tension was the fact that they were facing off in the national championship. Haines always tried to keep the two from competing head-to-head in major meets because he felt that a meeting would help neither.[23] Chavoor thought it was possible that if Spitz won that day, Schollander might quit swimming. Schollander joked that "some of the guys already call me 'the old man'" and said he clearly would be finished after the Olympics. But he still worked out hard every day and had not lost in the 200 meters in six years. "I feel as strong as ever," he said.[24] The rivalry was termed friendly but fierce, and many thought Schollander would win but Spitz would push him to a new world record.

The race itself turned out to be anticlimactic. Both swimmers went out slowly, eyeing each other for the first 50 meters. They were so focused on each other that they didn't notice a third swimmer in the far lane keeping even with them. Schollander's foot slipped on the wall as he made the turn at 100 meters, and Spitz pulled away from him but had no idea a third swimmer was in contention. When he finally realized what was happening, Spitz had to make a desperate surge and won the race, while Schollander finished a stunning fourth. Even though it was Schollander's first defeat in the 200 outdoor, he said he was not discouraged by the result.[25] His only concern was winning in the Olympics, and he had plenty of time to round into shape. The race had been so slow that Schollander's previously set world record still stood by a full two seconds.[26]

Haines was upset with his swimmers for not going out fast to start the race. "It was a good training race," Haines said sarcastically. "It was good for Mark because he is young and hungry, and it's good for Don because I think he needs a kick in the tail to work harder."[27] Despite the disappointing times, the press hailed the race as signaling the end of an era: "Spitz Sinks Schollander,"[28] one headline proclaimed, while another heralded, "Schollander's Reign Ends."[29] For *Sports Illustrated*, it was a "revolt of the palace guard" as the old order, represented by Schollander, fell to the next generation.

The psychological war that emerged was much more important than the race result itself. The battle that had started at the Pan American Games the year before was reignited. Spitz reportedly proclaimed he was going after five gold medals (later, some said he had predicted winning six or seven) in Mexico City. "The chances are I'll be able to make all three relay teams and the 100- and 200-meter butterfly events at Mexico," he said. The stories noted that such an accomplishment would surpass the four Olympic gold medals Schollander won in 1964. When asked if Spitz could win that many medals, Schollander agreed that he could. But he sought to downplay the importance of it. "Multiple medal winners won't be so rare at this Olympics because there are so many more events now," he explained. After saying he had been a bit out of shape for the Spitz race, Schollander matter-of-factly said he felt he could win the 200 free, three relays, and the 100 free and take home five gold medals himself.[30] Spitz countered, saying he was not in top shape and could go a lot faster in the Olympics. Picking up on the verbal exchange and the rumor mill that inevitably swirls in such hothouse events, the newspapers reported that "both men deny any idea of a personal vendetta." Haines said he was not trying to play them off against each other to stoke the rivalry, although it was clear to anyone who could look and listen that the feud was burning bright and hot.[31] Publicly, the friendly but fierce competitors spin held as the event ended, and the Californians left the thunderstorms behind and headed toward home and the calm, bright, blue Pacific.

The Arden Hills team arrived in Sacramento before the sun rose, tired but giddy from victory. Chavoor was "the man who most enjoyed the outcome," the *Sacramento Bee* reported. His charges had performed well, and they were coming home holding world records in five events, more world records than most nations held.[32] In the cool darkness of the predawn August morning, Chavoor told his team he was canceling the scheduled 9 a.m. practice later that morning. When news leaked out to the Sacramento press corps, they heaped faux outrage on the coach, accusing him of going soft on his swimmers and jokingly coming up with a list of imagined excuses for canceling future practices. Of course, they did this knowing Chavoor had a reputation for imposing torture on his swimmers that would have made the ancient Spartans look like marsh-mallows. Practices resumed that afternoon, and the Arden Hills swimmers returned to their familiar routine of sleeping, eating, and swimming. They were now ready for the Olympic trials, and no force on earth would get in the way of their preparations.[33]

Since Arden Hills had only twenty-five-meter pools, Chavoor trained his Olympians in the fifty-meter Olympic-size pool at the Corona Fitness Institute in rural Sacramento County. Unfortunately, the pool was an inviting target for critters in the area. Every morning Chavoor grabbed a hammer and assaulted gophers, snakes, and muskrats inhabit-ing the pool. Sue Pedersen sunk to the bottom to avoid witnessing the bloodshed. "Sherm is really horrible to those little gophers," Meyer remarked. "All that gore. Eech."[34]

In August, as the swimmers prepared for the Olympic trials in southern California, a *Sports Illustrated* reporter journeyed to "Sacramento's muddy waters" and found Meyer and Pedersen unaware of the seismic world events of the time. "It is an Olympic year, and all these girls are too young to have even known any other Olympics. From the time they first splashed through a race, this is the one thing, the one year, they have been after," reporter Richard Rollins wrote. He took some shine off the Golden State when he noted that California was a place where "the hot winds blow, and the divorce rate far exceeds the national, where one person in 38 lives in a trailer." The reporter thought Meyer and Pedersen were sheltered from the realities of the world, writing, "For the girls, there are only the blue pools filled season into season. Their hair is bleached by the chlorine and scorched by the sun into strands of gold tinsel, while their deep-brown bodies still carry reminders of baby fat. Swimming is their life, and they are unconscious of all but its demands." Meyer confirmed the story's thesis: "Gold medals," she sagely assured the reporter, "are the real reward in my line of work."[35]

In 1968, six women's swimming events were added to the Olympic competition: the 100 breast, 200 free, 800 free, 200 backstroke, 200 fly, and 200 individual medley. As coach of the U.S. Olympic women's team, Chavoor had considerable latitude in deciding which swimmers entered which events, the most challenging job for any Olympic swimming coach. It was an intricate task that involved considering the race schedule, the swimmers' strengths and weaknesses, and the opponent matchups. Who should swim, and which individual races? What four swimmers would be on each relay team? As the trials in Los Angeles approached, everyone joined in the parlor game of medal counting. As Chavoor saw it, there was no use having Pedersen and Meyer battling head-to-head in the same races. "Two months ago, we put Sue in an international meet at Santa Clara to give her confidence in the 100-meter free. She beat everybody. That's when we decided there's no use Sue and Debbie knocking heads in the 200-, 400-, and 800-meter freestyles," he said.[36]

Meyer was entered in her three world record events, while Pedersen was entered in five events: the 100-meter medley relay, the 100-meter freestyle relay, the 100-meter free, the 200-meter individual medley, and the 400-meter individual medley. She would be up against Claudia Kolb, five years older and one of the top swimmers in the world. Calculating all the factors, Chavoor thought the girls could win at least five gold medals combined, a fantastic haul for two teenagers from one club.

In the run-up to the 1968 Olympics, the gold medal count was an obsession not seen during previous games. The number of medals each nation won was tallied up and printed in newspapers daily. Don Schollander realized that his accomplishment in winning four gold medals in Tokyo had a lot to do with creating gold fever. The modern media machine had made him famous, putting him on magazine covers and making him the guest star of television shows.[37] Now others saw Olympic gold as paving the magic yellow road for themselves. How many gold medals would a nation win? How many gold medals would a swimmer win? And perhaps the most determinative factor in deciding what events the swimmers would race in was how many gold medals the coach thought his swimmers would win. Gold changed coaches' biographies. A coach is not described as coaching a particular school or club, but as the coach of gold medal–winning athletes.

In 1968, Schollander suspected George Haines, the men's Olympic coach, was maneuvering to get Spitz a shot at winning the most gold medals. Schollander felt he was capable of winning multiple gold medals once again but thought Haines's coaching decisions made his quest impossible: "George thought I was finished. The press was saying that Spitz could take five medals—or possibly six—in Mexico. Suddenly it hit me that George wanted very badly to have another four-gold-medal winner (or better) at the Olympics. I felt that George had made his choice; he had written me off; Spitz was a better bet. And the irony of it was that I was the one who had given him the taste of glory."[38]

11

THE AMERICAN GIRLS
WERE READY

A few hundred of the nation's top swimmers headed to the Olympic trials, and only sixty-nine would make the Olympic team. So Debbie Meyer and Mike Burton, among others, were wondering precisely why Southern California locations were chosen for the ultimate test to see who made the Olympic team. It's not that they had anything against the Los Angeles region, even though they were from Northern California. What mystified them was why the trials were held at sea level when the games would be held more than a mile high, at 7,382 feet. For years, the U.S. Olympic Committee had worried about how their athletes would perform at such elevations, so they had arranged for athletes to work out at high altitudes, conducted tests, and tried to figure out training regimens that would help their athletes' bodies best process the thin air. Testing results varied, but it seemed inevitable the high altitude would hamper some athletes' performance.[1] "It's kind of silly, really," Burton said. "They should have had them at altitude in Colorado Springs. We would have been better prepared and ready for the high altitude."[2] The U.S. men's Olympic track team considered the altitude, holding its trials at 7,377 feet in a ski area in the Sierra Nevada.

The men's swimming trials were held in an enormous new building in Long Beach so close to the ocean that waves almost broke against the walls. Standing on the beach and looking up at the imposing building, one swimmer asked a coach what the elevation was. The coach looked around with bafflement, then lay prone on the sand. Then, looking up at the swimmer, the coach said, "Oh, I'd say we're about six inches above sea level."[3]

The women's Olympic trials were first, at the historic Los Angeles Swimming Stadium, a beautiful art deco facility next to the Coliseum, where women's swimming history was made during the 1932 Olympics.

Chavoor had many special memories of the stadium, where his first great swimmers, Tak Iseri and John Stebbins, had competed in the 1949 national championship. Walking into the stadium, Chavoor regaled the press with a nostalgic story: "See that corner way up there? Thirty-six years ago, I sat up in that last row during the 1932 Olympic games. I'll never forget that. I was just a kid [he was twelve]. I sold 75 newspaper subscriptions to get that trip. The Japanese won almost everything. But we did have a few Olympic champions such as Helene Madison and Buster Crabbe."[4]

Helene Madison was the first female swimmer to win three gold medals in a single Olympics, winning the 100-meter freestyle, 400-meter freestyle, and 4 x 100-meter freestyle relay. The "Queen of the Waves," Madison was the first swimmer to hold every women's world freestyle record concurrently, a feat that has been matched only once, by Australian Shane Gould in 1972. Unfortunately, it was a disastrous year for the U.S. men's team, as Japan won five out of six gold medals. While Buster Crabbe's dramatic tenth-of-a-second victory in the 400-meter freestyle salvaged some U.S. pride and launched his movie career with roles as Tarzan and Flash Gordon, it was Madison and the women's team that allowed the United States to tie Japan, five all, in the total swimming gold medal count.[5]

Sacramento had never sent a swimmer to the Olympics, but Chavoor now led seventeen swimmers to the Olympic trials, including four "cinches" to make the Olympic team.[6] It was now time for the Arden Hills women to try to make history, but the intense pressure they faced while waiting for the trials to start took its toll on everyone. For two days after arriving in Los Angeles, they worked out so hard and so well that Chavoor worried they were peaking too soon. "Their sprint work here has been terrific, they haven't looked this good in weeks," he told the press. "I'm about to climb the walls."[7] While coming in first was important, swimmers earned a spot on the team if they finished in one of the top three spots in an event. Sue Pedersen told him that she would go out and swim for third place, just to make the team. "I said no, try and win it, and she said, 'I'm so scared I want to go in a corner and cry, is that all right?' I said no, everybody's scared."[8] Pedersen had good reason to be nervous, for the trials were packed with world record holders and former Olympians. Each had completed a lifetime of training and work that would now be tested as never before. An uneasy night's sleep, a family emergency, a sudden illness, or a slip in the water could be enough to throw them off the pace and cost them one of the twenty-nine slots on the team. Photo-finish races were decided by a bizarre combination of clocks and judges' eyeballs, and in at least one race, a vote was taken to determine the outcome.

In the days before the trials, the big TV cameras rolled in and were placed strategically to get the best camera angles. *ABC's Wide World of Sports* proudly proclaimed it would be broadcasting the trials IN COLOR. The trials were covered by famous announcers Jim McKay, Bill Flemming, and Howard Cosell. AAU officials from around the country arriving as a reward for volunteer work would use the opportunity to attend lavish receptions and parties. Former swimmers, kid swimmers, family members, and friends piled into town. Swimmers worked out, hung around the hotel during the day, and tried to sleep at night. The world fell away into a surreal mash-up of sounds and images as they struggled to shut everything out and focus on the competition. On the day of their races, swimmers were directed through the crowd to the starting blocks, and for some, it felt like they were on the way to their own execution. Seventeen-year-old Vicky King, who would earn a spot as an alternate on the Olympic team, described the emotions coursing through her as she prepared to race:

I sat nervously at the edge of the crowd awaiting the race. The spectators and officials drove me crazy. They were there for a good time, and they certainly were having it. Their gaiety and obnoxious laughter gave the scene the pervading air of a country fair. They neither felt nor cared to feel the underlying tension obsessing the participants. It was just like a horse race to them. I sat there amongst the gibbering fools, infuriated by their insensibility. "We are humans, not horses!" I shouted at them through my thoughts. Gradually I shut them out and turned to my world. I started thinking the same inadequate thoughts that I had come to know. "What am I going to do this time? God, I'm scared. Help me. Please! Is it going to be like last year? Am I going to choke on my own fear? Shit! Stop it! If you are going to think that way, you might as well not even get in the pool. I'm just as good as those other girls. Don't psych yourself out before you start. Just calm down. I can do it. I just have to keep cool." The hour of my event drew nearer. I felt the knocks of insecurity on the back door of my brain. This time a fog of calmness completely encircled me. It didn't matter anymore how I did. As long as I tried my hardest and didn't give up I would be satisfied. But my main objective was no longer the gold. Then it was time. As I headed for the blocks I signaled to my mother. A wave of guilt passed through me. I knew she was thinking of gold even if I was not. I would do my best for her, my father and my coach. I slowly loosened up my arms and turned to smile a plastic smile at the crowd, whom I despised for their detached frivolity.

"Smile at the cameras, Vicky," an official said.

"Isn't it great that ABC is covering the meet? You'll be on TV next week. How exciting. I hope they pan us timers. I told my nephew to watch for me."

At this point, I wanted ABC there as much as I wanted a cramp in my leg.

I gave my competition one last look of hate, which was meant to scare them into psychological depression. I dove into the pool and got out again to wait for the starter's call. A quick glance through the crowd to pick out my mother, father and coach. Then one quick look to size up my opponents. I took one, two deep breaths to hyperventilate, and I shook my muscles again. And then I waited . . . and waited. The starter blew the whistle, and I slowly stepped up on the block.

"Good stroke, keep calm . . ."

The starter called us to our marks.

"God help me now. Please, please . . ."[9]

Such thoughts haunted many a competitor, but Debbie Meyer, who had turned sixteen just ten days before the trials began, was as buoyant and exuberant as ever and had few worries about making the team. When asked how she became such a talented swimmer, she said, "I think I've got the greatest coach."[10] On the eve of the trials, Chavoor convinced her to change her breathing technique. She had a habit of breathing out of her mouth only on her left side, but Chavoor urged her to change that, and she agreed. "I alternated breathing on both sides. I was worried it might throw me off, but it worked good," she said.[11]

The fierce competition drove Meyer to even more incredible performances. First, she set a new world record in the 200-meter freestyle to stave off five competitors who also broke the world record. Then Meyer grabbed her second victory and world record of the trials in the 400-meter free, at 4:24.5, in a race that saw, for the first time in history, eight girls finish under 4:39. Meyer jumped out in front in the first 100 meters and was never threatened.

Meyer was poised for another world record in the 800-meter free, but she would face desperate competition since it was the last event of the trials. Seven girls were in the race; five had not qualified for the Olympic team, including Arden Hills' Vicky King. No matter how desperate the swimmers were, no one could head off Meyer, who sprinted out in the first 100 meters, erasing any doubt about her grabbing another world record. She was 1.5 seconds ahead of her record at the halfway point, leaving the rest of the swimmers far behind, and cruised in at 9:10.

Claudia Kolb, Sue Pedersen's nemesis, kept the pressure on as she lowered her world 400-meter individual medley record by more than a second and beat Pedersen easily. It was a case of inexperience for Pedersen, who said, "I was really out of it. I was so nervous." Her mom gave her a consoling hug after the race. "Don't cry, mother, I'm happy making the team," Pedersen told her. Pedersen reminded her mother that she'd beaten Kolb twice, and her second-place finish gave her another chance to defeat her in Mexico City.[12]

Pedersen and Kolb shared the 200 individual medley world record, and Kolb knew she would have to set a new world record to win, and did so in 2:23.5, with Pedersen in second, at 2:25.45. Pedersen had recovered from her anxiety and let it be known that she desperately wanted a victory in the 100-meter free. To do so, she would have to defeat twenty-one-year-old Jan Henne, the "old lady" of the team. Henne had been a breaststroke champion, winning four gold medals in that stroke in the indoor national championships earlier in the year. It was only in July, a month before the trials, that she switched to freestyle, but she was ready for the 100-meter sprint. In another blistering race, four women finished under a minute for the first time in history. Pedersen took a quick lead and held off Henne's finishing surge to finish a slap ahead at 59 seconds. One reporter was so impressed he wondered if Pedersen could swim without touching the water when she turned eighteen four years later. Pedersen's fans and family swarmed her with congratulations as she broke down in tears of joy and relief in the pool. Chavoor, who had told the press to keep an eye on Pedersen in the future, revised his assessment of his young swimmer. No longer was she just a potential future star; she had already arrived. "That was a great swim," he said. "She's great now."[13] "She'll be in the 100 free, both individual medleys, and anchor on the freestyle and medley relay teams, so you can see there is a possibility of her winning five golds," he told another reporter.[14] She earned the nickname "Baby Sue" and was not only the youngest swimmer but also the only female swimmer who entered five events.[15] *The Bee* noted that not even the infamous Los Angeles smog hindered the girls.

The trials were a triumph for Chavoor, his Arden Hills girls, and the women's swimming team. Many hailed it as the greatest amateur swimming team ever assembled. They held a combined seven world records, and while news reports focused on the swimmers' youth, the Olympic team had three returning Olympic stars and its average age was 16.8 years old, the oldest U.S. Women's Team since 1952. While there were concerns about Mexico City's altitude and how quickly the girls could return to peak condition after the trials, everyone in the world knew the U.S. team would be a dominating force. So as the team packed up to leave, ads began running in swimming magazines under the bold headline "Saludos Mexico." The American girls were ready.[16]

12

CHALK ONE UP FOR THE TALL MEN

Mike Burton, John Ferris, and Mark Shelley were Arden Hills' top male prospects in Long Beach. Burton was the overwhelming favorite in the 1,500, but Ferris would face top competition in the butterfly and individual medleys. At age seventeen, Shelley was thought to be one Olympiad away from making the team.

Forty miles south of Tinseltown, Long Beach lies in the considerable shadow of Los Angeles. The city seized on sports to raise its image, and in the 1960s, went on a building spree to enhance its sports facilities. The town hosted seven Olympic trials, and men's swimming was the effort's centerpiece. The Belmont Plaza Olympic Pool, built for $3.7 million, was completed just in time for the trials, a fantastic modern pool that drew rave reviews from swimmers and fans. The structure was so close to the ocean that people walking out of the building stepped right onto the beach. The Mediterranean California climate allowed the designers to create an open, airy five-story structure with a unique set of roof panels and windows that allowed brilliant shafts of sunlight to stream into the pool. The latest electronic scoreboard, electronic scoring and timing devices, and even an underwater video system provided fans with the ultimate viewing experience. It was another world from the cold Nebraska pool that had hosted the national championships and an epoch apart from the old stadium in Los Angeles where the women's team trials were held the week before. The new facility attracted raucous sold-out crowds who spurred the men to break seven world records and tie another. Much of the pre-event drama centered on Mark Spitz: Fans wondered how many events he would win and if he was ready to knock Don Schollander off as the king of America swimming. But Spitz would face many other rivals who were focusing their efforts on beating *him*.

At age twenty-two, holding a world record, two Pan American Games gold medals, a national championship, and high school and university All-American honors, Doug Russell was a man obsessed with failure. The only distinction he wanted was to be the fastest 100-meter butterfly swimmer in the world. His obsession focused on eighteen-year-old Mark Spitz, who had swiped his world record and beaten him nine consecutive times, all by the slightest of margins, all by sliced-up seconds that pierced his heart on the way to crushing his soul. It wasn't just the defeats Spitz imposed; it was the arrogant way Spitz refused even to acknowledge his existence that enraged Russell. That summer, he broke up with his fiancée, lived in a converted horse stable, worked out day and night, refused to take his mother's phone calls, and shunned his friends as he prepared for the Olympics—or so everyone thought. In reality, he didn't care where the showdown in the 100 fly came: "It could have been in Waxahachie, and it wouldn't have made a bit of difference. It could have been the 100 butterfly in the Brazos River. It didn't make any difference. I wanted to be the world's fastest butterfly."[1] Seeking a psychological advantage, Russell got up early every morning to work out, knowing he was working while Spitz was asleep. Then, late at night, he would get out of bed to do pull-ups, again reminding himself that he was working while Spitz slept.

But it didn't matter. All the effort seemed to run out of him like the sap from a tree when he faced Spitz. It was the same story at the trials. Sprinting from the start, Russell hit the turn barely ahead of Spitz, and the pack then pulled out almost a full body length ahead of Spitz. Russell held the lead with just 25 meters to go as he sprinted to the final wall. With just 10 meters left, Spitz surged and pulled even. Spitz suddenly burst ahead in the last three meters in a dramatic finish. Russell mistimed his strokes and had to take an extra stroke to make the wall. Spitz finished in 55.6 to break his world record in another eyelash victory. "I can't get out any faster," said Spitz of his start. "I knew he was ahead, and I just went after him." Russell realized he'd blown the finish. "I'm not taking anything away from Mark," he said. "I probably wouldn't have beaten him anyway, but I just wish I wasn't a 97-meter butterflyer."[2] As Russell dejectedly left the pool, he was reminded he would get another shot at Spitz in the Olympics. But after another close loss, he searched the dark corners of his memory, searching for the confidence he needed to beat Spitz.

Spitz's boyhood friend and Arden Hills teammate John Ferris's first chance to make the team was in the 400-meter individual medley, where he faced a pool full of world record holders. The top competitor was current world record holder Charlie Hickcox, a shy twenty-one-year-old seven-time NCAA champion at the peak of his career. Former world individual medley record holders Greg Buckingham and Gary Hall sparked Hickcox to another world record. Ferris finished out of the top three and failed in his first attempt to make the team.

Pressure was building as Ferris faced Hickcox and Buckingham again in the 200-meter individual medley. Chavoor rode him hard all week, using his diabolical combination of praise and stinging criticism to inspire in Ferris the courage to beat the world's top swimmers in a do-or-die moment. Ferris fought back the wave of nerves and fear that sought to devour him. As he entered the pool, Chavoor repeated the command he'd issued to Ferris since he had started swimming for him at age eight: "GO OUT FAST!" Ferris took the lead right away in the butterfly stroke. He'd concentrated on improving his backstroke, but Hickcox pushed past to take the lead. On the third lap, they switched to his specialty, the breaststroke, and he pulled even with Hickcox as they turned into the last lap and the freestyle. The powerful Hickcox turned on the jets as he sprinted to a win in world-record time. Now the threat to Ferris was from Buckingham, who was gaining on him. The two battled to the wall, with Ferris touching out for second place and a spot on the team. Ferris swam the backstroke lap two seconds faster than he ever had, which was the key to his finish.[3] When he was just ten years old, Chavoor had said Ferris was his best swimmer, and now, nine years later, after all the effort and tight losses to Spitz, the pressure was off. "He's a drill sergeant; gruff. He tries to scare you. But I sure do agree with his tactics," Ferris sighed in relief.[4] He was going to the Olympics.

With the pressure off, Ferris and Spitz squared off in the 200-meter butterfly. Ferris held the world record in the event, but Spitz reclaimed it thirty-nine days later. His confidence mounting, Ferris knew he had a shot at winning now. The field went out so fast that at 25 meters, Spitz was last. Ferris turned first at 50 meters, and Spitz was still last. Finally, at 150 meters, Ferris was the clear-cut leader. Then Spitz began making his famous finishing kick. Ferris held back a touch and later regretted it. "I should have sprinted to the end, but I didn't want to die." With 13 meters to the finish, Spitz pulled even with Ferris and made another incredible surge as they went to the wall. Spitz won, 2:05.9 to 2:06.17.[5]

After the race, Ferris reminisced about their days together at Arden Hills as ten-year-olds, when Ferris was the stronger swimmer. "Since then, I've never beaten Mark in the 200-fly, no never," he said. "But you took me in the individual medley in the indoor championships the last two years," Spitz countered.[6] Like Doug Russell, who had lost by a fingernail to Spitz in the 100 fly, Ferris would face off again with Spitz in Mexico City. And like Russell, Ferris was making a new plan.

Even though he was the world record holder, Don Schollander felt he had much to prove in the 200-meter freestyle. For months he had put up with questions about whether he was washed up, and while he assured everyone he was still a top contender, his private doubts chipped away at his confidence. Few records are set in the heats as swimmers conserve their energy for the final, but Schollander broke his world record by almost two seconds. The message sent rocketed around the world: Schollander was primed to equal his 1964 four gold medal performance. Facing the fastest field ever, he broke his world record again in the finals, by five-tenths of a second. He was still the best in the world, and he began dreaming of another gold medal bonanza.[7]

For many swim fans, the 100-meter freestyle is swimming's glamour event. In Long Beach, the crowd was enormous and cheered wildly. Packed with elite swimmers, it was the most tension-filled event of the meet. The top three finishers in the 100 individual event in Mexico would join the fourth-place finisher on the 4 x 100-meter freestyle relay team. Schollander, the crowd favorite, sent a message when he qualified first in the heat with a personal best time of 52.93. After his finish, reporters and fans mobbed him, speculating that the win indicated he could qualify to win five gold medals. Zac Zorn, the 100-yard freestyle champion from UCLA, also cracked 53 seconds for the runner-up spot, while Spitz qualified third. That evening at the finals, the swimmers were introduced to thunderous applause and took off their warm-ups, ready to hit the water. But the seconds ticked off and turned to minutes. No one understood why the swimmers were not started. The cool ocean breeze rolled in, and Schollander began to shiver.

The starter finally assembled the swimmers on their blocks. Schollander tensed. When the gun finally went off, he was one of the last men in the water. He wondered if there had been a false start, but no one was called back. He was the slowest at 50 meters.[8] He made up time after the turn, but Zorn touched in at 52.58 to tie the world record, with Ken Walsh second. In the battle for third place and a spot on the relay team, Spitz and Schollander finished simultaneously. "I saw Don and I thought he was ahead of me, and I think he was," Spitz said immediately after the race. The swimmers waited while a committee of officials huddled to decide one of the most consequential third-place finishes ever. Finally, after a long delay, the decision was rendered: Spitz had come in third and Schollander, somehow, fifth. "I was pretty surprised Don didn't get in there [in third place], and I'm disappointed too, especially after Schollander did so well this morning," Spitz said. "We both went out slow and had fast finishes. But I think he might have gone out a little too slow."[9]

Schollander's great heat in the morning meant nothing. He was devastated by what he felt was an unfair ruling that consigned him to the fifth-place finish, knocking him off the relay team. He thought his coach, George Haines, had something to do with the verdict because Haines felt Spitz was the better bet for success at the Olympics. Schollander went to the locker room as Spitz collected his third-place medal and the crowd squirmed in silence. Many fans felt Schollander had finished third and been cheated. That night Robert Riger, a journalist who covered sports for ABC and *Sports Illustrated*, handed him a note that read, "The loss hurts tremendously, I know. I think the silence in the crowds during the awards when you were missing was a tribute to you. Have faith that life changes, and a chance for one gold medal this year can mean as much as four did in '64. I wish I could do something to pick you up on a night like this but know that we care. And chalk one up for the tall men. It is the price you pay for having been there so long."[10] Instead of a possible five medals, Schollander qualified for a chance at two. For most swimmers, that would be a fantastic accomplishment. For Schollander, it was a disappointing denouement with one agonizing act to be played out.

Mike Burton was always thoroughly prepared for any race he entered. His preparation for the trials had been intense, even by his demanding standards, and he was determined to finish first in the long 400- and 1,500-meter events. Burton won the 400 in near world record time, then had to wait until the evening of the last day of the trials for the "grand finale" 1,500-meter final. That afternoon he went to his hotel room to relax and prepare for the race. With him were his fiancée, Linda, and John Ferris, his Arden Hills teammate. Lying on the bed with his eyes closed, he visualized each part of the race: how he would glide into the turns, making tight, smooth underwater somersaults, his feet planting flatly and firmly on the pool wall, thrusting his body forward, then breaking the surface, thrusting his right arm forward into the air, cupping his hand into the water and pulling it past him. He visualized his pace and how many seconds every 100 meters would take. At a compact five-foot-nine, his form was not elegant or pretty, and his damaged leg did not contribute much to the effort. Still, his enormous arm strength thrust him through the water, pulling his 153 pounds along with the force and power of a "pocket battleship," which had been one of his many nicknames. He saw himself powering through turn after turn, pulling inexorably away, leaving the sixteen-year-old wunderkind John Kinsella and the rest of the pack bobbing far behind. He visualized growing stronger and stronger and exploding through the 800-meter mark in record time and gliding to victory. He envisioned every second of the race.

Suddenly, like a man awakening from a trance, he sat straight upright on the bed and blurted, "I'm going to go 16:08 tonight." After a few seconds of stunned silence, Linda replied quietly, "That's impossible." Ferris couldn't find any words and started laughing so hard he rolled around on the floor, holding his sides. Such a feat was impossible, absurd, ridiculous. Burton had predicted he would beat the world record by almost twenty seconds. He felt so strong he leaped out of bed and grabbed his gear. The three headed quickly to the Belmont Plaza Olympic Pool, and Burton tumbled into the water for warm-ups. He began ripping off 100-meter sprints so fast that Assistant Coach Mike Hastings cautioned him to slow down and conserve energy. "I feel fine, Coach," Burton replied, once again announcing his vision of going 16:08. The coach laughed and made him an offer he thought could never be realized: "Mike, if you do that, I'll take you and Linda to dinner after the race."

"You're on," Burton replied.[11]

Enthusiastic crowds had packed the trials all week. They had been rewarded with upsets, record times, and frenetic races, and they hated seeing the meet end. On the day of the last race, silent sonar moved through the fans, coaches, and journalists, portending that something epic was going to transpire in the last night's final event. Many fans thought the rising star John Kinsella would upset Burton, as he had almost done at the nationals in Lincoln. An immense crowd turned out, filling every seat in the enormous stands. Some with bad seats managed to work their way out onto the diving platforms overlooking the pool for a bird's eye view of the race.

Burton entered the water in the calm, confident manner felt by great athletes on the brink of stellar achievement. At the crack of the starter's gun, he flowed smoothly through the water. Chavoor recognized that he was tuned to perfection and was making beautiful turns in rhythm. Kinsella stayed within reach early in the race. At 200 meters, Burton had just a body-length lead. The vast glass squares on the ceiling fifty feet above the pool sent streams of diffused bluish light into the pool. The light projected through the water, creating bright, pulsing squares of azure sunlight on the bottom. The squares were fifteen yards apart, separated by dark shadows. He swam from square to square, guided by wayposts that seemed somehow to silently urge him on. He felt like he was in a magical undersea world on an alien planet. During the turns, he heard the crowd roar for a few hundredths of a second before his head plunged back below the surface. As he ripped off lap after lap, the crowd grew increasingly louder as they realized Burton was not only setting the record, he was obliterating it. At 1,000 meters, he had opened up three and a half lengths on Kinsella and 40 meters on the field. Two hundred meters later, his lead had grown to five lengths. The crowd lost its mind as Burton was "cutting through a bedlam of screams."[12] With 100 meters to go, he led by almost half the pool. Triumphantly he brought the last 100 meters home in 1:02.5. The building shook with ovations as Burton stepped out of the pool and was swarmed by swimmers and coaches congratulating him, awed by his accomplishment. Another colossal ovation erupted as the time flashed on the new scoreboard: Just as he predicted, it was 16 minutes, 8.5 seconds—chopping 19.6 seconds off Echevarría's world record. Kinsella, who also came in under Echevarría's time, finished second. Spectators searched for adjectives to describe it: "amazing, unbelievable, astounding. Possibly never before in the annals of swimming had one race completely drained all descriptions from its awestruck spectators," Don Bloom of the *Sacramento Bee* exhorted. "I knew he could do it. That was the greatest swim by any person in history," Chavoor said. "You just don't beat a great record in over 19 seconds."[13] Still, Chavoor thought Burton could go faster. "We were trying for a 16:10. Now [we're aiming for] under 16 minutes!"[14]

The crowd surging around Burton was so strong that it threatened to shove officials, swimmers, and coaches into the water. "It'll take a little more training to get under sixteen minutes, a little different training," Burton said, again thinking about the altitude in Mexico City.[15] Even more impressive than his endurance was his character. Chavoor, not given to lavishing praise on anyone, called him "the kind of boy you'd like to have for a son, an inspirational boy, trustworthy, ethical, morally sound and grateful for everything he has in life. He never complains."[16]

Finally, after the awards ceremony, as the crowd calmed and filed out of the building, Hastings came by. "Well," Burton said, "I told you the time I was going to swim and swam it."[17] It was time for the coach to pay up, and off they went to dinner at an upscale restaurant that sat on stilts built over the Pacific Ocean. In the darkness, exhausted by the race and humbled by the moment, they listened to the waves break powerfully on shore, one after another, rumbling on relentlessly.

Burton's impressive victory immediately sparked renewed conjecture about what it meant for the 1,500-meter Olympic showdown with Echevarría. Bloom, the *Bee* reporter, shared some information on the pressure that was building on the Mexican swimmer: "Echevarría is so popular down south of the border they stop bullfights when he enters the stadium. Then they cheer and dedicate the bull to him." Bloom wrote that Mexican sports fans "have been known to push down wire fences and trample spectators" when their favorites lost. If he lost, Echevarría "had better have a cab at the gate" to make a getaway. Bloom said that Echevarría would still be the favorite because of his familiarity with the altitude, which some coaches believed could be an advantage of as many as twenty-five seconds.[18]

The highlights of the trials were Burton's outstanding swim, Hickcox's overall performance, Spitz's clutch finishes, and Schollander's 200-meter victory. Now George Haines would take the men's team reins. With five veterans returning from the 1964 team, three proven swimmers would be in the water for each event. But the press was focused on one swimmer. Spitz had qualified in six events, and Haines was contemplating putting him in one more race if he could schedule it. Spitz was young, handsome, charismatic, confident, and exciting, and the prospect of Spitz winning seven gold medals was a favorite topic on the world's sports pages during the long wait before the Games began. The stories did not make much of the fact that Ferris and Russell had pushed Spitz to the absolute limit before losing to him by the tiniest of margins or that competitors in Canada and Australia were posting near world record times in training. All competitors love to aim at a target; in the fall of 1968, that target was on Mark Spitz's back.

13

EVERYBODY HAD AN AGENDA

While the men and women's teams and their coaches were supremely confident of victory in Mexico City, U.S. Olympic officials took no chances. They imposed a prison-like regimen on their young swimmers in the weeks before the Olympics. The five weeks of training started on September 7 at the U.S. Air Force Academy, located on the east side of the Rocky Mountain Rampart Range, at an elevation of more than seven thousand feet. The athletes' immersion was to be complete. "The world will not see or hear of this great team until they formally enter the Mexico Olympics," an Olympic official announced in a draconian statement. "The public and press will be barred from the training site."[1]

Most athletes despise training camps. The hours of repetitive training, the isolation from friends and family, and the rivalries that build from being confined with their competitors every day for weeks invariably raise tensions. Thirty-two swimmers were in the men's camp, and "everybody had an agenda," Doug Russell, Mark Spitz's archrival, said, "and everybody's friends had an agenda."[2] Cliques developed, and swimmers tried to psych-out opponents. The swimmers quickly became tired of the media hype about Spitz winning six gold medals.[3] After all, they were all there to train to win their own gold medals, and many would be competing directly with Spitz. "We trained harder than he did every day," Russell said. "If he was going to win six gold medals, it was going to be over our backs."[4]

Spitz didn't have a friend on the team and claimed he was the victim of anti-Semitic actions by fellow swimmers. If there was a cabal formed against him, it might have had its origins with the other members of the Santa Clara Swim Club who were at the training camp. Arnold Spitz claimed that while at Santa Clara, his son had been kicked and spat upon because he was Jewish, and the younger Spitz felt like he was again a target of anti-Semitism. Chavoor was coaching the women's team, which was also training at the Air Force Academy, and he heard rumors that Spitz was struggling emotionally. To cheer up Spitz, Chavoor said he set up a golf foursome with himself, men's coach George Haines, sixteen-year-old women's swimmer Susan Shields, and Spitz. Chavoor said male swim team members followed Spitz and Shields on a miniature golf course. "I don't know who said what," Chavoor wrote five years later in his 1973 book, but he said both he and Haines both heard a "constant barrage" of anti-Semitic insults hurled at Spitz, including: "Five gold medals? You'll be lucky to win one, Jew-boy," and "Hey, Jew-boy, you ain't gonna win nothin." Chavoor's account of the incident ends there, with no indication that he or Haines reprimanded the allegedly insult-spewing swimmers.[5] Spitz's account of the incident, published thirty-five years after Chavoor's book came out, directly quotes the anti-Sematic slurs Chavoor listed. Spitz said he "tried to ignore the taunts, but they hurt."[6]

Why didn't the coaches take action to control the team? I was unable to find any account of Haines's actions that day. Chavoor described Haines as a swimming tactician who did not get involved with his swimmers on a personal level. Don Schollander thought Haines seemed tired of coaching, was uninvolved with the swimmers, and had lost his enthusiasm to coach.[7] So perhaps Haines didn't notice if harassment was going on. But Chavoor had a completely different personality than Haines. He wrote that he liked to be involved in the personal lives of his swimmers and abhorred racism. He said that if he had a "Jew or an Oriental or a Black on my team" and someone insulted them, "I'd kick that someone's ass out of my club."[8] If such behavior had occurred, it seems inconsistent with his statements on race relations and his sometimes-belligerent character that Chavoor would have let such slights slide without confronting the offenders. So what was the truth? While Spitz's and Chavoor's versions of the incident were printed in their respective books and quoted in news articles for years, no one asked Susan Shields, who was supposedly one of the golfers that day, if she had heard the racist taunts. When I contacted her, she was adamant in refuting the tale. "No, no, no," she said "That never happened. I totally refute it. I don't even golf, not even put-put."[9] She wondered why Spitz and Chavoor would create such a story. Years later, after reading both Chavoor's and Spitz's accounts of the incident, Russell said, "Spitz played the Jewish card" to deflect criticism of his performance in the Games. "I never witnessed it," Russell said. "I come from Midland, Texas, and I could give a good damn about what your religion was . . . it's so far from being an issue with me it was just ridiculous."[10]

The camp wore on tediously, day after day. Swimmers missed training on the slightest pretense, claiming they suffered from an ache or a cold. Spitz, always fussing about minor ailments and pains, came down with tonsillitis and struggled with the altitude. He missed several workouts due to his maladies and was accused of goldbricking by some teammates. Spitz said he was the butt of jokes and taunts and crude pranks. "The team's treatment of Mark had nothing to do with competition," said Ken Walsh, a twenty-three-year-old Michigan State graduate and 100-meter sprint champion. "He was easy to kid."[11] By the end of the camp, Spitz's confidence was low, and the tension with his coaches and teammates was high. He was "distracted and depressed" that Haines had not intervened and defended him from the other swimmers' actions.[12] On the contrary, Russell was training hard and beating Spitz regularly in practice by a comfortable margin.

Schollander was appalled at how the camp was run. "This was the most lackadaisical team I had ever seen," he said. Haines and his assistant, Don Gambril, took breaks to return home for a week at a time. "Nobody seemed to care very much," Schollander said.[13]

The women's camp, under Chavoor's tutelage, was far less dramatic. Sue Pedersen's workouts were stress free and gravity defying; her split times were as fast as they had been at sea level. Picking up on the popular *Peanuts* cartoon strip and its famous "happiness is a warm blanket" line, Debbie Meyer's dad sent her a card that read "HAPPINESS IS A GOLD MEDAL." The card came back, its message altered in Debbie's handwriting: "HAPPINESS IS THREE GOLD MEDALS."[14]

The U.S. swimming team arrived in Mexico City on October 10, two days before the opening ceremonies. Their arrival at the new airport was festive, and the women were adorned with flowers while mariachi bands belted out brassy tunes full of excitement, hope, and expectation.[15] Looking slightly embarrassed in her red Olympic team blazer, Meyer was serenaded in the terminal while a crush of photographers surrounded her. Boarding the buses to the Olympic Village, they soon saw another side of Mexico, a vast cardboard encampment that encroached on the airport. Mexican troops, spaced ten meters apart with weapons unslung, lined both sides of the street. They arrived at the fenced-off Olympic Village to the sounds of construction as the crews finished the apartment building they would be living in for the fortnight.

The swimming events began on October 17, so the swimmers had to wait a week before competing. They nervously tried to fill the time by working out, shopping, eating out, and watching other Olympic events. The days passed and the tension mounted as they witnessed the effect the altitude and Mexican food had on the U.S. team. They began worrying about being healthy enough to compete at their highest level once they finally got in the water.

14

AN ABSENCE OF ORDER

In October 1963, Mexico City was awarded the XIXth Olympiad, beating out Detroit, Buenos Aires, and Lyon, with a significant boost from International Olympic Committee president Avery Brundage, who had an "early and outright embrace of Mexico City as his preferred choice for the 1968 Games."[1]

Brundage and other Olympic officials wanted to expand the Games' reach and took huge and unprecedented risks in awarding the event to Mexico. For the first time, the Games would be held in a developing country, a Spanish-speaking country, and a nation in Latin America. In addition, the Games would be conducted in a "nonaligned" nation. In that period, much of the world was aligned politically either with the democratic governments of the West or the Communist countries of the Eastern Bloc. Olympic officials hoped tensions would be lessened if the games were held in a politically neutral nation. All of these "firsts" led to speculation in the world media that the games would be a disaster. Nevertheless, the Mexican public was ecstatic when it was announced Mexico had won the competition to hold the Games. Still, the euphoria was short-lived. Critics questioned whether it was realistic for an economically developing nation to stage such an expensive event. Japan had spent $2.7 billion to prepare Tokyo for its games, a figure Mexico could not dream of matching. Mexico would spend just $176 million, a sum many felt was still too high. Critics felt the money would be better spent on social programs to reduce poverty.

Like the United States, Mexico experienced a wave of economic prosperity following World War II and sought to use the Games to showcase Mexico's cultural and artistic achievements. Yet despite the progress, many viewed Mexico as a backward nation, a sunbaked land of *mañana*. Mexican officials saw the Games as a giant advertisement for the country and thought they would help foreign investment and stimulate tourism. So they hired two young American designers to create a daring new graphic design look that transformed Mexico City for the international stage. Mexican Olympic Committee chairman Pedro Ramírez Vázquez, a renowned architect and artist, gave orders to his graphic design team on what *not* to produce: "Create an image that isn't an image of a Mexican wearing a sombrero sleeping under a cactus," he told them.[2]

The designers spent their first week on the job at the Museum of Anthropology, immersed in Mexico's native art. Incorporating the Olympic rings into Aztec art allowed them to create a dazzling visual array across the city. Posters, directions in bus terminals, arenas, and stadiums were festooned with bold, arresting designs. Workers wore striped uniforms with vibrant psychedelic colors. The integrated design scheme transformed the look of future Olympics and many other future events.[3] As the war in Vietnam wore on, Mexico promoted a theme of peace. The graphic designers created a dove, depicting Mexico's role as a peacemaker in the world, and that image became the centerpiece visual image of the games. Giant banners featuring the dove image decorated the thoroughfares, and dove stickers were prominently displayed on the windows of stores large and small. Everything from the plaza surrounding the main stadium, the Estadio Azteca, to the slums was painted in bright, psychedelic colors.[4] For the first time, the Olympics had a cultural emphasis equal to the athletic competition. Twenty spheres of activity encompassed music, art, poetry, and science. Mexico proudly presented *baile folklórico*, featuring performers from throughout Mexico displaying Mexican culture's costumes, dance, and music. Folkloric programs were vital because they involved many young people and college students in designing and presenting the shows. Vázquez emphasized Mexico's noninterventionist position in global geopolitics with slogans like *"Todo es possible en la Paz"* (All is possible if you have peace). As the vision gained traction, the world began to look beyond its problems and warmed to the idea of participating in a transcendent event in Mexico. Vázquez hoped it would be a big world party. *Look* magazine, a major publication of the day, presented an issue loaded with aspirational high-image photographs and featured an attractive woman in a bikini resting in a hammock on an Acapulco beach. Inside was a "Journey to Mexico" section with seventeen pages of color photos illustrating everything from beach resorts to bullfights. "To us, Mexico seemed not only foreign but almost completely unpredictable," the *Look* reporter commented. "The absence of order in the European or American sense is what exasperates. It is also what delights and rejuvenates."[5]

But as the fiesta was gathering, the Games faced enormous political threats from many directions. The Associated Press reported that the eighty-one-year-old Brundage, the "ramrod-straight champion of amateurism, had the most difficult year of his career."[6] Olympic politics, heightened by Cold War tensions and the Vietnam War, were more intense than ever. When South Africa and Rhodesia were reinstated to compete in the Games, some forty African nations and Russia immediately announced a boycott unless the South African nations were prevented from participating. If they boycotted, the Mexican Organizing Committee envisioned total devastation of the XIX Games.[7] In the face of a boycott, the IOC voted to ban South Africa and Rhodesia from competing and the boycott threat dissolved.

Another threat to the Games came from Eastern Europe. The world expressed horror and outrage when the Russian army invaded Czechoslovakia that spring and violently suppressed student protests. Voices were quickly raised, demanding that the West boycott the Games. Another issue arose from Black U.S. athletes who threatened to not participate in the games due to racial inequality. The proposed boycott fizzled, but several top Black athletes, including basketball player Lew Alcindor (who later changed his name to Kareem Abdul Jabbar), stayed home. That spring and summer, the assassinations of Dr. Martin Luther King Jr. and Robert F. Kennedy stunned the nation. King's murder sparked civil disturbance that required National Guard troops to go to troubled towns throughout the country.

Mexico also faced antigovernment protests that summer. Thousands of students staged a massive rally at the Plaza de las Tres Culturas (Three Cultures Square) in the Tlatelolco neighborhood on October 2. Troops and police clashed with students, and machine-gun bullets rattled off building facades. The government initially reported that four people had been killed and twenty wounded. But witnesses told a much more tragic story, saying they witnessed hundreds of bodies loaded into trucks and driven quickly away. Rumors spread that the bodies had been dumped in the ocean. There remains wide disagreement about how many protestors were killed that day.

Leaks in the press attributed to U.S. Olympic officials led to speculation that the Games might be canceled due to security concerns. Still, in a statement that many saw as insensitive, Brundage quickly assured the public that the Games would go on.[8]

The U.S. team arrived not just with self-imposed pressure to win but also with public pressure to beat the Russians. The United States had not won the overall summer medal total since 1956, and the Soviets had prevailed in the intervening years. Analysts thought that if the United States were to regain supremacy in the medal count, it would have to win not just a majority of the swimming events, but almost all of them.

Adding to the pressure was that for the first time, the athletes' friends, families, neighbors, and millions of people throughout the country and around the world would watch them as they competed. ABC would air an unprecedented forty-four hours of events, and while the athletes would certainly enjoy stories about their "thrill of victory," they were not as keen to be shown in the "agony of defeat." Another Olympic first was random drug testing for all athletes and gender testing for women. Chavoor confronted all these rules as an Olympic coach for the first time in 1968. For the up-from-the-streets Chavoor, the nature and character of the IOC officials were an affront. Olympic officials were usually depicted as elderly gentlemen, noblemen and millionaires who had little in common with the athletes and coaches. Chavoor called them "a small army of inept officials freeloading at their cocktail parties and endless receptions."[9] The leader of these officials was IOC president Avery Brundage. A fierce advocate of strict amateurism, he was often viewed as an autocratic aristocrat who was out of touch with modern times. A former Olympic track competitor, Brundage was a self-made man from tough circumstances, raised by relatives in Chicago after his father abandoned the family.

In an era when Olympic athletes were not supposed to be paid, shoe and clothing manufacturers supposedly slipped thousands of dollars to athletes who displayed their brands. Many called for an end to "shameuterism," but Brundage, IOC president from 1952 to 1972, fought to preserve amateurism. When asked why paid athletes shouldn't be in the Olympics, he replied bluntly, "Because he doesn't belong there! Let him join the circus."[10]

The wars, invasions, political protests, and boycotts failed to stop the Games. On the eve of the opening ceremonies, Mexican president Gustavo Díaz Ordaz contemplated the magnitude of the achievement. Bold, colorful logos, posters, banners, and displays gleamed under the Mexican sky. In their colorful costumes, the folkloric artists were ready to display the nation's diverse cultures to the world. Huge crowds from around the world were arriving to participate in the Olympiad. The lively, animated scene, televised in magnificent color to millions of people around the world, replaced the land of *mañana* with a brilliant modern Oz.[11]

The Olympic torch arrived the night before the opening ceremonies. The torch bearers were cheered on by enormous crowds as they ran on streets covered in flowers. They followed the route Spanish conquistador

Hernando Cortés took from his ships on the Gulf of Mexico to Mexico City when he arrived in 1518. The world watched as twenty-year-old hurdler Norma Enriqueta Basilio, a farmer's daughter, sprinted up the stairs of Estadio Olímpico Universitario and became the first woman in history to light the Olympic flame. The amplified whoosh of the igniting flame was drowned out by an ovation from the immense crowd that stood as one as all of Mexico beamed with pride.

Athletes ate in dining halls separated by nation, served the food they were used to eating at home to try and avoid digestion issues. Debbie Meyer's training diet consisted of three jars of peanut butter, Fig Newton cookies, soda, cake, and ice cream.[12] After meals, athletes from different countries congregated in social halls, speaking to each other through translators. There was little discussion of the geopolitical issues that seemed to absorb the world's attention. Walking through the Olympic Village one day, Sue Pedersen was awed when she saw two of the most enormous human beings she had ever seen. Vladimir Georgiyevich Andreev, the center on the Soviet basketball team, was listed at seven-foot-one and seemed unsteady when he walked through crowds of gawkers. And at six-foot-four and 359 pounds, Leonid Ivanovich Zhabotinsky, a Ukrainian Cossack, cut a wide swath around the Olympic Village as he prepared to pluck the gold medal in the super heavyweight weightlifting competition.

While most of the athletes' pre-Games apprehension was about adjusting to the altitude, they perhaps should have focused on the infamous malady known as *tourista*, which comes from eating local food and drinking unpurified water. They were also susceptible to colds, and the flu swept through the Olympic Village. By the end of the Games, it was estimated that half the U.S. athletes suffered from upper respiratory illness or diarrhea. Other Western nations also suffered, but somehow the athletes from behind the Iron Curtain were immune. Team physicians were cautious about the drugs they used to combat the diseases. The doctors were concerned that some of the medications traditionally used to combat those maladies were now considered illegal under the IOC's new anti-doping rules. Diarrhea, abdominal cramps, nausea, fever, and bloating swept through the village.[13] Sue Pedersen came down with *tourista* after attending one of the many embassy parties and sampling the mushroom hors d'oeuvres. Debbie Meyer also came down with it, and it hit her hard on the morning of one of the biggest days of her life.

After eating at a pizza parlor, Mike Burton got very ill. He broke into a fever and sweats and threw up. Alarmed, his coaches decided to hustle him to the infirmary. With no elevators in the dormitory, his Olympic teammates had to carry him down four flights of stairs to get medical attention. Those who hadn't contracted it were hoping they would not be struck down the day of their event. *Swimming World* noted that if swimmers got sick, "Years of hopes, training and readiness could end in frustration without an opportunity to compete at maximum condition."[14]

Pedersen turned fifteen the night before the swimming competition began. When the press asked her what she wanted for her birthday, she replied, "A gold medal." Chavoor quickly interjected, "No, two gold medals!" That evening Pedersen was lured to a "team meeting" outside her dormitory. When she returned, Claudia Kolb, her chief rival, burst into the room where the athletes were relaxing. She rolled in a super-sized birthday cake decorated with gigantic candles for a surprise birthday party. The U.S. Olympians, dressed in their Olympic warm-ups, gathered around and sang "Happy Birthday" and wished her well in the upcoming races. "Sue will get her gold and a birthday party, too," Chavoor said. Associated Press writer Murray Rose's story about the tall, fun-loving girl who wanted a gold medal for her birthday generated headlines and pictures of the birthday party worldwide. As if there wasn't enough pressure on Pedersen, the stories ran under the heading, "What about three gold and two silvers?"[15]

But another story out of the Olympics that day set a more somber tone. It reported that the U.S. athletes were steadily moving ahead in their quest for gold medals and said that more medals were expected from the swimmers. But the medal count, the story said, was growing "as the dark cloud of racial unrest overshadowed the record-breaking performances of the U.S. athletes."[16]

The first notice the swimmers had of this unrest was the night of Pedersen's birthday party. U.S. track stars Tommie Smith and John Carlos took the medal stand after winning gold and bronze medals in the 200-meter sprint. As the national anthem played, Smith took out black gloves. He and Carlos dropped their heads as the flag rose and raised their fists in the Black Power salute. They stood draped in beads, barefoot on the medal podium, framed by a lit night sky and bright green grass. The pictures taken that night would become among the most well-known photographs and images in the world. The first the swimmers heard of the protest was when they saw hundreds of journalists shouting and waving at the men's dormitory, hoping to get Smith and Carlos to come out for interviews. At the time, most of the swimmers were confused about what was happening, and many had mixed feelings about it. They fought to maintain their focus and tried to block out the uproar over the protest as their long week of waiting was ending and they would finally get to compete.

15

THE INVINCIBLE AMERICANS

The fast times and world records held by the U.S. women had intimidated many swimmers from other nations before they even showed up in Mexico City. The only threat they seemed to face was overconfidence. The first race, the women's 400-meter medley relay, was expected to be an easy win for the U.S. team, and the question was not if the U.S. women would win but by how many seconds they would shatter the world record. The team consisted of Kaye Hall, Catie Ball, and two Arden Hills swimmers, Ellie Daniel and Sue Pedersen. All of them held or would hold world records. Pedersen had the honor and the pressure of swimming the anchor leg. But it turned out to be no easy go, as the feisty Australians were ready to give it their "Aussie all" in the pool. Although a much smaller nation, Australia, with thirty-five thousand kilometers of coastline, is a nation of swimmers with a proud Olympic swimming tradition.

As the teams warmed up, the loud Mexican crowd was clearly behind the underdog Aussies, cheering them and waving stuffed koalas as they were introduced. The race was close from the instant the starting gun went off. After the first 100 meters, the U.S. team led by less than a body length. The Aussies had their own young star in fourteen-year-old breaststroker Judy Playfair, who beat her American rival by 0.4. The United States had only a narrow lead after the butterfly, and Pedersen knew the race for gold was tight as she dove into the water for the final 100 meters. The crowd rose, hoping for an upset, urging on Australia's anchor, Jenny Steinbeck. They were neck and neck at the turn with the crowd screaming and waving koala bears, hoping to witness a dramatic Aussie win. The girls were even with 50 meters to go when Pedersen dug as deep as she could and edged out her rival. The U.S. team won, but it took setting a new world and Olympic record to best the proud Australians by 1.7 seconds.

The Australians had served notice that they would challenge the Yanks in every event. Chavoor was a little stunned and surprised at the narrow victory, muttering that the challenge was a good wake-up call for his team, but he felt his squad had been nervous, and he hoped they would go faster in the following days. The relief at winning the first race was enormous for the "invincible" Americans, who wept as the anthem was played, the flag raised, and their medals awarded. Holding her medal high and kissing it, Pedersen gushed, "I'd like to eat it, I cannot believe it; it's a dream." Her birthday wishes were starting to come true.[1]

Even though she had already claimed gold, Pedersen was swimming scared in the 400-meter free relay. But the United States took an early lead and never looked back, with Pedersen swimming the third leg, opening a lead of a body length and a half. Then, her teammate and rival Jan Henne brought it home for the Americans in an Olympic record time.

Once again, Pedersen's main rival for the 100 meters would be Jan Henne, whom she had narrowly beaten in the U.S. nationals and the Olympic trials. Pedersen, the pre-race favorite, felt if she could match her trial time of 59 seconds, she would win—and she was right. But Henne, an experienced twenty-one-year-old, pulled a psych job on fifteen-year-old Pedersen. "Just because you beat me in that race doesn't mean you'll win in the final," she told her young adversary.[2] The two were side by side during the entire race. But when Pedersen made the turn, something didn't feel quite right. Did her foot slip on the wall? Did she fail to plant her foot firmly enough to push off with maximum power? It was just a feeling, a nudge, and she would never be able to tell for sure what had happened. They came to the finish line together. "I didn't know I'd won and then Susie Pedersen told me to look up at the little red dot [signifying the winner on the scoreboard], and I knew it was me," Henne said. She finished at a minute even, with Pedersen three-tenths of a second behind. Chavoor told the press that a tactical mistake prevented Pedersen from recording her third straight win over Henne. She was "coached to breathe on alternate sides [of her mouth] as Debbie does, and she forgot to do it in the last 25 meters," Chavoor said. "She didn't see Jan until it was too late. I think she would have responded to the challenge and won the race if she had known Jan was coming up on her, but she just forgot to look over on that side," Chavoor said. Pedersen disagreed with her coach's assessment. "The 100 is a full-on sprint from start to finish," she said. "I never lost sight of Jan. I was healthy, and I swam my very best, and as hard as I could, I just got beat."[3]

It was Pedersen's fate to come up against one of history's greatest medley champions in the 200- and 400-meter individual medley. At age eighteen, Claudia Kolb was in her prime and already held an Olympic silver medal in the 200-meter breaststroke, which she won in the 1964 games. George Haines called her one of the greatest swimmers he ever coached. Pedersen mounted the only challenge to her and took silver, finishing 4.1 seconds behind Kolb in the 200 individual medley, and was ready to make a strong bid in the 400, her last Olympic event. But it was then that the burden of competing in five events hit her. She, too, felt the impact of the *tourista*. Asked about the altitude, she made no excuses: "I blew the individual medley completely. I was just plain tired. I wanted to go all out, and I tried so hard I just couldn't do it."[4] Nevertheless, she finished strong and was barely edged out for the bronze medal. She finished with two golds and two silvers, a haul few Olympic athletes would ever match. But it was another Arden Hills swimmer who would capture the imagination of the world.

At age sixteen, Debbie Meyer came to the 1968 Olympics as perhaps the most famous swimmer in the world. She held fourteen world records, and her record-shattering performances in the national championships and the Olympic trials sent an unmistakable message to the rest of the world's swimmers: Meyer was the one to aim for in Mexico City. With all the media pressure on her, she showed she had as much talent in public relations as she had in swimming. Her smiling personality had enthralled *Sacramento Bee* reporter Don Bloom, whose stories over the previous two years formed the basis for profiles in national magazines and newspapers as well as television and radio profiles. He had personalized her as the easygoing, peanut butter–eating girl next door. *Life* magazine, shadowing her during the Games, proclaimed her as "Debbie the peanut butter kid" in a glowing profile.[5] But when she arrived, she couldn't find any peanut butter in Mexico City and was desperately craving it. She had such an addiction to peanut butter she once ate thirty-four Reese's Peanut Butter Cups the night before a race. Sacramento television sportscaster Creighton Sanders was able to corral a jar and took it to Meyer in time for her first events. Media reports rarely mentioned her confidence, the outstanding balance in the water, or her massive shoulders and muscular arms built on a solid torso that rocketed her through the water.[6] Instead, she was described as friendly, shy, and cuddly. Parents, coaches, fans, and reporters loved her. But the attention she received was a little much for some of her competitors who murmured, "Here comes the queen" when she walked past.[7]

For Chavoor, the Olympics were the *thing*. "They are the World Series, Super Bowl, world championship golf, all the great sports events wrapped into one."[8] The elegant, refined world of dignitaries, celebrities, galas, and embassy parties was another world from anything he could have imagined growing up during the Depression. He was not one for polite small talk. In conversations, he was blunt and to the point, never afraid to share his opinions about the food, the accommodations, or the peccadilloes of minor Olympic officials, whom he derided as "pipsqueaks."[9] The glare of the television lights, the pressure of coaching the women's team while helping Mark Spitz and John Ferris, and the constant requests from the media kept him on edge for the fortnight.

It had been four years since Meyer first showed up in his pool with the stopwatch that bore the inscription "Mexico City 1968" on the back. The words were more of a hope and a prayer than a prediction. She and Chavoor had built a complex relationship that now had her on the brink of immortality. Meyer described it as a "love-hate relationship, more love than hate." He had become a second father to her, and she "worried about his head colds, baked him cakes and sent him Father's Day cards."[10] He thought of her as his third daughter. Despite the affection, he never stopped pushing her, badgering her to do better, and always the praise was faint.

As the swimming competition approached, rival swimmers began to shorten their workouts, but Chavoor pushed Meyer harder than ever. He was merciless in the daily workouts in the Mexico City pool and exploded in anger at any sign of weakness she displayed. A parade of coaches from other Olympic teams came to watch her work out and were shocked at what they witnessed. He worried about her mental attitude and railed at her constantly. Using one of his well-known pet words, he said her performance was driving him "fruity." "Now show me some guts; get moving in that water," he constantly bellowed during workouts. Nevertheless, Meyer gritted through the week of activities, dealing with sniping competitors, meddling reporters, and worshiping fans. Four days before her first race, she broke down in tears after a Chavoor tirade but did not give into self-pity. Instead, she steeled herself in her crowded dorm room and forgave her coach: "I kept telling myself not to worry. I told myself to stop fighting Sherm. He was uptight about this meet as anyone."[11]

On the eve of her first race, she ran into Donna de Varona, the female star swimmer of the 1964 games. Meyer shared her anxieties, and de Varona told her she'd had similar experiences at the Tokyo games. She recounted how she felt like she had been "swimming in molasses"[12] right before the competition began. It was a feeling Meyer was experiencing, and it helped her cope with the pressure of knowing that de Varona had overcome her fears to become an Olympic champion.

Her first race was the 400-meter free, and she was happy to finally be in the water, away from all the commotion, and quickly "proved beyond doubt that she alone is the world's queen of freestylers."[13] Her race day psych-up routine was now well established. First, she imagined a rival swimmer boasting how she would destroy her in the pool. Next, she worked herself into a wave of boiling anger at the imaginary insults and vowed that she was going to stomp her rivals and "beat their guts out." Then, hitting the water as the race began, she told herself, "Okay, now get going."[14] Any pre-race jitters or concerns were quickly allayed. Chavoor trained his swimmers to go out fast, and she held a two-length lead through 300 meters. Despite the lead, Chavoor was fretting on the pool deck, worried the altitude would somehow reach down and slow her. "Breathe on both sides of your mouth, you little nut," Chavoor yelled at her from the pool deck. Her pace was perfect, and she felt dull pain and exhaustion, the result of her peak performance as she finished. Chavoor slumped against a concrete pillar in relief. The victory he had predicted for the past two years had finally come true. "Mexico City 1968" had become a reality.

Meyer woke up at 5 o'clock the morning of the 200-meter freestyle "sicker than a dog.[15] Adding to her predicament, she had to swim a qualifying heat in the morning in the 800-meter free. She spent the morning shivering and wrapped in blankets to keep warm as the stomach cramps from the *tourista* swept through her. "Debbie is ill, may miss two events," read the headline in the evening *Sacramento Bee*. Chavoor took her out of the pool building and laid her on a bench behind the arena. Her parents raced out of the stands, and her mom comforted her, cradling her head in her lap. Regaining her strength she made it to the ready room, where her father asked, "Are you going to guts this one, kid?"[16] She recovered and finished first in the 800 qualifying heat, then continued to feel better as she awaited the 200 final that night. It looked as if she still might be scratched up until race time, like her teammate and friend Catie Ball, who withdrew from the competition due to illness. The bid for her second gold medal would be challenging even without the sickness, as she had to face Jan Henne, who had upset Pedersen in the 100 a few days earlier. Meyer led by only a head at the 50-meter turn as Chavoor wriggled in agony, worried that she was holding back too much, and shouted at her to get going. As the swimmers moved down the pool for the last 75 meters, it looked like Meyer was faltering. Somehow she held a slight lead with 50 meters left: "The three Americans came plowing for the finish and were almost swimming like one, but Debbie continued to fight off her challengers." In the stretch, Henne felt her arms tire and her legs die. "I had a weird feeling I wasn't going anyplace," she said.[17] Meyer won in a touch, 2:10.5 to 2:11, for her second gold medal. After the race, she said she felt fine, but a coughing fit on the medal stand illustrated how ill she was.

Meyer's bid to make history by becoming the first swimmer to win three individual gold medals in a single Olympics came on October 24, the eighth day of the competition. She showed little effect from her recent illness, but she thought she would have to set the world record to win the grueling 800-meter race, the longest women's swimming event in the Olympics. The world had long forgotten U.S. swimmer Helene Madison, the first swimmer to win three gold medals in a single Olympics, winning the 100-meter freestyle, 400-meter freestyle, and 4 x 100-meter freestyle relay during the 1932 Games in Los Angeles. Now Meyer would better her feat, winning three individual gold medals and captivating the world. Meyer ended the suspense quickly, winning as "easy as water running off a duck's back."[18] At the seven-minute mark, she was "out of sight" of the rest of the field. Meyer made her final turn, leading by 18 meters as the rest of the field struggled for silver and bronze. While Meyer celebrated her landmark victory, the crowd's attention was focused on the battle for the bronze medal, and they cheered wildly as Mexico's Maria Teresa Ramírez took third place.

But it was Meyer's day, even if the scale of her accomplishment didn't hit her right away. "I just swam it; I didn't have any real definite plan," she said. "I didn't try and hit any particular splits. I just paced it all the way. It felt easy! The altitude didn't bother me a bit," the champion said.[19] Headlines worldwide hailed Meyer's feat, and the media reported she was the "top American heroine" of the Games. Moreover, her three gold medals came on the day it was announced that the United States recaptured the "unofficial team championship" in overall medals from the Russians, the first time that had occurred in twelve years. So what was Meyer going to do with all her medals? Her first words to the media were that she would give one of the medals to Chavoor, who she called "the greatest."[20] Chavoor momentarily shed his gruffness and was near tears when Meyer hung the medal around his neck.

There is little doubt that she would have won four gold medals if the antiquated Olympic rules were not biased against women. Meyer's dominance in the longest event, the 1,500-meter free, was impossible to translate into Olympic gold. Although it was routinely swum at national championships, Olympic officials did not allow women to swim the mile race. "I probably was better at the 1,500 [than in her other gold-medal-winning events]," Meyer told the *New York Times* in 2014, "because I really didn't get tired. I pretty much held the same pace the entire race. It really was all about the thinking at that time which was women were the weaker sex, and because men were stronger people, they could last the distance. [It] definitely gnaws at me a little bit more now than it did at the time I was competing."[21] Finally, in 2017, the IOC announced that women would be allowed to swim 1,500 meters. Unfortunately for

Meyer, it came nearly fifty years too late for her to compete for the fourth gold medal she almost certainly would have won in Mexico City.

Despite fears about the altitude and the sickness that most swimmers dealt with, Chavoor's "naiads" won ten of a possible fifteen gold medals, eight silver out of twelve possible, and eight bronze out of twelve, a total of twenty-six medals out of a possible thirty-nine. The U.S. women won all three relays and scored sweeps in the 100-meter butterfly and 200-meter individual medley. Debbie Meyer and Sue Pedersen had five gold medals and two silver medals between them, and the pair combined won more gold medals than any nation other than the United States. The 1968 U.S. women's Olympic swimming team is regarded as one of the greatest swim teams in history.

16

"I GOT DOWN ON MY KNEES"

With expectations of a record gold medal bonanza for Mark Spitz and the men's team, Coach George Haines constructed a schedule that saw Spitz potentially competing in eight races in five days. From the first race on, the world would be counting how many gold medals Spitz won—and how many opportunities slipped away. Spitz's first event went perfectly for him. He was swimming with Zac Zorn, Steve Rerych, and Ken Walsh on the 4 x 100 freestyle relay team, which had set the world record in the Olympic trials. There was little pressure as the veteran squad romped to victory. Spitz swam the fastest leg of the race as the United States set another world record, trouncing the Soviet Union by almost 3 seconds. The result of his second race, the 100-meter freestyle, would not be so satisfying for him or the United States. It was Spitz's first individual test, and he was pitted against a challenging field, including fellow Americans Zorn and Walsh, both world record holders in the event. The U.S. swimmers were confident one of them would win swimming's marquee event. They had overlooked Michael Wenden of Australia, who had trouble adjusting to the altitude and had been sick much of the week.

Spitz was still upset from the perceived slights he had endured during the training camp, and in the seconds before the race, Spitz said he "heard his teammates encouraging Walsh and Zorn but not him." He felt like it was another stab directed at him, one he tried to ignore.[1] Spitz got out fast and threatened to put the race away early, as he had often done. He turned first at 50 meters, three feet ahead of everyone else, but he had gone out too fast. He faltered 20 meters from the finish as the other swimmers sprinted past him. Wenden blasted home in world record time to win by a length as Walsh took silver and Spitz settled for bronze. The Americans watched disconsolately as his Aussie teammates hoisted Wenden in the air and paraded around the pool in victory. Spitz kept up a good front for the press. He had not been feeling well and was coughing and sneezing but did not mention it. "I'm pretty happy with the way it came out," he said. "I tried my hardest, and it's my best time. I was going to go as hard as I could tonight, and I had a feeling I would be either the first or second American."[2] The loss also had consequences for his shot at another gold medal. Because he finished third, he did not earn a place on the freestyle leg of the medley relay team, an almost certain gold medal for the Americans. However, he did have one chance left to make the relay; if he won in the 100-meter butterfly, he would be placed on the medley team on the butterfly leg. Since the fly was his best event, his chances of making the relay squad and winning that gold still looked bright.

For the first time, the 100-meter butterfly, one of the most complex and painful swimming strokes, was an Olympic event. For Spitz and Doug Russell, mastering it was an immense point of pride and evidence they were among the toughest swimmers in the world. How is it done? Coaches advise watching dolphins swim to visualize the stroke and see the wave action it produces. It requires precision timing, flexible strength, and relaxation. "To watch Olympic swimmers do the butterfly is to witness a metamorphosis: half-human, half-fish, wholly mesmerizing," wrote journalist Marie Doezema.[3] The butterfly uses more than fifty of a swimmer's muscles to execute the stroke, and a strong body core is the control center. The shoulders and glutes are timed to work together with the legs and abs to create a powerful stroke. The stroke contorts the entire body, the arms lifting the head out of the water as the body moves forward. Then the head drops to the water as the arms rise and plunge through the surface. The arms spread in the way a butterfly's wings spread. Finally, the swimmer joins the legs together, kicking in unison as if they were one leg, like a dolphin's tail. During the stroke, the swimmer uses the dolphin kick twice. "It's a tough kick to master because it works really well if you can pass that wave down your body very smoothly—the smoother that wave is as it passes down your body, the faster you will cut through water," said Rajat Mittal, a mechanical engineer who analyzed the butterfly. "Everything has to operate in unison in order to do this properly."[4] Coaches love to use the stroke in training because it requires the use of all the muscles.

While Spitz was the world record holder in the 100-meter butterfly, he would have to contend with Russell, who had come close to beating him many times, most recently at the Olympic trials. Spitz had so many come-from-behind wins against him that Russell told himself Spitz would run him down and beat him every time. An hour before the race, the swimmers were ushered into the dark-paneled ready room. Carefully avoiding looking at each other, each swimmer plumbed the depths of his psyche, alternately calming his secret fears and searching for inspiration that would power him to peak performance. Russell thought back to his days at the pool in Midland, Texas, when we would splash his hand in the water, sending ripples through the pool, and race the ripples to the pool's edge. Now he imagined the ripples weren't his competitors; they were his guides. They were showing him the way to victory. He remembered the football games he played as a kid on the rough Midland playgrounds, going out for a long pass, his only chance at glory. He always told himself he had to make that catch. Now he had to win the gold, and this was it, his big chance. He remembered growing up poor, fighting to protect his mother from being beaten by his alcoholic stepfather. He had given everything to get to this point, even breaking up with his fiancée and cutting off his friends to concentrate on training. Spitz was the best in the world. Beating him was "the essential thing," Russell thought as he stared at the floor.

In their prior races, Russell usually took the early lead, sprinting as hard as he could. This time Spitz moved quickly into the lead. As they approached the halfway mark, ABC Sports commentator and former Olympic champion Murray Rose intoned, "Watch Doug Russell in lane four, Russell will have to have a lead here [to have a chance to win]." But Spitz took the lead by a little less than half a length at the turn, and Rose knew something was up. The excitement in his voice rose as he announced, "This is a switch. Mark Spitz rarely goes out this fast; whether he can hold on and have his usual finish in a race by going out this fast, I don't know."[5] An image flashed through Russell's brain: He was at the finish line, his feet up on the pool deck relaxing as he watched Spitz and the others finish. Coming off the wall at the turn, Russell took five massive, powerful strokes and caught Spitz. He pushed into the lead with a few more strokes, and Spitz could not answer. Russell felt a burst of strength he had never experienced before. This time it was he who won by a stroke. There were no fist-pumping or high fives. Instead, Russell realized the biggest competitor he faced had been himself. The images of his troubled youth, of the adversity he met his whole life, flashed through and overwhelmed him: "I got out [of the pool], and I got down on my knees because I literally saw mental pictures and voices of all the people that had helped me growing up."[6]

It had been Spitz's seventh race in five days, and the defeat knocked him off the 400-meter medley relay team. The loss shattered Spitz, who lapsed into a dreamlike mood, so unaware of what was happening around him that he had to be nudged off the medal stand after the medal ceremony.

He had little time to recover, and a half hour later he was mounting the starting block for the 4 × 200 freestyle relay. Many of his teammates noticed how tired he was and thought he should have stepped aside for a fresher swimmer. After all, they had a full bench of great swimmers who were alternates. The United States built up a healthy lead, but Spitz swam the third leg much slower than his time at the trials, and the Australian Wenden almost caught him. But the hero of 1964, the man many thought was washed up, rose to the challenge, and Schollander finished strong to hold off the Australians and win the gold medal. In the locker room after the victory, his teammates criticized Spitz for jeopardizing their win by not giving his spot to another swimmer and said his "medal greed" had cost them a world record.[7]

Although Spitz was faltering, the rest of the U.S. team performed brilliantly. Charlie Hickcox won the 200-meter individual medley and established himself as the Games' U.S. star. Arden Hills' John Ferris and Greg Buckingham waged an intense battle for silver, with Buckingham prevailing by three-tenths of a second, and the effort exhausted Ferris. He began to feel woozy as he walked uncertainly to the medal stand. Then, as the national anthem began, his knees started to buckle. Hickcox and Buckingham grabbed him and held him up for a few seconds, only to see Ferris's legs go out from under him as he stood on the medal stand. An Associated Press wire photographer captured the instant, and Ferris received more publicity from the picture than from his swimming exploits.[8]

It seemed Ferris might be deprived of his main Olympic goal for a while: winning the 200-butterfly. He fully recovered and was ready to challenge Spitz, the favorite, the kid he had competed against since they were ten-year-olds at Arden Hills. Spitz had beaten Ferris for years, but often by very narrow margins. In those races, Ferris had usually sprinted to the lead, only to see Spitz pass him in the last ten meters. In sports, some coaches say, "Never change a winning game; always change a losing game." With Olympic medals on the line, Ferris and Coach Don Gambril decided to change strategy. Instead of sprinting to the lead, he would ignore the other swimmers and stay close to Spitz, conserving his energy for the final surge. That switch in tactics may well have worked if Spitz had employed his usual strategy. But he was exhausted, worn down by a cold, and depressed by his performance. At 75 meters, "much to everyone's astonishment," Spitz was last, and Ferris was next to last as Ferris continued to track Spitz, falling ever farther behind the pack. Finally, with just 75 meters left, Ferris realized his error and sprinted wildly and somehow was able to catch the group. But it was too late to win gold, and despite going as hard as he could, he finished third, just six-tenths of a second out of first place. Ferris was resentful after the loss, knowing he had so much energy in his tank he could have won if he'd gone all out from the start. He knew that if Spitz had swum his typical race, he would have beaten him and the rest of the field for the gold medal. "I was swimming against Mark Spitz," he said. "I had everything left after the race."[9] Spitz never did get going and finished in last place, and the loss stuck with him for years, creating a psychological wall in the 200 fly he found almost impossible to breach.

Winning two gold medals, a silver, and a bronze is a remarkable achievement for any Olympian. But his failure to win two events in which he held world records stung him. As the great *Los Angeles Times* sportswriter Jim Murray put it, "He did a belly flop. He finished dead last in a race he held the world record in, took a second and third in two other specialties, and got gold medals only as part of a relay team."[10] Instead of Spitz dominating the men's swimming events, the American hero was Charlie Hickcox, the Indiana University star. Sandwiched between Don Schollander's four gold medals in 1964 and Mark Spitz's seven gold medals in Munich, Hickcox's gold medals in the 200- and 400-meter individual medley and the 4 x 100 medley relay and his silver in the 100-backstroke are often overlooked. But in a time of stress and strife, his performance had held the team together.

Why did Spitz underperform? A biographer explained his performance this way: "The slights at training camp, the shock of the student massacre, the intensity of the black power incidents, and the lack of any real friends on the team distracted and depressed Mark."[11] Spitz placed some of the blame on Haines for failing to help him navigate these obstacles during the ordeal. His performance shocked many in U.S. swimming, and it would have been easy for him to quit the sport at that point. But as time passed, he knew he wasn't finished, and his Olympic performance burned within him. It would become the fuel that would propel him for the next four years.

Many struggled with the altitude, and the 200-meter free final showed just how dangerous the situation was. Wenden and Schollander raced neck and neck, but the Australian had the closing edge and snatched victory in an Olympic record time. But far from being able to celebrate his second gold medal, Wenden lost consciousness and was saved from drowning by teammate Robert Windle, who pulled his head out of the water. Schollander was also exhausted and had to be given oxygen after the race. John Nelson, who had trained at Arden Hills that summer, took bronze.

It was the last race of Schollander's career. He had competed in only two races in Mexico City, so he had a lot of time to contemplate his career and the Olympic movement that week. When he won four gold medals in 1964, it was the first time anyone had won so many in the modern era of global television and mass communications. In 1964, he'd been a naive eighteen-year-old high school student. At twenty-two, he'd seen the world, gone to Yale, and experienced the transition from golden boy to old man. He contrasted the Olympic ideals he heard so much about with the boycotts and the controversies over banning nations from the Games. He was upset about what he saw as rising commercialism and exploitation of athletes. He'd won five gold medals and one silver medal in his two Olympiads, but it all seemed empty to him. With all the controversies, the Games tarnished the Olympic ideals he had once cherished: "The fact was that the smoke of international politics over the Olympics was so thick nobody could even see the original ideals anymore." He worried that the Olympic Games would die if the political leveraging continued in the future.[12] Little did he know how valid his fears would turn out to be.

Mike Burton hadn't eaten solid food for two days and lost fifteen pounds the week before his first race, the 400 meters. Already a trim 165 pounds, he vomited the night before the race and almost missed qualifying. If he'd swum five-tenths of a second slower in the qualifying heat, he would not have made the final. He was so bad off that Chavoor considered keeping him out of the race. But he was called "Iron Mike" not just because of his physical stamina but also because of his mental strength. He steadied himself, as he often did, by visualizing the race. Someone said he would have to finish in 4:11.0 to win it. "Well, I'm going 4:09 tonight," he replied.[13] He planned to go out fast. If anyone was going to stay with him for 400 meters—a length of about four and a half football fields—they were going to hurt. Burton sprinted out hard and took a stroke lead over the field at the turn. Ralph Hutton, a Canadian who had upset him at the national championships in Lincoln a few months earlier, made his move and took the lead. Burton and Hutton remained close until the last 100 meters, when Burton pulled in front by a second. Burton's iron will cast nausea aside, and he held the race in his hands. He sprinted to the wall, winning by 2.7 seconds over the gallant Canadian. Raising his arms triumphantly, he felt the pressure roll off his shoulders. He felt exhilarated, relieved, the long hours of preparation finally over. The anthem played, and he felt so proud to be an American he had to fight back tears. As the medal was draped around him, he felt its weight tugging at his neck. He held onto it the rest of the evening and curled up with it in bed that night.

On the final night of the swimming competition, the long-awaited duel between Burton and Guillermo Echevarría in the 1,500 was finally at hand. But Burton faced one last obstacle before he made it to the pool. He was supposed to take one of the Olympic buses to the arena, but when he went to the pickup area, no buses were there. Coach Haines emerged from his room and said the swim team had a car that could take him. But the car was in the hands of one of the team managers, who had decided to take his wife on a shopping outing that evening. They thought about walking to the pool but worried they would not make it in time. Burton, clad in his U.S. Olympic team warm-ups, calmly walked across several lanes of traffic and stuck out his thumb. He and Haines were picked up by a surprised and excited Mexican fan who recognized Burton. The driver stomped on the gas to deliver the world's greatest distance swimmer and his coach just in time to make the Olympic final.

Waiting for him was Echevarría, who had been a national hero since the previous summer, when he set a world record while beating Burton in California. Since Echevarría trained in Mexico City's high altitude, the experts predicted a gold medal for Mexico. Certainly the Mexican fans believed it, and the pool was sold out weeks in advance, with ticket scalpers enjoying brisk business. President Gustavo Díaz Ordaz, eager to share in Mexican glory, joined many dignitaries cheering their hero on. Finally, Burton could step into the pool and forget about his years of worry—Chavoor had called it a "phobia"—about how the altitude would affect his swimming. His win in the 400 had taken much of the pressure off his shoulders.

Conversely, the pressure had mounted on Echevarría. He was a national hero, his picture on every newsstand and magazine. A comic book foretold the story Mexicans wanted to see: The panels showed Burton and Echevarría battling side by side in the pool, with Echevarría slowly pulling in front, holding on to win a glorious gold medal in front of his adoring countrymen. In a corner panel, Chavoor consoled a crestfallen Burton.[14] Now the fanciful cartoons were put away and the noisy reality arrived, the pressure pounding on the swimmers as the crowd roared, "Meh-i-co, Meh-i-co" and the swimmers made final preparations. The starting gun went off, barely audible above the din, and Echevarría blasted into the pool and took the lead. Burton did not back off his trademark fast start, and they set a formidable pace as they made the 200-meter turn so close together they looked like synchronized swimmers. The crowd was on its feet, urging Echevarría to go ever faster. Instead, it was Burton who surged ahead as the Mexican began to falter. Burton's lead steadily mounted every 100 meters, and the crowd grew more and more muted. Finally, at 500 meters, Burton was in command, three body lengths ahead, and it was "apparent that unless he died, the race for the gold medal was over."[15] Burton won by 27 meters, and Echevarría finished sixth, almost a minute behind the leaders. The home crowd turned quickly and savagely against him. *Swimming World* called the rousing jeers "one of the most repulsive exhibitions of poor sportsmanship by a host nation. The loss by Guillermo Echevarría in the 1500-meter freestyle provoked a spontaneous outburst of derision toward an amateur athlete that can never be equaled."[16] Burton knew how the intense pressure could affect swimmers, and he felt terrible for what the Mexican swimmer had endured. Burton never boasted or gloated about his victory or said a bad word about Echevarría, and they became lifelong friends.

The U.S. men's and women's swimming teams accomplished what they came to do: almost total domination in the pool, helping the United States to the most Olympic medals, 107–91 over the Soviet Union overall, and a 45–29 advantage in gold. It was the first time the United States defeated Russia for the "unofficial" Olympic championship since 1956. U.S. swimmers won 52 of the 87 swimming medals, with the women winning 26 of a possible 39. For Arden Hills, Debbie Meyer's three gold medals and Sue Pedersen's two gold and two silver medals were Mike Burton's two gold medals, John Ferris's two bronze medals, and John Nelson's gold and bronze.

Back in Sacramento, the swimmers' accomplishments were being closely watched. Then, in an editorial that sounded like it was written during Sacramento's halcyon days of the Gold Rush, the *Bee* proclaimed in soaring rhetoric that "the name of Sacramento has sounded like a stuck record at the Olympic Games in Mexico City, simply because it has [been] featured so often in the names of the winners in the swimming events. And none more than Debbie Meyer, who has kept the name of this city before the world as she became the first swimmer in Olympic history to win three gold medals." Praising Chavoor for his coaching, the *Bee* concluded that not even the greatest coach in the world could have "planted such genius in any human body as that displayed by Debbie Meyer." There is no better word to use than hagiography to describe the paeans of praise that gushed from the *Bee*; Meyer "gave herself a secular baptism in Mexico City as Neptune's bride and the glorifier of America, Sacramento and herself." In the two weeks of the Olympics, Meyer had ascended from mortal swimming queen to eternal goddess.[17]

The Olympic fortnight wound—or, depending on the point of view, staggered—to its conclusion, but officials managed to make even the majestic closing ceremonies controversial, ruling that only six athletes per country would be allowed to march in the celebration, and the rest would sit in the stands. The reasons for this decision were never fully explained, but Olympic officials sensed the athletes might get out of control. Jesse Owens, an Olympic official himself and the star of the 1936 Olympics, could not understand the decision. "I can't help thinking something important is being lost, it's a highlight of the human Olympic experience."[18] The U.S. team selected Meyer as one of the six allowed on the field. Mike Burton sat with Meyer's parents in the stands and watched the unfolding celebration. Pedersen skipped it and went out to dinner with some friends.

Many films and documentaries costing millions of dollars would be produced about the 1968 Games. They would focus on the Smith and Carlos protest, the great competition, and the fabulous artwork created for the Games. In the official Olympic documentary, IOC president Brundage wanted to cut out the Black Power protest, but it was kept in the film on the insistence of the Mexican Organizing Committee and the president of Mexico. As a result, it became, and still is, the single most dominant image of the 1968 Games.

One film about the closing ceremony of 1968 tells the story of what the Olympics really mean. It captures Olympic magic without narration and flashy edits in just under two minutes in length. It opens with a white flash, a starburst exploding in the dark late October sky. The glowing embers tumble slowly back to earth. The next scene shows a young boy looking skyward, his wide brown eyes reflecting the sparkling fireworks. A big grin spreads on his face as he grips the edges of his hat and pulls them over his ears. A brocade of light descends behind the stadium, highlighting the enormous Olympic torch and the flags that ring the stadium. The athletes are sitting in the infield as the marchers carry their flags around the circular track. The banners are just a few feet apart, moving slowly and giving the appearance of unity among the nations. Both stadium decks are packed with fans, all standing, waving white handkerchiefs and saluting the athletes. The excitement builds as the athletes on the track wave back to the fans. The marchers begin beckoning their teammates to join them in the parade. The athletes edge forward like water gathering before a dam. Suddenly they burst forth, inundating the track from the infield, where they are joined by a waterfall of people from the grandstand. It is unbridled joy, delightfully out of control. The march disintegrates. Marching Boy Scouts break their ranks and begin jumping up and down in excitement as people belly laugh in surprise. It seems like everyone has a hat, and everyone is tossing it into the air. The camera shows three young women, their hair newly coiffed, wearing heels and dressed in uniforms of different countries, standing smiling and talking unconcernedly as fans and athletes race around them. The flags are lowered; there are no nations. The athletes wear an exotic combination of suit coats and ties, native dress, and Olympic tracksuits. People of all races dance, jump, and play ring-around-the-rosy and children's games. They swap hats, notes, and buttons; shake hands; kiss and hug. Cowboy hats and sombreros bob above the crowd, mixing with Africans and Asians dressed in traditional clothing. Seventeen-year-old Felipe Muñoz, who had won a gold swimming medal for Mexico, is hoisted onto his teammates' shoulders and carried around the track, waving to the home fans. Suddenly other athletes are lifted onto shoulders. Folkloric dancers abandon their posts and run around the track, their broad skirts billowing. Green-robed Nigerians dance, engaging all who come near. The nine-hundred-member orchestra, led by a battalion of violinists and guitar players, wanders in an unregimented circle. One performer looks at the camera smiling and nodding as if to say, "Yes, this is what the Games are about." The film ends with the celebration in full flower, thousands of people running, jumping, and smiling so broadly their cheeks must have ached for a week. It couldn't have been more impactful if Walt Disney had choreographed it. For one evening, the national rivalries, illnesses, medal counts, protests, scandals, and tensions were gone. The youth of the world had come together and shown the world how to get along. The lights dim, and the crowd dissolves into the Mexican night. High above the crowd, the scoreboard blinks a final message: "Munich, '72." In a private box far from the field, Brundage frowned at the undisciplined melee. Sitting next to him, President Gustavo Díaz Ordaz smiled at the exuberance.[19]

On October 28, Chavoor and his swimmers triumphantly returned to a waiting crowd of a thousand people at the new Sacramento airport. Stuck on a makeshift riser, John Ferris fidgeted as Meyer and Pedersen made brief remarks. Tired and happy, their talk dissolved into tears of joy. They piled into convertibles and drove into Sacramento, proudly circling the downtown business district and ending up at the lawn in front of the magnificent California Capitol, where fans mobbed them. They were presented with flowers, plaques, and keys to the city.[20] That day *Life* magazine hit the newsstands with eight pages of color photos that followed Meyer through the Games. She was bumped from the cover by the wedding pictures of Jackie Kennedy Onassis and her new husband, Aristotle.

If Arden Hills had somehow seceded from the United States, it would have finished second in the swimming medal count with thirteen, far ahead of Australia, which had only eight. The gold medal count was even starker: Arden Hills, eight; Australia, three. The rest of the world's swimmers tied Arden Hills in gold with eight. But the number that captured the world's attention like no other was Meyer's three individual gold medals, the first time a woman had accomplished that feat.

In describing women swimmers, sportswriters sometimes referred to them as naiads. In ancient Greek mythology, the naiads were beautiful maidens who frolicked in fresh water, scampering over fountains, pools, and lagoons so quickly it was difficult to catch more than a glimpse of them in the water's spray. Even before her three gold medals, the press was referring to Meyer as the queen, and now that she was crowned, the awards from around the world began to pour in. Meyer was the cover girl of the November edition of *Swimming World* magazine, flashing a confident, friendly smile at the camera, twirling her three gold medals attached by blue ribbons around her neck. She was nominated for the 1968 James E. Sullivan Award, presented to the top amateur athlete, male or female, in the United States; *Swimming World* named her Swimmer of the Year, the Amateur Athletic Union gave her its 1968 swimming award, and Genoa, Italy, named her its Outstanding Person. Cuba selected her as the athlete of the year. The *Los Angeles Times* named her one of California's "Women of the Year," along with Nancy Reagan and author Joan Didion. She was honored by *Mademoiselle* magazine and invited to go to Europe, swim in exhibitions, and conduct clinics. While not gaining nearly as much attention, Pedersen was invited to swim in South Africa in early January along with Jan Henne, her conqueror in the 100 meters at the Olympics.

Mike Burton told the press he did not think he would be in the 1972 Games. Instead, he was content to continue swimming at UCLA, where he would be a junior in the upcoming winter quarter. In the meantime, he would have to find a means to support himself. "I'll need to get a job and earn some money," he told a reporter. "Know of anything?"[21] So much for the rewards of being a two-time gold medal winner.

Sherm relaxing during his days as an Army Air Force pilot. *Courtesy Chavoor family*

Chavoor's YMCA swim team featured boys from many racial backgrounds. *Courtesy Chavoor family*

Mark Spitz, second from left, faced stiff competition as an Arden Hills age group swimmer. *Courtesy Chavoor family*

Sue Pedersen, right, was a superstar at a young age. *Courtesy Chavoor family*

Chavoor with his great distance swimmer Mike Burton. *Courtesy Chavoor family*

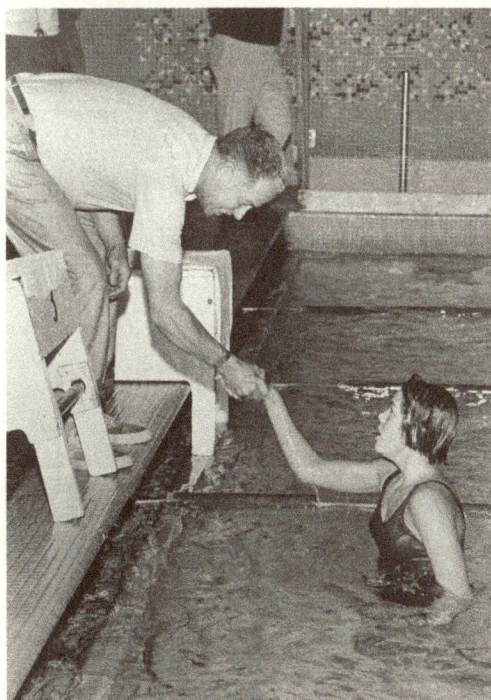

Chavoor congratulates Debbie Meyer after a race. *Courtesy Chavoor family*

Swim meets drew big crowds to Arden Hills. *Courtesy Chavoor family*

From left to right, Sherm Chavoor, Sue Pedersen, Claudia Kolb, Jan Henne, and George Haines at the 1968 Olympic trials in Los Angeles. *Courtesy Chavoor family*

Chavoor kept a close eye on his swimmers during the 1968 Olympics. *Photo by Michael Rougier*, Life

Debbie said she and Chavoor had a love/hate relationship but mostly love. *Photo by Michael Rougier*, Life

Chavoor trains Spitz before the 1972 Olympics. *Photo by Erhardt Krause,* Sacramento Bee

Chavoor and Mark Spitz after the 1972 Olympics. *Courtesy Chavoor family*

Chavoor, left, and Spitz, right congratulated by then California governor Ronald Reagan after the 1972 Olympics. Reagan's daughter, Patti, third from left, looks a bit starstruck. Reagan lived a few blocks from Arden Hills. *Courtesy Chavoor family*

Jeff Float, Chavoor's last gold medal winner. *Courtesy of Jeff and Jan Float*

Chavoor's daughters, Shelley, left, and Sheron, with a portrait of their father. *Photo by Steve Batz*

17

BEAT 'EM, MURDER 'EM

"Gee, I don't think I want to swim anymore."[1] Those words from Debbie Meyer in early January 1969 stunned Chavoor. At sixteen, Meyer was at the top of her game, the acknowledged queen of world swimming. Chavoor thought she was just approaching her peak years, and she could win seven gold medals at the next Olympics. So he was relieved when she showed up for practice the next day. He did everything he could to psych her up and keep her interested. He had her work on her butterfly and train in the individual medley to vary her workout routine and give her new goals. But he knew it would be a struggle to keep her swimming.

Coming off the highs of the Olympic victories, the exciting foreign trips, and the warm holidays full of gifts and congratulations, the return to normal in January was particularly deflating for Meyer and Sue Pedersen. The new year rolled into Sacramento cold and wet, with one storm after another billowing in off the Pacific Ocean. Right after New Year's Day, the swimmers were back at it, conforming to Chavoor and his murderous schedule. The warm, sunny days in Mexico City seemed like a million years ago. The swimmers rose in the chilly predawn darkness at six every morning to make their way to the pool, where the temperatures could dip into the mid-30s with occasional frost. Farmers might protect their fruit crops with smudge pots, but no such luxuries were afforded the swimmers who scampered off the icy deck into the warm pool water, where they worked out from 6:50 to 8:15, swimming five thousand yards. Then it was off to school, with barely time to catch a quick breakfast before the first bell. After school, they were back at Arden Hills for another workout, this one for more than eight thousand yards. When their day finally ended after four, the shadows were lengthening as sunset approached, and they headed home through the gloaming for dinner, homework, and bed. It was an exhausting schedule, and the swimmers didn't get any favors from their teachers, one of whom gave Meyer a grade of B in precision swimming.

There were no easy days for the swimmers as Chavoor kept to his "constant pressure" method. Meyer's ideal swimming weight was 120 pounds, and when she reported in at 121 pounds after the holiday break, she encountered Chavoor's disdain until the offending sixteen ounces evaporated under the workload. "I goad them with constant chatter, insults, and innuendos—with occasional interspersed praise," Chavoor said, a recipe that somehow kept them motivated. He explained his method a little more colorfully when giving a swimming clinic at Sacramento State College. Asked how he kept his swimmers motivated, he answered, "Like anybody else. I beat 'em, murder 'em, hang 'em, kill 'em, bribe 'em, that's how." To some, it was unclear if Chavoor was kidding or really felt that way. After watching the punishment the swimmers endured, a PhD observing the clinic felt compelled to speak up, saying, "I don't agree with that philosophy," to which Chavoor replied, "Oh, and doctor, how many gold medalists have you coached?"[2] The conversation suddenly and awkwardly ended.

Since late December 1968, excited rumors about Meyer winning the Sullivan Award circulated in Sacramento, but the gossip was that she would not win it. The Sullivan Award had been dominated by track and field athletes for years, and 1968 had produced two outstanding candidates, Al Oerter, a four-time Olympic discus thrower, and Bill Toomey, the Olympic decathlon gold medalist. Meyer was a teenager and female, attributes that also seemed to weigh against her. Nevertheless, in the closest vote in the award's history, Meyer received 1,237 votes to Oerter's 1,165 to take the prize. Meyer became the youngest and only the fourth woman to win the award. Chavoor broke the news to Meyer during practice. "I thought Sherm was putting me on," she said. "I called mom. She started crying right away."[3] The *Sacramento Bee* said she was on her way toward being the most respected female athlete since Mildred "Babe" Didrikson Zaharias. This was quite a compliment, since Zaharias had set four world records, winning two gold medals and one silver medal in track and field in the 1932 Los Angeles Olympics.

Arrangements for Meyer's award presentation were quickly made, and it was announced it would be presented at the Scottish Rite Temple in Sacramento on March 9. The meal would be the heavy fare featured in the early 1970s: baked potato, prime rib, string beans, and lemon chiffon pie. "Sacramento, which hardly is recognized nationally as a major sports center, will be exactly that when the gracious Debbie Meyer receives the 1968 Sullivan Award," the *Bee* enthused. The event quickly sold out all tickets at $7.50 each. About the only person in town who would not be there was Sue Pedersen; she would be in Germany, competing in the Bremen International Swimming meet.[4] In February, his peers in the American Swimming Coaches Association named Chavoor 1968 coach of the year, but he knew his coaching would now be tested as never before.

While some wondered if success would spoil him, he worked and worried as hard as ever, keeping a sign on his desk that read "Ulcers Department." Mike Burton was focused on his final semester at UCLA, and the women were not rounding into shape. He told them the Olympics were over, and they had to prepare for the post-Olympic competitions. Chavoor felt Meyer was a little frightened by her success and the challenges she would face, since all the swimmers would be out to beat the Olympic champion. There were so many requests for Pedersen and Meyer to appear at events that Chavoor felt like he was their full-time manager. He spent hours on the phone calling the Amateur Athletic Union office in New York and vetted all the requests for his swimmers' participation in events. The rules about what events were allowed and which weren't were confusing and sometimes contradictory. Rule 26 of the Olympic charter could have banned athletes who "received any financial rewards or material benefit in connection with his or her sports participation, except as permitted." All arrangements, from travel to meals, lodging, and any spending money or free hats and shirts, for example, were subject to approval by the International Olympic Committee. Athletes faced possible revocation of their amateur status if the AAU or Olympic authorities deemed a private entity benefited financially from the girls' participation in an event. Some of the offers were presented as benefits for charities but turned out to be of little benefit to anyone other than unscrupulous event organizers. "Hell, you have to draw the line somewhere," Chavoor said after turning down some of the more dubious requests.[5]

Chavoor just wanted to get everyone's mind back on preparing for the national short course championships in April. But first was "Debbie's Big Party" on March 8 at the Sullivan award banquet. Governor Ronald Reagan proclaimed it "Debbie Meyer Day" in California. City leaders, including Mayor Richard Marriott, gathered to honor their teenage star, and *Bee* sports editor Marco Smolich and reporter Don Bloom covered the affair. Bloom's lede said, "Sacramento's prize 'Peanut' became an athletic immortal last night." The star-studded guest lineup included former Olympic swimming champion Johnny Weissmuller and Olympic track star Wilma Rudolph, who was the last female winner of the Sullivan award, her reward for winning three gold medals in the 1960 Olympics.

The speakers praised Meyer for her "poise, beauty and self-discipline" as much as they lauded her swimming achievements. Weissmuller urged her to stay in shape for the next Olympics and said, "You'll be the greatest medal winner in history."[6]

The next day, the *Bee* played the story on page one of the news and sports pages, a total of three long stories with large pictures of Meyer and the celebrities.

Underneath the stories was another swimming story. The headline read, "Sue Pedersen's Double Victory Helps U.S. Swimmers Lead German Meet." Pedersen had won the 400-meter medley and the 100-meter freestyle. The wire story did not include any quotes or pictures of her.

The first significant appearance for Meyer and Arden Hills in 1969 was at the National AAU Short Course Championships in Long Beach that April. Concerns that all the distractions and awards would hurt their performance were quickly allayed, although there was an upset when her teammate Vicky King narrowly beat her in the 500-yard freestyle. The press described the race as an Arden Hills training drill. "I'm not on top anymore," Meyer said, perhaps a bit facetiously, as she went on to win the 1,650 free, tying her own U.S. record. Mike Burton set yet another record in the 1,650 free but got more media attention when he announced he was getting married and said he probably wouldn't be swimming in the 1972 Olympics.[7]

18

INDIANA CALLING

Mark Spitz spent the months following his disappointing Olympic performance recovering mentally. While he was blasted in the media, college coaches who attended the Games were not discouraged by his showing and were eager to recruit him. Spitz first said he would attend Long Beach State, a natural choice since its head coach, Don Gambril, had been the assistant Olympic swimming coach. Before Spitz had to make a final decision about where he would attend college, he and a group of Olympians went on an excursion to South America for some swimming exhibitions. For Spitz, the relaxing Latin scene, far away from the American media, was a release from the criticism and pressure he had been under since the Olympic trials. The swimmers enjoyed a warm camaraderie. For the first time in years, Spitz felt like he fit in and was accepted by his companions. While their stomachs still had not adjusted to foreign food, they were happy. "We are all sick with diarrhea but having a great time," Spitz wrote in a letter home.[1] Like many young people at that stage of life, they discussed their futures, where they wanted to go to college, and what they wanted to do in their lives.

The swimmers talked about the coaches they knew and liked. Invariably the discussion turned to Doc Counsilman and the innovative coaching system he had established at Indiana University. When Spitz returned from the South American trip, his plane stopped in Florida, where Indiana University coincidentally happened to be conducting its holiday break workouts. Spitz, who had been criticized for being immature and controlled by his father, took the initiative and tracked Counsilman down for a one-on-one meeting. Indiana had dominated college swimming for a decade, was the defending NCAA champion, and was loaded with new talent. After a quick campus stop in Bloomington, Indiana, he was sold.

Counsilman said Spitz was "the greatest swimmer ever to come out of high school," and would be enrolled in the pre-dentistry school.[2]

Still, there would be challenges. The king of the Hoosier hill was Olympic hero Charlie Hickcox. Indiana fans wondered if the pool was big enough for both of them and if Spitz could fit in with his teammates, as he had often failed to do. For the first time in his life, Spitz would be living away from his father, away from California. For the time being, he maintained his relationship with George Haines at the Santa Clara Swim Club and returned there in the summer to train and compete in the national championship. But Spitz was growing and changing, and he would be making more of his own decisions from now on.

Spitz's move to Indiana University proved to be exactly the tonic he needed. Gone were the infighting and cliques he had endured at Santa Clara and on the Olympic team. Counsilman, rightly renowned as a technical genius when it came to swimming, was also a master psychologist and motivator. In an era when most college coaches were authoritarian figures who ruled by fear, Counsilman found out what made each swimmer tick and appealed to it. His swimmers enjoyed joking around with him, wearing T-shirts that read, "What's up, Doc?" stenciled on the front.[3] Well aware of Spitz's past controversies, he handpicked Spitz's roommate and assigned his son, an Indiana swimmer, to help Spitz feel welcome on his new team. Relaxed and swimming better than ever, Spitz dominated his first NCAA Championships held at Indiana's home pool. He won victories in U.S. record times in the 200- and 500-yard free and the 100-yard butterfly, becoming the first freshman to win three titles. Also an NCAA champion was his old friend John Ferris of Stanford, who set the American record in the 200-yard fly. Spitz set the record for most points won by an individual swimmer in the meet as Indiana won nine of the eighteen events, prompting Counsilman to call it the greatest college swimming team ever. "Having this team," said one Indiana fan, "is like having an atomic bomb while everyone else just has a water gun." Concerns about Spitz getting along with Hickcox and the other Hoosiers never materialized, and Hickcox won two championships. A senior, he dedicated his last victory to Counsilman. After his swimmers gave him the traditional victory toast of tossing him in the pool, Counsilman reflected on how much Spitz had grown in just a few months: "He fights for the team as much as he does for himself now, and the kids all like him. He's actually learned to smile and laugh."[4]

With the collegiate season over, most swimmers returned to their home clubs to prepare for the summer's international events and the national championships. Spitz returned to Santa Clara and Haines. It would be a test to see if his personal growth during his time in Indiana would extend through another pressurized season with his old coach and some of the swimmers he said had tormented him.

In the wake of the Olympics, the Santa Clara International Invitational shone brighter than ever that July. The meet drew a record number of competitors, including Olympians from thirteen nations. In 1969, there were three major television networks, and with such limited airtime, it was quite an accomplishment when an event was put on television, ensuring a substantial national audience. Haines had negotiated coverage of the meet with ABC, which proudly televised some of the races live and in color. Spitz returned to Santa Clara in time to enter the meet but was exhausted from a year of almost constant competition.

Debbie Meyer won three freestyle events, but the big news was not her victories, which were becoming rather mundane, but her statement that she could not get "psyched up" for the freestyle races and would be switching to the individual medley. Headlines like "Debbie Meyer says she's getting tired of freestyle event"[5] and "Debbie Meyer looking for new fields to conquer" ran in newspapers around the world.[6] She beat Vicky King in the 1,500 but was off her world record by ten seconds, saying she knew when she got in the water that the adrenaline wasn't flowing. Next, she won the 400-meter free but was off her world record mark again. Then, without announcing it, she switched from the 200-meter free to the 400 individual medley and won that as well. The press said it was good news for rival freestylers, who would not have to face her in the freestyle races.

Spitz was frustrated when he tied but did not break two of his world records, but he still made a strong impression on observers who agreed that he had climbed back from the depths of his Mexico City performance. In the wake of his invitational results combined with his college showing, many said he was now the top swimmer in the world.[7]

Haines was banking on Spitz swimming for his Santa Clara team at the national championships in Louisville that August. His team needed the points Spitz would provide to win the title. But Spitz and his sister Nancy, four years younger, instead accepted an invitation to participate in the 1969 Maccabiah Games in Israel. Spitz was very fond and protective of his sister, who was rapidly improving as a swimmer, and the event would allow them to swim and spend time together. Spitz had swum in the Maccabiah Games as a fifteen-year-old in 1965 and attributed much of his later success to his performance in Israel. "Coming here in '65 was how it all began. I had finished fifth in the 1,500 at the U.S. Nationals [that year] but getting all those firsts did something for me," he told nationally syndicated writer Murray Olderman. The Spitz kids dominated the event, and fifteen-year-old Nancy won multiple gold medals and established herself as one of the top female swimmers in the world. But the real news from Olderman's piece filed from Tel Aviv was Spitz's surprise declaration that he would not swim in the upcoming U.S. National Championships in Louisville. "This will be my last swimming for the summer," he said.[8] When Haines learned he would not enter the meet, Spitz said Haines flew into a rage and yelled at him about shirking his responsibility to the club. Describing him as "headstrong," Spitz said Haines lost his cool and "blew up" at him.[9] Haines told the press that "my boys aren't very happy about Mark's decision, and I'm not either." Nevertheless, he vowed to soldier on in Spitz's absence and defend Santa Clara's national championship. "Our boys are pretty dedicated. They're not going to roll over and play dead," he said.[10]

Without Spitz, Santa Clara lost the championship for the first time in six years. "Spitz is a good boy," Haines said, "but he is going to have to learn that there are certain meets you don't pass up, and this is one of them."[11] Haines sent a letter to the Spitz family notifying them that he had dropped Mark and his sister Nancy from the Santa Clara club. For Haines, it was a matter of a swimmer's loyalty to his teammates. However, Arnold Spitz was outraged when he saw the letter. To him, it was an epic betrayal of the most precious thing in his life: his family.

For the Spitz family, the obvious choice for a new home, pool, and coach was Sacramento, Arden Hills, and Chavoor. In his book, Chavoor reported that Haines said, "If his father had stayed out of it, we could have worked it out. I figured they'd go back to Sherm. With his background in psychology, I figured he could handle it." Chavoor realized in addition to getting Mark and Nancy on the team, he was also inheriting their father.[12]

Seven months later, Haines told *Sports Illustrated*,

> I probably knew Mark as well as anyone, and I probably still do. I understand that he has matured a lot, and I hope so because that was his biggest fault. His trouble with his teammates came because he would say something before he thought. Immaturity. I think he was kidded a lot, and razzed, but down deep every kid was glad he was on this team. Whatever problems he had with his teammates was a 50–50 proposition. If a kid in high school is great, there is a lot of jealousy. I'll say this for Mark; whenever he said he could do something, he could do it.[13]

What, then, to make of this emotional mess that so roiled swimmers, coaches, and media? Spitz collaborated on a book with his biographer, and Schollander and Chavoor both wrote books. They delved into their complicated relationships with Haines in great detail. It would be easy to paint Haines as the evil stepfather of the saga. But unfortunately, George Haines died without writing a book, so other than a few statements made to the press, his side of the story is not presented. After he died on May 1, 2006, the *New York Times* obituary said, "To many, he seemed a dour disciplinarian with a biting sense of humor. When Spitz broke three world records in one night in the Santa Clara pool, Haines was asked if the main reason was a fast pool. 'Yes,' he said. 'The water flows downhill in both directions.'"[14]

What did those who knew him well say? Don Gambril, who coached with Haines on five Olympic teams, said, "The level of respect and confidence he inspired among the swimmers was obvious, and a large factor in our teams domination of world swimming in that era." Claudia Kolb, one of his great Olympic swimmers in the 1960s, said, "I cannot separate my thoughts about George from my everyday life. For over 40 years now, he has been a part of who I am. I cannot tell you how many times, when faced with a decision about something large or small, I have thought about George and what he would do or think. He, along with my mom and dad, have been the most powerful influences in my life and have helped shape the person I am." For Stephen E. Clark, who swam for Haines from age nine until he was twenty-one but never became a star, Haines's best ability was to "understand and help swimmers of all types and ages. Somehow it was his basic personality. He had almost a unique way about him which made each swimmer feel like he was that swimmer's personal and almost exclusive coach, I knew that he genuinely wanted me to do my personal best, just like he wanted my teammate competitors to do their best." Other terms of endearment include statements like "he was a role model," he "oozed honesty and fair play, a man who knew how to deal with people, with straightforwardness, respect and integrity."[15]

Like Arnold Spitz and Sherm Chavoor, George Haines was a World War II veteran who grew up in a rugged, no-nonsense era and was engaged in a challenging, competitive business. That his baby boomer swimmers did not always understand and agree with his decisions is not a reflection of his character. At one point or another, Spitz, Schollander, and Chavoor all thought Haines favored their competitors over them. A baseball umpire knows he's done a fair job if both sides are unhappy with him. Bluntly, George Haines called balls and strikes, despite the gripes from all sides. There is no dispute that he was one of the greatest swimming coaches in the history of the sport.

With Spitz sitting out, Meyer became the star attraction of the national championships in Louisville and did not disappoint, winning the 400-meter individual medley and the 400-meter free. Once again, it was Meyer who drew headlines with a stirring performance in a repeat duel against Vicky King in the 1,500 meters. Meyer took the early lead, but Vicky was determined to take the crown. She closed in the last 250 meters in world record–setting time, but Meyer was somehow able to hold her off by a tenth of a second.[16]

Arden Hills was proving it was still among the top teams in distance swimming as Mike Burton broke his record in the 1,500, setting the new standard at 16:04.5, but he missed his personal goal of becoming the first person under sixteen minutes. Burton had recently married, and he brought his wife, Linda, to the meet, allowing the irascible Chavoor to crack wise with the media: "It's his own fault [Burton didn't break the sixteen-minute mark], I told him not to allow his wife to come along."[17]

With her rival Claudia Kolb retired, Sue Pedersen was putting on a show as well, winning the 200-meter free and the 100-meter free and coming in second in the 400 free and the 200 individual medley. She won the award for scoring the most individual points of any swimmer in the U.S. indoor and outdoor national championships that year. It was also a time for Pedersen's Olympic revenge. Jan Henne had beaten her in the 100-meter free race in Mexico City. That loss had stayed with Pedersen for almost a year. Now they would be set against one another again, this time for the national championship. It was no contest, as Pedersen finished in 59.07 to Henne's 1:01.

The miasma that enveloped the team earlier in the year seemed to be lifting, and Chavoor expressed his appreciation with his usual sarcasm. He claimed he expected victory, "and if they hadn't delivered, they'd have gotten a good kick, you know where."[18] His girls won the championship, and Mike Burton was getting stronger, becoming the first swimmer to win the 1,500-meter race in the outdoor and indoor national championships four years in a row. Better yet, Burton was now starting to believe he had a chance of making the Olympic team in 1972. King was getting better every day, giving Meyer all she could handle and set to join Pedersen and Meyer as elite swimmers. Chavoor figured he could have ten swimmers in the 1972 Olympics.

Chavoor didn't know it, but the first chip on the team he was building was about to fall off the team and dim Arden Hills' 1972 gold medal hopes.

Still just fifteen years old, Pedersen won her sixth U.S. National Championship with her win in Louisville. She was swimming effortlessly, without the pain other girls her age were beginning to feel as their bodies matured. But she wondered about the future and where swimming was leading her. The Olympics were three long years away, and even if she won more gold medals, there was little opportunity for endorsements—not that she cared about that. There were no college swimming scholarships for women. She had been in the pool since age three and was loaded down with awards. She realized it was time to quit. She did everything quietly and modestly, and that's the way she ended her career.

There were no big announcements, no newspaper editorials urging her to stay. Chavoor never approached her for a heart-to-heart about her future. She was just suddenly gone. At age ten, she was so well known the *Sacramento Bee* referred to her in a headline using just her first name: "Only Ten, But Susan Is Swim Star Already." She was almost always the youngest girl in the pool and among the most reliable. For five years, Chavoor had plugged her into relays, sprints, and distance races, and she routinely came through with a first- or second-place finish. Sprinkled through the years were three world records and nine American records. She was at her best in the cauldron of international competition and won three silver medals in the Pan American Games.

When experienced athletes succumbed to the illness, confusion, and controversies in the Mexico City cacophony, "Baby Sue," the youngest Olympian, won two golds and two silvers. She never complained or said a bad word about anyone. When twenty-one-year-old Jan Henne pulled a subtle psych job and upset her in the 100 free by a fingernail, Pedersen immediately responded that she had lost to a good person. More than fifty years later, she would give the same answer without a trace of regret or bitterness. Her favorite memory of the Olympics was when her brother, a U.S. Marine serving on an aircraft carrier, was flown in on a navy helicopter just in time to see her swim.

She got married after she stopped swimming and worked as a CPA in Washington State. In 1977, Meyer, Spitz, Chavoor, and Burton were inducted into the International Swimming Hall of Fame together. Pedersen was not invited and did not enter the hall until 1995.[19]

19

"EVERYBODY'S SON"

After moving back to Sacramento, Mark Spitz faced the skepticism of his Arden Hills teammates, who did not like his cocky and arrogant attitude.[1] Chavoor said that he "Svengalied" Spitz's acceptance by the other swimmers by hosting cookouts and get-togethers. The swimmers warmed up to him, and Chavoor noted, "He was no longer a loner, in constant conflict with his teammates. He was enjoying being part of the team." While his psychological outlook was improving, his practice regimen was still lacking. Chavoor said he had first sensed Spitz was lazy when he was just ten years old.[2] Spitz was not looking forward to Chavoor's brutal over-distancing workouts. Instead, convinced he knew his body well enough to forge his own training program, Spitz occasionally played hooky, called his cousin, and headed for the nearby rapids of the American River for a day of rafting in the sun. To get him to train harder, Chavoor instituted a regimen of constant butterflys for him and the team. Meanwhile, his sister Nancy fit in and was training with Debbie Meyer, Vicky King, and Sue Pedersen. She improved rapidly and was seen as a possible Olympic champion, a prospect that gave her brother great delight.

Sacramento Bee reporter Don Bloom was a fixture on the Arden Hills beat and never missed a move. In September, he buried a bit of news deep in one of his occasional opinion columns, disclosing that "Mike Burton of Sacramento, the [UCLA] Bruins' two-time Olympic swim king, said he probably will swim for Sherm Chavoor at Arden Hills through the '72 Olympics and possibly try some individual medleys."[3] Bigger news came in November when the AAU's Pacific Division unanimously nominated Burton for the Sullivan Award. Bloom perceptively noted that Debbie Meyer had won the last award, beating discus thrower Al Oerter and de-cathlete Bill Toomey, both 1968 gold medal champions. It was unlikely that another Sacramento swimmer could beat out the two respected track and field men.

Burton's accomplishments certainly made for a strong case: Following his two gold medals in 1968, he set world records in the 800 and 1,500 meters in 1969. He was called the most incredible distance swimmer ever, famous for his torturous workouts that amazed rival coaches and competitors. UCLA's athletic director called him the "toughest Bruin athlete of all time," quite an accolade considering that Bruin athletes included Jackie Robinson and his classmate Lew Alcindor, who went on to NBA fame as Kareem Abdul Jabbar. Chavoor said he was a "nut," his idiomatic name for those he most admired. Indiana coach Doc Counsilman used the obscure word "agonist" to describe Burton's pain-filled workouts and endurance at the end of races. Bloom heaped praise on Burton's character, impressed by more than his toughness and swimming ability: "He should be my son. And yours. Everybody's son." Bloom said the country and its college campuses were being ripped apart by antiwar protests and riots. "Burton was planning on being a coach and influencing our youth," who, Bloom said, "more than God only knows can use some direction. They have it made and, for some unknown reason, refuse to believe it, appreciate it or accept it." Bloom concluded that if Mike Burton were everybody's son, "there would be no youth rebellion in America today," a sentiment many people shared.[4]

But soon, Burton himself would have reason to consider rebelling, for something fishy was going on in the Sullivan Award process. On December 30, 1969, the headquarters of the Amateur Athletic Union mailed ballots to a panel that would vote to decide the winner of the Sullivan Award. The procedure had been to place candidates on the ballot during the AAU's annual convention, which had concluded in Miami earlier that month. There were nine "final" nominees for the award, including Burton. Bill Toomey, who had won the Olympic decathlon, was not placed on the ballot. A few days after the convention adjourned, Toomey participated in another event, where he set the world decathlon record for points in a time trial—an event held without any other athletes on the UCLA campus on December 10.

In the 100-meter sprint, Toomey finished in 10.3 seconds, helping him break the all-time world record for points scored in a decathlon. Burton, a UCLA student, attended that decathlon and wondered about the veracity of Toomey's recorded sprint time. "There were a bunch of 80-year-olds [AAU officials] holding stopwatches," Burton said. "It was all a setup, a political deal."[5] There is evidence for this claim. The *New York Times* reported that when New York track clubs heard of Toomey's world record performance, "they immediately put pressure on the AAU executives" to put Toomey on the ballot, even though it had already been printed and mailed. These track clubs were not identified by name or affiliation, and apparently materialized spontaneously from the track club enclaves of New York City. The Sullivan Award Committee conducted a telephone poll that "produced an overwhelming vote for adding Toomey to the ballot." The *Times* praised "sports leaders here [in New York] for taking 'prompt and effective action' to put Toomey on the ballot" at the last minute, despite the obvious and blatant irregularities in the process.[6]

An AAU official in New York told Don Bloom of the *Bee*, "We presumed Mike had it wrapped up until that special telephone vote was taken to add Toomey to the list [of candidates] last month. [Toomey] got the advantage of all that late publicity."[7] When the votes were counted, Toomey was the overwhelming winner; Burton finished second.

The year came to an end with even more awards for Meyer. She was named World Swimmer of the Year for the third straight year by *Swimming World* and was nominated for the Associated Press Athlete of the Year, an award she won in January 1970. In addition, Italian newspapers selected her as the sportswoman of the world, a sign that her Olympic renown lived on around the world.

The decade of the turbulent 1960s was coming to an end. It had been a time of unprecedented social change and violent protest in America and the world. Many hoped the Vietnam War was coming to an end. Neil Armstrong walked on the moon, raising hopes for a new decade of tranquility and international cooperation. But life had changed dramatically in many other ways. A short list of some of the latest technological developments gives a picture of the sweeping changes altering the nation. By the decade's end, television had gone from a novelty to the dominant medium of the age and one of the most profound communication tools ever. In 1961, the laser was perfected. In 1965, the Houston Astrodome, the world's first roofed stadium, was built. In 1967, the first heart transplant was performed by Christiaan Barnard in Cape Town, South Africa, opening up remarkable new vistas in medicine.

In 1970, the organizers of the Munich Olympics announced they had received one million requests for tickets to the opening ceremonies, which posed a problem since the stadium only had eighty thousand seats. The Associated Press reported that the "roar of bulldozers and the staccato of builders' drills fills the Munich air these days as the Bavarian capital gets ready for the 1972 Games." Officials said they were right on schedule, and the new stadium would be completed by the end of 1971, well before the

August 26, 1972, opening ceremonies.[8] But even building the Olympic facilities was loaded with the emotional symbolism of Germany's Nazi past. Journalist Peter Gyallay-Pap noted that Oberwiesenfeld, the area in Munich where the Games would be held, had once been the airport British prime minister Neville Chamberlain flew into in 1938 to sign the "peace in our time" agreement with Adolf Hitler. Unfortunately, peace did not prevail, and Munich was bombed into rubble during the war. Clearing the fields for the Games created a 250-foot-high hill that was covered with shrubs and grass and offered a commanding view of the Olympic grounds. "The Germans' attempt to bury—if not forget—the past is thus symbolically represented," Gyallay-Pap observed.[9]

Arden Hills sent twenty-eight swimmers to the 1970 national championships in Los Angeles that August. At the halfway point between the 1968 and 1972 Olympic Games, Chavoor saw the meet as an essential measuring stick for his star swimmers. The championships were held in the Los Angeles Swimming Stadium at the Los Angeles Coliseum, a venue Meyer said was the fastest pool in the world and the scene of her outstanding Olympic trials performance two years earlier. But Meyer was not the same person. She was growing up, mentally and physically. Before the meet, Chavoor acknowledged that Meyer's enthusiasm was waning. "In practice, that spark she needs as far as motivation is concerned hasn't been there. But this happens to most athletes who are on top," he said.[10] Entering the 400-meter free, she thought she could set the new record, but "I knew it was going to have to hurt. I could feel the strain down to my toes."[11] Determinedly, she dug deep and set the world record in 4:34.3. She also won the 1,500-meter race, her ninth national outdoor championship, but did not break the world record. Afterward, she said she was just happy she'd won. She also joined Nancy Spitz, Vicky King, and Evelyn Kossner to win the 800-meter relay for Arden Hills. Despite his concerns, Chavoor's female swimmers came through for him again, and his reputation for developing female distance swimmers continued to be enhanced by these performances.

That summer, Meyer graduated from Rio Americano High School. She went through the graduation ceremony like any other kid, except she was followed around for a few days by *Sports Illustrated*. In August, she turned eighteen, and *Sports Illustrated* reporter Jerry Kirshenbaum noticed how she had changed, physically and mentally, from her Olympic year. "While nobody was looking she has sneaked up to 5'7½", nearly three inches taller than when she set her first world record at fourteen," he wrote. Relaxing in her backyard after the graduation ceremony, she mused about the young swimmers she would have to contend with: "There are a lot of girls who'd love to beat me, that puts pressure on me. But I just try to stay calm and set goals for myself. I'm glad I decided to keep swimming. If I hadn't, I don't know what I would've done with myself." Her training at Arden Hills had slackened a bit, and Chavoor wondered what he should do about it. He tried to push her but worried he was torturing her. But he couldn't get the dream of more gold in 1972 out of his mind. Reporter Kirshenbaum watched a few workouts and perceptively sized up the dilemma:

> Unfortunately, swimming is not fully compatible with growing up, this being a clear case of two kinds of pain competing jealously for the same victim. Despite her determination to continue swimming, Debbie has lately been balkier ("how come no rest between laps, huh, Sherm?") than obedient. That may sometimes strain but has never actually impaired the affection that exists between Chavoor and herself. Asked not long ago whether theirs was a love-hate relationship, she answered softly, "Yes, but the hate is temporary and the love is permanent."[12]

Time was fleeting and eroding the magical memories of 1968. Sue Pedersen had retired quietly, and Vicky King was going to attend Stanford. Many of the kids Meyer had grown up swimming with were out of the pool and getting on with their lives. It seemed like all that remained the same was Chavoor yelling and the crushing boredom and pain of swimming endless laps.

The last meet of Debbie Meyer's swimming career came in January 1972 in an AAU meet in San Francisco. Meyer easily won the 500 but was not close to her record time. "When the race was over I couldn't breathe for the pain," she said. Meyer went back to Sacramento and went to her usual Monday workout. About halfway through the workout, Chavoor waved her to the side of the pool. It was clear Meyer's motivation was lacking. Chavoor told her to go home and discuss the situation with her parents. After a three-hour talk, her mom said, "Darling, when it becomes a chore, and the fun is out of it, it is time to quit." She went back and told Chavoor she was done. "I knew it was killing him inside but he kind of hugged me in that gruff way of his, and he said, 'I'm glad.'"[13]

The news went worldwide. The headline in the January 25 *New York Times* read, "19-Year-Old Debbie Meyer Calls It Quits as Swimmer." The brief item said, "Miss Meyer had been a leading candidate for a berth on America's squad for the Summer Olympics in Munich. But she said, 'I just don't seem to have the drive anymore. I have been to the Olympics and don't want to work that hard to get there again. My mind tells me to get moving, but my arms won't go.'"[14] The *Sacramento Bee* announced the news on page one and lauded her in an editorial as a woman who "raised endurance swimming to a performance art, who has been a model athlete, a credit to her community."[15] While Chavoor took the news well, he reflected on how his women's team was being decimated. Sue Pedersen had retired, Vicky King was leaving, and Nancy Spitz was struggling to recover her swim stroke. At the time, many "experts" believed girls quit swimming because they peaked physically at age fifteen or sixteen. But Chavoor understood the real reason the girls generally stopped earlier than the boys—there were no college scholarships for them. College swimming programs, if they existed, were more recreational than competitive.

Chavoor always considered Meyer his third daughter, and she thought of him as a second father. Her devotion to him grew no matter how hard he pushed her or how many barbs he tossed her way. Their partnership gave both Meyer and Chavoor lasting renown.

Her most outstanding achievement was becoming the first female swimmer to collect three individual gold medals at the same Games when she won the 200-, 400-, and 800-meter freestyle events at Mexico City in 1968, a feat that has been matched only by Janet Evans and Katie Ledecky. In many ways, that epic achievement has been overshadowed by the non-athletic events of the Mexico City Games: The Black Power protest of John Carlos and Tommie Smith, the bloody riot on the eve of the Games, and the controversy over the Soviet invasion of Czechoslovakia conspired to partly obscure Meyer's remarkable feat. Even today, the dominant image of the Games is that of Carlos and Smith with fists raised in the air.

In 1968, Olympic officials were neurotically fixated on controlling their athletes. Olympic athletes were not allowed to benefit financially in any way from their accomplishments. There were few product endorsement deals and limited paid speaking engagements. The offers would have rolled in for Meyer, whose good looks and personality would have made her a mega-celebrity. While Meyer did some promotional work after her retirement, the monetary rewards were modest compared with what star athletes receive today. Nevertheless, she never grumbled about what could have been. She worked with young people, operated a swim school, and enjoyed recognition in the swimming world, even when some of the young swimmers' parents were more excited to meet her than the kids were. The happy kid turned into a happy adult.[16]

With her newfound free time, Meyer took to the nearby Sierra Nevada ski slopes, where she promptly broke her left leg. "It took her eight years to learn to swim," Chavoor quipped. "I hope it doesn't take her eight years to learn to ski."[17]

Observers saw evidence that Mike Burton would soon be eclipsed by rising star John Kinsella, who beat Burton in the 400 free while setting a new world record. Kinsella also broke Burton's world record in the 1,500 meters. But Burton was not conceding anything and stubbornly battled to the end, finishing a close second. Reporters noted that Kinsella stood six-foot-three and weighed 200 pounds, all muscle. Beside him, the five-foot-seven, 150-pound Burton looked small and scrawny. Kinsella was sure and confident. "I realized after the 400 that I was a bit stronger than Mike," Kinsella said. "He was always stronger than me. I never had the endurance to beat him before, but now I realize I do." Kinsella was headed to Indiana University to join Spitz and Gary Hall in Doc Counsilman's thriving program, but he was looking farther ahead. "I'm hoping by 1972 that I'll be a little bit stronger. I'll have about reached my peak in two years. I'll be twenty then, and I plan on being ready."[18] Burton was a marked man. *Los Angeles Times* sports writer Jim Murray humorously noted, "As swimmers go, he's the Old Man and the Sea—[at age] twenty-three." But Murray also realized that Burton had an indefatigable will and work ethic, and rival swimmers should have taken the sports writer's humor as a prophetic warning. He "spent more time in the water than the *Titanic*, and when he quits, he will drip for ten years," Murray quipped.[19] Burton was far from quitting, and he would spend as much time as he could in the pool to get ready to fend off his young challengers.

Mark Spitz's collapse in the 200-meter fly at the Olympics continued to psych him out at the nationals. He set a world record in the 200 preliminaries but faltered badly in the final when he finished fourth and saw his world record eclipsed by nineteen-year-old Gary Hall. Chavoor saw this as a significant psychological setback for Spitz. Chavoor had been grooming Spitz for a win in the 200 and worked hard to restore his confidence, and he thought a national championship win would pave the way for future success. When Spitz lost, however, Chavoor thought he was still psyched out by his poor performance in the 1968 Olympics. Spitz set another world record in the prelim of the 100-meter free, only to come in second in the final. He managed to win two events, the 100-meter fly and 200-meter free, but Chavoor knew Spitz still had to overcome the psychological impact of his Mexico City performance to succeed in Munich.

Entering 1971, Mark Spitz was on the knife's edge of excellence. Counsilman and Chavoor had worked relentlessly to restore his confidence, which had been so severely damaged in Mexico City. Now a twenty-year-old college student, he was developing his own identity. He was overjoyed when his younger sister Nancy won the 200-yard freestyle at the national indoor championship. Mark had won two championships in the outdoor nationals the previous August. With sister Nancy's win, the Spitz kids became the first siblings to hold AAU National Championship titles simultaneously.

Arnold Spitz seldom interfered with Chavoor when he coached Mark. But he was deeply involved with developing Nancy. Chavoor said Arnold Spitz changed his daughter's swimming stroke and that it took months to get it straightened out again. Nancy's progress was too slow for her father, and Chavoor said the elder Spitz "became so incensed at his daughter because she wasn't going as fast as he thought she should that he threw a rubber training tube at her." According to Chavoor, Mark witnessed the scene and said to his father, "If you did that to me, I'd tear you apart."[20]

In 1971, Mark Spitz erased any doubt that he was the world's greatest swimmer. At the start of the summer season, he began to make his case at the Santa Clara Invitational, where he won the 100 free and the 200 butterfly. Then he went on a rampage in late August at the AAU National Outdoor Championships in Houston and became the first person to win four individual gold medals in the event. Overcoming his perceived psychological hang-up, he set two world records in the 200 butterfly, the event that had so troubled him after his performance in Mexico City. Next, he set another world record in the 100 butterfly and won the 100- and 200-meter freestyle races. "The audience in Houston was half stunned, half screaming and yelling" at his performance, Chavoor remembered. But he wondered if Spitz had really overcome his fears of the 200 butterfly and said, "I still wasn't sure he had overcome some of his old abrasive social habits."[21] The Houston pool was "one of the worst I've ever competed in," Spitz told the press after the event, sparking an unneeded controversy and news stories once again portrayed him as the talented, arrogant, and spoiled swimmer.[22]

Spitz and his fellow AAU national champions left for a series of meets in Eastern Germany and Europe, where Spitz continued his historic world record spree. The competition marked the first time a U.S. athletic squad competed inside East Germany. In a stop in Leipzig, Spitz set the world record in the 200 free, breaking Schollander's record that had stood since 1968. In the 400-meter medley, Spitz swam the butterfly in the race's third leg. The American team was behind, but Spitz's blazing lap pulled the United States to victory in world record time. The team moved on to Minsk, where Spitz again set the world record in the 200-meter free while leading the American men to a world record in the 800-meter freestyle relay. Spitz set six world records in less than two weeks while traveling more than twelve thousand miles.

Now that he was at his peak, people began asking what made Spitz such a great swimmer. Many factors led to his success. He was raised in Northern California, one of the hotbeds of swimming, and was pushed by intense competition. Many of his teammates and competitors from that region grew up to become Olympic contenders and champions. Early on, Arnold Spitz was convinced his son was a great swimmer and saw to it that he belonged to the best clubs with the best coaches. From the day he entered the pool, he benefited from great coaching. When he started swimming at the YMCA, he was spotted by Paul Herron, an accomplished college and AAU swimmer. He moved on to Chavoor at Arden Hills, then George Haines at Santa Clara, and finally Doc Counsilman at Indiana. These men are among the greatest coaches in history, and each imparted tactics and wisdom to Spitz. Coaches and rivals spent years figuring out the biomechanics that propelled him through the water at record speed. Chavoor said Spitz's greatness started with his anatomy; he had long arms, elongated and sinewy, Chavoor noticed. Chavoor always said any swimmer's power came from the upper torso, not the legs, and said Spitz had tightly packed muscles in his arms, shoulders, and back, similar, Chavoor thought, to baseball slugger Hank Aaron. Chavoor noted that Spitz frequently slouched when not in the water, standing with his head bent forward like a coiled spring. Others noted the smoothness and flexibility in his entire body, a characteristic that made him such a devastating butterflyer. The press made a big deal out of what they saw as an unusual conformation of his knees, and rival and Olympic medalist Jerry Heidenreich explained it this way: "Did you ever look at his legs?" he asked a reporter.

"Yes, they're pretty long," the newsman answered.

"Long!" Heidenreich exclaimed. "He's so hyperextended (meaning that his knees are so supple that his legs flex slightly forward and backward) that he can kick six inches deeper than anyone else. His legs are like a bow. When he puts on a pair of pants, the stripes seem to go in different directions."[23]

Chavoor acknowledged the unusual shape of Spitz's knees but saw a different result. "What the unusual knee conformation did for him was give him perfect balance in the water."[24] Chavoor said that outstanding balance was one attribute all great swimmers enjoyed.

Sportswriter Joe Falls covered Spitz during the 1972 Olympics and described what it was like to see him in a race:

Spitz swims spectacular races. He is the first into the water, the first to begin his strokes, his turns are faultless, and his finishing kick. Well, the notion here is that a swimmer is a swimmer. You get them all into the water, and they all look alike. A lot like horses. You can tell the difference with Mark Spitz. He's the one far out in front, knifing straight ahead with a power that is awesome to behold. You look for weaknesses. Does he favor his right arm over the left arm? Does he weave? Does he ever get tired? He is a machine. Each stroke is like a piston hammering into an engine.[25]

Spitz was immensely talented, but from his earliest days swimming, he did not possess a superior work ethic and often displayed bizarre phobias. For example, he had an odd ritual about getting into the water. He would stand by the poolside, refusing to get wet. Some of the younger kids would see this and begin spraying and splashing him with water until they finally got him wet enough to jump into the pool. Not wanting to get wet, Chavoor observed, was odd behavior for a world-class swimmer. Spitz also had special talismans and superstitions. He would insist on wearing blue whenever possible because the blue ribbon signified winning. He would only train in the middle lanes because that's where the top finishers in the heats swam.

Teammates often questioned his commitment to swimming and his resistance to working out. Indiana teammate and world champion John Kinsella wondered at Spitz's approach. If you watched Spitz practice, he said, you would have no idea he was a world-class swimmer. The criticism had little effect on Spitz. He had the casual arrogance of a champion and said he would rely on his physical and mental ability to reach the top. He said he didn't need long, hard workouts; he was a sprint racer, knowing how much work he needed to win and when to take it easy. Spitz admitted he sometimes did not go all out in practice but justified it by saying he felt he knew his body better than anyone else. He'd run the rapids if he had to skip a day of training and go river rafting.[26] It did not please Chavoor, but the coach lived with it. Spitz would never train with the intensity of Mike Burton, but as he got older, he grumbled less and began to embrace Chavoor's grueling workouts.

Spitz was named the 1971 winner of the AAU's Sullivan Award. When notified he'd won, Spitz was asked about the Olympics and said he was not 100 percent sure he would compete in them. He said he had been admitted to the Indiana University School of Dentistry, noting that the Olympics and the start of class that September conflicted, and he'd miss three weeks of school if he competed. In addition, he was thinking about his future, and while grateful about winning the award, he was concerned about life after swimming. He said there was no money in swimming and noted that while college Heisman Trophy winners got pro contracts, there would be no such lucrative offers for him.

With the Olympics approaching, the press noted that Spitz, a Jew, would be possibly the most famous athlete competing in Germany in the first Olympic Games held there since the Holocaust. When Spitz set a world record in Berlin it was reported that he said, "I'll bet Hitler turned over in his grave tonight." On the night of the Sullivan Award, U.S. Olympic team manager Ken Treadway said, "I predict in Munich not only Hitler, but Khrushchev, Stalin, and Lenin will all turn over in their graves."[27] Treadway announced that Chavoor would return as the women's coach again, and Pete Daland, head coach of the University of Southern California, would replace Haines as the men's coach. Chavoor thought the women would have a strong contingent but acknowledged that Australia, led by its star Shane Gould, would provide tough competition.

20

THE GOAL OF ANY ATHLETE

Mark Spitz's most important collegiate victory came in 1970, when he avenged his Mexico City Olympic loss to Doug Russell. "I have a lot of respect for Russell. But he never broke my records, and to me the best swimmer is the most consistent one. This was very satisfying to me, because I proved to myself I could beat him. I can't forget losing, and I never will. My worst moment was at the Olympics, and my best, maybe, was tonight," Spitz said after the race. [1] The victory gave Spitz confidence to begin thinking about a gold medal in Munich in 1972.

Spitz began his Olympic year with more victories in the NCAA Championships. He set the U.S. record in the 200- and 100-yard fly. The meet, Indiana's fifth consecutive NCAA title, marked the end of his collegiate career, during which Spitz won thirteen Big Ten and eight individual NCAA Championships. His years at Indiana transformed Spitz from a cocky, insecure teenager to a man ready to assume the greatest challenges of his life. He won the recognition and admiration so desperately sought since his humiliation at the 1968 Olympics. He was cocaptain of the swimming team and honored at "Mark Spitz Day" at his final home meet with standing ovations. He waved farewell to the adoring crowd with tears in his eyes as Indiana sportswriters proclaimed the end of an era. [2]

Spitz dominated the AAU Short Course Championships the following month in Dallas, winning three gold medals and narrowly missing a fourth. While he was the top swimmer, strong performances from Gary Hall, Genter, and Heidenreich showed that they would be factors in the Olympics. Newcomer and rising star John Kinsella won the 500- and 1,650-yard events at the meet, further solidifying his claim as the top U.S. distance swimmer.

As the year progressed, it was clear that Heidenreich would be Spitz's chief U.S. rival. Spitz and Heidenreich were born within six days of each other in 1950—Heidenreich on February 4 and Spitz on February 10—but temperamentally, they were poles apart. Heidenreich helped make Southern Methodist University (SMU) a college powerhouse that challenged Indiana. Like Spitz, Heidenreich's father pushed him hard. But unlike Spitz, who never smoked or drank, Heidenreich was "the most intense swimmer—and the most intense reveler—S.M.U. had ever seen."[3] But he was one of the fastest sprint swimmers in the world and had beaten Spitz's time by a second in the 200-meter free, and he was the man seen as most likely to knock Spitz off in Munich.

After graduation, Spitz returned to Chavoor and Arden Hills and, along with Mike Burton, joined fourteen other Arden Hillers to prepare for the Olympic trials held in Chicago starting July 29. Mark's sister Nancy and 1968 Olympic silver medalist Ellie Daniel were favorites to make the women's Olympic team. On the men's side, Spitz kept his eyes on young challengers. He feared fellow Arden Hills sprinter Dave Fairbank, who was "drop dead fast," a sobriquet he earned because he would go out with every last ounce of energy he had in the 100 but then "drop dead" after 75 meters and lose the race. But Spitz could see the eighteen-year-old's pure speed and knew if the youngster became more strategic in his race approach, he could threaten any swimmer.

Spitz knew there were many young swimmers like Fairbank who, on any given day, could rip off a world record. If that day happened during the Olympic trials or the Olympics, it could cost him a gold medal—a concern that added to the doubt growing in his mind. One day, rafting on the American River with his cousin Sherman, his mind wandered, and he thought again of his future. What did he have to gain by swimming in another Olympics? He'd won the Sullivan Award, already had two gold Olympic medals, and held national championships, world records, and collegiate records. If he failed to win every Olympic race he entered, he'd be branded a failure. He had proved that he was a great swimmer the year before by winning four championships at the nationals in Houston. Having lived the disastrous Olympic experience once, he did not want to endure it again.

Chavoor recognized that Spitz's indecisiveness was turning into one of the biggest crises of his career. Chavoor and Arnold Spitz kept pounding the message that his past accomplishments meant little. "Burton, Schollander, Debbie Meyer all say the only thing that counts is Olympic gold," Chavoor told him.[4] Chavoor accused Spitz of malingering in practice, hounded him relentlessly, and criticized him for taking too many sunbaths; some days, he had to spend hours coaxing him into the water.[5] It took a visit to his former home pool to get him over his final qualms. In less than top shape, he won the 100-meter butterfly and the 100-meter free at the Santa Clara International in late June. Encouraged, he finally committed to going all out, putting in the work during practice, and seeing just how great a swimmer he could be.

Chavoor's goal was to have his swimmers mean and edgy by the time they headed to the Olympic trials, now just a month away. Somehow, he conjured brutal weather conditions that aided his quest to make their lives miserable and toughen them up. Sacramento is hot in the summer; 100 degrees is not unusual. In 1972, 100 degrees seemed cool. A heat wave enveloped the valley and baked the region. The thermometer rose day after day. Finally, it reached successive near-record levels of 108, 110, 112, and 114 degrees in late June. In the countryside surrounding them, chickens died from the heat and ponds that provided water for cattle evaporated.[6] Ranchers packed their pickups with water jugs and raced to the cows' relief. Pear orchards withered under the relentless sun. The thin skins of tomatoes and grapes were scorched and sunburned; the crops yielded little fruit. It seemed like a disaster straight out of the Bible. Power companies struggled to meet the demand for air conditioning, and short energy supplies led to outages.

Tens of thousands of people broiled in the heat, and even the pool could not protect the swimmers. The sun baked their backs as they drove through lap after lap. Chavoor employed a brutal schedule. Yelling, cajoling, and insulting, he drove them daily until their bodies shrieked in protest. Chavoor used every trick he had gathered in thirty years of coaching. Dangling his stopwatch, he promised them he would end the practice and let them get out of the pool if someone could come close to beating a world record.[7] At the end of the race, Chavoor invariably proclaimed that the time had been met and everyone could go home. One day Spitz arrived late, looked over the scene, hopped in the water, and ripped off a world record time in the butterfly. Jumping out of the pool, he told Chavoor goodbye as a stunned Burton looked at Chavoor and asked, "How am I supposed to compete with that?"[8]

Finally, the heat wave broke. The pleasant Pacific marine layer overcame the blanket of hot air, and a cool breeze pushed over the coast range into the valley. The nights fell into the 60s and 70s, and Chavoor orchestrated team-building outings. They went to the Spitz and Burton homes for cookouts. The coach set his insults and jibes aside and listened as they spoke about the upcoming games. Layer after layer, the bravado peeled off as they talked about their insecurities. Chavoor understood that only Spitz and Burton, the holders of two gold medals each, had enough experience to conceal their fears.

Chavoor arranged for several former Olympic greats to visit his swimmers. Don Schollander came and stayed a few days. With the fierce fires of rivalry banked, Schollander spoke about the focus they needed to attain to be Olympic victors. He left impressed with the maturity Spitz now displayed. He said Spitz could win six gold medals "if he keeps his cool and doesn't psych out like he did in '68. His mind is his biggest problem, not his body."[9]

By the last week of July, a very confident Chavoor had his contingent ready to head to Chicago for the Olympic trials. "Eight, maybe ten, will make it to Munich," Chavoor told the *Sacramento Bee*. He predicted that Arden Hills swimmers would win "10 Olympic gold medals."[10] Spitz was in the best shape of his life and armed with new confidence. The trials were held in Portage Park, a working-class neighborhood on Chicago's northwest side. The facility was no glitzy glass-walled natatorium like the sparkling new structure in Long Beach that hosted the 1968 trials. The pools had been built for the 1959 Pan American Games and resurfaced for the trials, a city park dressed up for the occasion. Chicago weather is never dull, and a cold front descended from the north, bringing wind, rain showers, and temperatures in the 50s.

At the pre-meet news conference, Spitz quickly pronounced the pool "inferior" and said it wasn't as good as the Sacramento pool where he trained. "The AAU and the Olympics are all politics. The trials are here because of politics. AAU Swimming does not have enough former swimmers on committees, and most of the swimmers on the committees are stupid," he stated bluntly. But Spitz had grown bigger than swimming. He was becoming a superstar on the level of American chess champion Bobby Fischer, who was captivating media attention by dueling with Russian chess grandmaster Boris Spassky for the world championship. Some writers saw similarities between Spitz and Fischer: They were both Jewish and outspoken and had their eccentricities. The press asked if Spitz played chess, and he said he occasionally did. "Chess is all in the head, but so is every sport," he said. But when it came to making pronouncements about how many gold medals he would win in Munich, Spitz proved he'd learned from his 1968 experience and repeated platitudes. "I'll just try to do the best I can," he repeatedly recited in response to the media's constant questions. "I never swam for glory, only the satisfaction of being recognized as the best in the world. That's the goal of any athlete, isn't it?"[11]

But the biggest news wasn't about swimming; it was about the mustache he had grown. The mustache gave his handsome, suntanned face a perfect frame, setting off his deep-set, flashing eyes. The press, without irony, immediately compared him to the mustachioed Hollywood film star Omar Sharif, one of the world's most handsome and famous men. Sharif, the Egyptian star of the movies *Lawrence of Arabia* and *Doctor Zhivago*, was a Muslim, and Spitz was a Jew.[12] Spitz's handsome dark looks stood out even more when contrasted with the other swimmers, all of whom were white and many of whom were blond. Spitz had grown his mustache as a mild protest against Indiana University coach Doc Counsilman, who thought swimmers should look like all-American boys. Even a thin mustache was seen as tipping an athlete dangerously toward nonconformity, even though professional quarterback Joe Namath had sported a robust and daring Fu Manchu mustache. Spitz had nursed his growth for five or six months before the trials and was prepared to shave it off until he noticed his competitors were talking about it to the media. Always looking for an edge, Spitz thought the mustache issue was distracting his rivals' focus. At the news conference, all the questions were asked of Spitz until a coach finally interrupted and said there were many other accomplished swimmers at the meet and they might enjoy a little attention.

Despite the weather and the less-than-glamorous facilities, Chicago, the adopted hometown of Olympic swimming great and Tarzan actor Johnny Weissmuller, turned out in large and enthusiastic numbers to watch seven hundred swimmers compete for sixty-one Olympic team spots. With U.S. swimming dominating the world, everyone knew the trials would be as competitive—or more—than the Games.

David Russell, a former Chicago city champion, did not compete in the trials, but he got a job covering them for a suburban newspaper and painted a superb portrait of the competitors. He was impressed by the young swimmers' poise, professionalism, and perfectionism. The U.S. swimmers, Russell wrote, reflected country club culture: "highly competitive, individualistic, young, white, rich, middle-class, with a certain kind of adolescent sophistication and a growing sun-and-fun culture." He explained that swimming is an expensive sport confined to wealthy all-white areas that could support private clubs. "All are the product of age-group swimming having begun . . . as early as four and five years of age." He noticed Arden Hills' Mike Burton, age twenty-five, and Ellie Daniel, age twenty-two. He detected "a fatigue of spirit, possibly burned down at some earlier age, a symptom of age group swimmers who were seasoned veterans at sixteen, tired bodies at twenty-five after twenty years of competition." For most of the competitors, victory and defeat were taken with subdued equanimity: "For many, there was only a small chance of becoming a member of the team, yet there was honor enough in competing with the best in the country." Spitz stood out as the star, "an idol particularly for younger girls . . . the Omar Sharif of the swimming world. His aloofness, his near boredom with breaking word records, and concern over camera lighting for pictures of himself are exceeded only by his raw talent and skill at being the best there is." He found an array of characters: shy and comfortable talkers, scared and cool kids. They were, he concluded, "indeed excellent, possessing calculated confidence, superior athletes in skill, training and attitude."[13]

In five days, eleven world and seventeen American records fell. Spitz set three world records and won four events in the trials. There was no holding back or conserving energy, Chavoor said. Spitz was so relaxed that he dipped into his camera collection to take snapshots of the action when he wasn't swimming.

In his first event, the 200-meter fly that had haunted him since Mexico City, he broke West Germany's Hans Fassnacht's world record twice, first in a preliminary heat and then in the final that evening. The victory loosened him up, and he drew more energy from the crowd of five thousand that got behind him and pushed him to faster and faster times. There was noise and excitement everywhere, from the squealing teenage girls who followed Spitz to the boisterous blue-collar crowd that cheered like they were at a Cubs game.

In the 200 free, Spitz faced rivals Jerry Heidenreich, the NCAA record holder in the event, and UCLA great Steve Genter. Both had beaten him in the college season and were capable of world record times. Many thought Heidenreich would win in Chicago and take gold in Munich. Like Spitz's Mexico City antagonist Doug Russell, Heidenreich was a Texan, and Russell had taken him under his wing and coached him on how to beat Spitz. But the cool weather got to him, and he couldn't get loose for the race. The cruelty of the Olympic trials method of win or go home was on full display; not only did he lose to Spitz, but he also didn't make the cut for a spot on the team in the 200. Spitz won handily but looked around so much during the race some thought he was playing in the pool.

There were no flaws as Spitz set another world record in the 100 butterfly before moving on to face his final challenge in the 100 free. This time Heidenreich was ready, and he and Spitz swamped the field. The crowd now realized it was seeing one of the best swimmers in history. Wanting to see a peak performance, they urged Spitz on, chanting, "Go, go, go" as

Spitz sprinted to the lead with Heidenreich beside him the entire way. Spitz had to set another world record to win by inches, and Chavoor named Heidenreich as Spitz's archrival for Munich.[14]

The possibility of winning seven gold medals came within sight as Spitz qualified for four individual races and three relays. "Well, I guess I accomplished something this summer after all," Spitz told Chavoor. But Chavoor laughed: "You accomplished a good suntan, Buster. Just think how much better you might have done if you'd have worked."[15] Spitz was happy with his performance but begged off making predictions on how it would translate to Munich.

While Spitz was enjoying his run as the king of the Windy City, Mike Burton was struggling to make the Olympic team. Even though he was the defending Olympic gold medal champion in the 1,500 and the 400, his few mentions in the media revolved around his age (twenty-five) and how many years he'd been swimming (ten). Some viewed him as a gimpy over-the-hill swimmer who had not set a world record in three years. John Kinsella lived in a Chicago suburb, and many in the crowd had come to witness his anticipated ascension to the throne as the world's greatest distance swimmer. At age twenty, Kinsella was in his prime. He had already won the Sullivan Award and was the first person to swim 1,500 meters under sixteen minutes. Yet even he was being threatened by a young rival, the "sudden sensation," sixteen-year-old Rick DeMont, a high schooler from Marin County, California. Despite struggling to control his asthma, DeMont made a solid bid to make the team. Aficionados marveled at his beautiful technique, finishing kick, and excellent balance.

Burton was eliminated in the 400 free and the 200 butterfly, and it looked like he would not survive the preliminary heats in the 1,500. He barely wiggled into the finals by finishing seventh. It seemed unlikely he would finish in the top three the next night in the finals in a pool full of younger rivals, and likely his long Olympic career would end. The final was held on a cool and blustery Chicago evening as the city lived up to its Windy City nickname. Dark clouds descended from the northern prairies, bringing the scent of impeding rain. DeMont and Kinsella looked to leave the field behind and went out fast, with Kinsella taking the early lead. But at the 800-meter mark, DeMont started pulling steadily away on his way to breaking Kinsella's world record. Sprinting up past Burton came another teenager, a 125-pound wisp named Doug Northway. It came down to a battle between Burton and Kinsella for third place, the final spot on the Olympic team roster. The crowd roared and chanted, trying to will Kinsella to push past Burton, but Kinsella could not gain any momentum as Burton pounded inexorably ahead. Burton did have one enthusiastic fan who ran on the cement curtain alongside the pool, shouting, "Go, go" and wind-milling his arm. The dark mustachioed figure was Mark Spitz.[16]

Kinsella had failed to finish in the top three in the 200 and 400 free earlier in the week, and now his will was collapsing in his last shot at earning a spot on the team in an individual event. Burton managed to hold on to finish third, earning a spot on the team. There to help Chavoor coach the women's team, Debbie Meyer broke into tears of joy when Burton touched out.[17] Burton choked up as the crowd rose and applauded his victory over time and youth. In the top rank of world swimming, Kinsella suffered a shattering defeat. "He had lost his world record and nearly everything he hoped for," the *Chicago Tribune* said of its home-town hero. Blinking back tears, "he stood waist-deep in the water like a wounded bull as the clouds swept over the pool like a curtain falling on a three-act tragedy." At least that's what the reporter wrote. By some magic, the "s" was left off the word "swept," so the line read, "the clouds wept over the pool."[18] Thus, the heavens displayed the emotions of the mortals below who had witnessed the drama.

While Burton's last, desperate shot rang true, Arden Hills' sixteen-year-old sprinter Dave Fairbank made the team as an alternate, which meant he would swim in the relay heats but not the finals, and would not, according to the rules in place at the time, be eligible for a medal. Heiden-reich rebounded from his close loss to Spitz in the 200 free, qualified in the 100 free and the 100 butterfly, and made the medley and freestyle relay teams. But he really wanted to finally notch a win over Spitz in his final chance in Munich.

With the addition of Gary Hall, an Olympic silver medalist and but-terfly world record holder, the U.S. men's Olympic team was once again the most potent squad on earth, its only weakness being it was not quite as experienced as the 1968 version had been. Along with Burton, the seasoned veteran was Spitz, who would have to set an example for the younger swimmers to follow, putting even more pressure on his shoulders. Rival coaches immediately unleashed their psych tactics and began trying to unnerve him. Spitz was a great swimmer but was "vulnerable and unpre-dictable," former Australian Olympic coach Sam Herford told the Australian press. Spitz had been shaken before, and he could be shaken again, he added hopefully.[19]

Chavoor and his assistant, George Haines, were concerned about how inexperience would impact the women's team. Debbie Meyer was there to help coach, not swim. She, Sue Pedersen, Jan Henne, and Claudia Kolb had accounted for eight gold medals in 1968, and not one was returning. Chavoor was looking to replace some of the lost firepower from his own Arden Hills pool. Nancy Spitz and Sandi Johnson fought through the preliminaries and into the finals of the four freestyle events. Few of the tens of thousands of competitive swimmers ever accomplished such a feat, and in almost any other country, the women would probably have qualified for the Olympics in at least two of the events. But they finished just seconds short of finishing in the top three and had to return to Sacramento to watch the Games on TV. The "new Debbie Meyer" Chavoor had hoped for and predicted did not materialize. Ellie Daniel was the only Arden Hills girl to make the team, qualifying in the 200 fly.

The U.S. women's coaches knew they faced tough competition in the Olympics. Sixteen-year-old Australian Shane Gould held five world records, including every world freestyle record, and was peaking as the Games approached. "Shane Gould is generally regarded as the first [top] girl swimmer in the world," Chavoor said of the champion from New South Wales.[20] But his concerns were soon allayed as Shirley Babashoff and Jo Harshbarger broke Gould's records during the trials. The fifteen-year-olds were part of a wave of new U.S. swimmers proving that they were utterly unawed by the competition. Babashoff, a five-foot-nine-and-a-half freestyler from California, broke Gould's record in the 200. Harshbarger, from Seattle, swam twelve miles a day in the heavier, denser water of a saltwater swimming pool to push herself into unrivaled shape for the distance races, and in the 800, she shattered Gould's record by more than four seconds. Chavoor saw in them the one thing he prized most in swimmers: guts. Joined by backstrokers Melissa Belote and Susie Atwood, Santa Clara star Karen Moe, and sprinter Sandy Neilson, the U.S. team was deep and talented in every stroke, which meant Gould would be challenged by a fresh American swimmer every time she got in the pool. "There aren't any superstars on this team like we had in 1968, but we have more depth and balance and better [relay team] speed," Chavoor said.[21] With the trials ended and the team selected, Chavoor led the women to the University of Tennessee for final pre-Olympic workouts, where he imposed his tried-and-true formula of overdistancing on them and had them swimming twelve to thirteen thousand yards a day to get ready.

In 1968, the U.S. Olympic swimming teams were sequestered for five weeks at the U.S. Air Force Academy to prepare for the Games. In 1972, the time was cut to just two weeks, this time at the U.S. Military Academy at West Point. Spitz felt that he had been bullied and humiliated in 1968 and said it had hurt his performance. Coach Pete Daland and his assistant,

Don Gambril, ensured no hijinks went on in 1972. Spitz's fellow Arden Hills swimmers Mike Burton and Dave Fairbank formed a protective layer around him to ensure no one harassed him and no horseplay got out of hand. But they couldn't protect him from the dreams that haunted him in his sleep. He dreamed that giant balloons with "Mexico 68" written on them were floating in the air, descending and suffocating him. Bad memories of the training camp and his last-place finish in the 200 fly flashed through his dreams, but Spitz did not let the dreams unnerve him, and he dismissed them when he woke up, vowing to avenge his defeats.[22]

There was little apprehension as the U.S. Olympic teams gathered to fly across the Atlantic to Germany. They were headed to a modern, Western nation. Unlike Mexico, there was no concern about drinking the water, eating the food, or encountering the dreaded *tourista*. Germany was calm and peaceful, with no hint of the violent civil disturbances that struck Mexico City on the eve of the 1968 games. World geopolitical tensions were easing as well. In May, Richard Nixon became the first U.S. president to visit Moscow, where he and Soviet leader Leonid Brezhnev reached agreements to limit the possibility of nuclear war. The press called the time of easing tensions "Détente," and many hoped the Cold War would soon end.

21

THE FRIENDLY BAVARIAN CAPITAL

By 1972, the Olympics had established itself as more than just an athletic competition in the world's consciousness, they were a cultural phenomenon. "The Olympics are the most frustrating and strange and wonderful and overwhelming and complex and joyous and sad and beautiful experience I have ever had," explained *Chicago Tribune* sports editor Cooper Rollow.[1]

Gesamtkunstwerk. That was the ideal the planners of the Munich games were seeking. The word means to synthesize and combine different components to create an all-embracing work of art. It was a similar concept to the one employed by Mexico, where folkloric dancers, stunning art posters, mod clothing, and even transit directions combined to transform the ancient city of the Aztecs and project the image of a vibrant, young, dynamic nation. Germany deemed its event "The Happy Olympics" and rolled out Waldi the Dachshund, the first time the Olympics employed a mascot.[2] The cute, stumpy-legged little dog's image was plastered on posters and artwork and emblazoned on buttons, stickers, and pins. There were no images of brawny athletes struggling and sweating in competition against each other. "We are aimed at a festival dedicated to a peaceful encounter among nations," a city official said.[3] A lot of that encountering went on in the *Schwabing*, an area of three hundred bars and "plentiful sex bazaars." The U.S. swimmers, wandering through Munich, were stunned at the open display of flesh peddling. The beer gardens were packed soon after breakfast, and the swimmers were amazed that alcohol drinks went down before noon.

Huge, enthusiastic crowds poured into Munich from West Germany, the rest of Europe, and around the world. Concerns about a lack of lodging had been expressed ever since the Games were awarded to Germany in 1966. Although rooms were scarce, people kept arriving, even without room reservations. Accommodations were so hard to obtain that even Mark

Spitz's parents couldn't get a space in town, and they had to take an hour-and-a-half train trip from the mountain town of Garmish-Partenkirchen, on the Austrian border, to watch him swim. Chavoor's animosity toward Olympic officials emerged again. While the athletes had modern rooms in Munich, Chavoor was annoyed by the disparity between the rooms the athletes slept in and those of the Olympic officials. Chavoor said IOC president Avery Brundage was being put up in a Munich palace while the U.S. team and coaches were "relegated to beds in kitchens and foyers of half-completed apartments." The buildings would be converted to housing after the games, but for now, "they were calling it the 'Olympic Village,'" Chavoor said disdainfully.[4]

A waitress told a reporter that Munich was the city with a heart, an image the city worked hard to establish as it tried to overcome its dark past as the scene of the Beer Hall Putsch and the birthplace of Nazism. The planners strove to present Munich as the modern and welcoming "friendly Bavarian capital." Munich had suffered dramatically from Allied bombing during World War II, and bomb squads were still finding unexploded ordnance in the soil. They carefully detonated them to cheers and applause from the crowds of *Muenchner* and *Muenchnerin* who assembled to watch the fireworks. They had either forgotten the horror of the bombing, wanted to ignore it, or didn't experience it. Sixty percent of the town's 1.3 million residents were less than forty years old as the Games began.[5] Memories of Nazis, Adolf Hitler, bombs, World War II, the Berlin Olympics of 1936, and the Holocaust were overawed by the festival of youth, sport, lust, and art that enveloped Bavaria. Olympic flags flapped in the breeze along the *Ludwigstrasse*, the city's grand old boulevard designed to be worthy of kings. Visitors marveled at the ancient buildings with Italianate red roofs, forgetting that Nazi banners once obnoxiously covered the fronts of the buildings.

In an era of student protests, few of the young hippie radicals bothered to visit the memorials to the students who resisted the Nazis during the war. A group of Ludwig-Maximilians-Universität students were guillotined for peacefully protesting against the Nazis. They did it openly, writing anti-Nazi leaflets and distributing them to people on the streets. Sophie Scholl and her brother Hans, two of the movement's leaders, had the youthful good looks and vitality of the athletes streaming into Munich. Their heads were cut off in February 1943. With Teutonic efficiency, the Nazi kangaroo court billed their family 300 Reichsmarks each for the executions.

The ghastly reminders of the past were hard to ignore. The Dachau concentration camp, where the Nazis murdered thousands of Jews and other "undesirables," stands silently just ten miles outside of Munich. Although it was only twenty-eight years after the war had ended, the enormity of the Jewish persecution was difficult for the athletes to comprehend. During the Olympic week, Spitz sat down for an interview with Ray Kennedy of *Time* magazine. After discussing Spitz's swimming accomplishments, Kennedy asked if he felt any irony as a Jew competing in Germany. "Actually, I've always liked this country," Spitz said. Reaching out to a lamp, he tapped the shade and continued, "even though this lampshade is probably made out of one of my aunts."[6] The quote referenced reports that Nazis had used human skin from those they had murdered in concentration camps to make household goods. Later, Spitz said it was a godsend that *Time* was a weekly magazine, and the story with the quote was not published until a week later, when dramatic events obscured the comment.

The overriding purpose of the Olympic planners was to show the world that West Germany had evolved after the horrors of World War II and was now an open and modern republic. The planners did not just make cosmetic changes to bolster Germany's image. In Mexico City, the athletes had been surrounded by layers of security, strong walls, and soldiers carrying their rifles unslung. Munich's police chief trained his officers to be polite and courteous to the throngs attending the Games. There was not a soldier with a gun in sight. The Olympic Village was protected only by a short fence that many of the athletes effortlessly bounded over when returning from an evening of drinking in the *Schwabing*. Few guards were on hand to challenge them. "Strangers keep wandering in and out of our quarters, there is no restraint whatever, no protection for the athletes," U.S. track coach Bill Bowerman complained to the press. U.S. Olympic Committee president Clifford Buck asked the Olympic organizers to tighten security around the village, but little was done to address the situation.[7]

The scenes of Hitler and Nazi officials strutting around in the Berlin Olympiastadion would live forever thanks to Leni Riefenstahl's documentary *Olympia*. The massive, ugly, gray concrete stadium was built so solidly that it was one of the few buildings in Berlin to survive the war. In sharp contrast, the Munich architects put their facilities in a park setting featuring hills, streams, and small lakes. Inspired by dew-covered cobwebs, Munich's Olympiastadion was light, airy, and whimsical. Viewed from a distance, it suggested a giant sailing ship straining to rise from the sea. It and the nearby *schwimhalle* sat under enormous drapes that appeared to float in the air.

The men's swim team arrived at 11 p.m. on August 21, and head coach Pete Daland marched them straight to the pool for a ninety-minute workout; he later said, "It was just 6 o'clock U.S. time, so we figured a workout wasn't a bad idea."[8] A news conference the next morning turned into a "Spitz conference" where the swimmer said he was eager to get in the pool and away from all the media attention. "The heat's on me," he said, "but I believe I can take it. I'm four years older and four years wiser and four years better than Mexico City." Spitz stayed away from predicting how many medals he would win, only venturing that he had "good chances" in his four individual races and the three relays.[9] Others weren't shy about heaping the expectations on him. Don Schollander said he "can, and should win seven gold medals." But, reminding the media that Spitz was a "total failure" in 1968, Schollander noted that "all the world records don't mean a thing if you can't produce in the big one, the Olympics."[10] After having swum in what he felt were "inferior" pools in Houston and Chicago, the Munich *schwimhalle* was a revelation for Spitz, who found the pool to his liking and thought several world records would be broken. Chavoor said the pool was the best he had seen, a true manifestation of genius: "The gutters extended for several feet under the pool's concrete deck. They were so wide—almost a buffer reservoir—that they reduced any returning waves to near zero." He said there was nothing like it in the United States.[11]

Spitz was fortunate in that he had his quartet of coaches on hand to assist him. Daland was the men's coach and directed all the workouts and team activities. Doc Counsilman, Spitz's Indiana coach, was also on hand to provide assurance and advice. Chavoor had his hands full coaching the women but seemed never to be more than a body length from Spitz. And George Haines, his old Santa Clara coach, was Chavoor's assistant coach. There were still lingering bad feelings from the fissure they experienced in 1969 that resulted in Spitz leaving Santa Clara and returning to Arden Hills, but when a reporter tried to dredge up the story, Spitz refused to criticize Haines and credited him with turning him into a great swimmer.

These were the coaches who had spent a significant part of their lives helping Spitz attain the rank of world's greatest swimmer. They saw him set world records as a sixteen-year-old, saw him rise to be the U.S. national champion, and witnessed his fall in Mexico City. They knew his strengths and weaknesses as a swimmer and as a person. They knew how to goad him into training harder and working longer, tapering him to a fine pitch. They understood how to motivate him, how to stifle the arrogance that could still arise in him. They helped him confront his fears and phobias and knew he still needed coddling and fussing over. So now, at the precise moment he needed them most, they assembled in Germany and formed the phalanx he needed to push through the distractions and obstacles to true greatness.

Chavoor, the master media manipulator, used all his communication skills as the Games approached. Spitz kept away from the press as much as possible, turning down dozens of interview requests. But Chavoor was media savvy, and he cultivated a few top reporters to gain the best possible coverage for Spitz. One of the privileged few to have access was Jerry Kirshenbaum of *Sports Illustrated*, who had covered Spitz closely for years. Kirshenbaum, Chavoor, and Spitz went out to dinner one night, and Spitz's usual array of phobias began to appear. He was sniffling and coughing and worried he was coming down with a cold. He complained that he was feeling tired and sleepy. As dinner was served, he turned to Chavoor and asked, with concern in his voice, "You know something about those antibiotics I took? They made me dizzy." Without looking up from his dinner, Chavoor replied: "Dizzier." His "cold" vanished the day before the opening ceremonies. It was a masterstroke in communications by Chavoor. In a word, he had illustrated for Spitz how petty his worries were, how he was exaggerating and perpetuating his fears and insecurities. For the reporter, it was a revealing but not harsh look into the phobias and insecurities Spitz faced. The resulting story presented Spitz as a mature athlete who, while still subject to gaffes, had overcome his demons to mature and develop as a great swimmer.[12]

The swimming competition was held in the first week of the Olympic fortnight, beginning on Monday, August 28, and concluding Monday, September 4. When swimming finished, the other events continued until the closing ceremony on Sunday, September 10. Spitz had fourteen races packed into eight days, and counting the preliminary heats and the finals, he would swim every day but one. However, he said there was no question he could handle the workload.

Spitz was the focus of global media attention in the last few days before his first race. His mustache was now internationally famous and whether he would shave it off was the subject of much speculation. After practice one day, Spitz met with some Russian swimmers and coaches. Surely, they thought, he would shave off his mustache; how could he keep it when most swimmers shaved as much hair off their bodies as possible so that nothing impeded their progress through the water? "Doesn't it slow you down?" they asked. "No, I'm not going to shave it off," Spitz replied as a Russian coach translated. "I'm much more smooth in the water," Spitz explained with a straight face, claiming the mustache actually made him faster. "It deflects water away from my mouth, allows my rear end to rise, and makes me bullet-shaped in the water, and that's what had allowed me to swim so great." The Russian swimmers were soon sporting mustaches.[13]

The opening ceremonies projected carefully crafted gaiety, harmony, and hope. In contrast to the heavy military presence at the Mexico City

Olympics, where armed troops ringed the stadium, there was little sign of a police presence. "The older generation remembers very well the games of 1936 in Berlin, which were abused by the-then rulers in Germany for their purposes," West German president Gustav Heinemann said.[14] There was no emphasis on nationalism. Displays of swastikas and pictures of Hitler, even in bookstores, were against the law. Restructured Germany had forged a new identity.

Eight curved wooden alphorns, twenty feet long and carved from trees from Bavarian forests, sent their centuries-old harmony over the stadium. Three thousand cheerful boys and girls clad in green-and-gold costumes flocked like so many tiny birds onto the red crushed brick track. They waved flowers to the crowd as the music transitioned from ancient to modern and musicians played popular tunes. Finally, the athletes marched into the stadium clad in their nations' uniforms, waving their hats and smiling at the crowd under the blue sky and white clouds of a perfect Bavarian late summer day.[15] A loud roar cascaded through the stadium at the sight of the stars and stripes as the U.S. team—men dressed in red pants and white sports jackets and the women in red coats and knee-length white skirts—marched into the stadium.

After the ceremonies, the magnitude of the Olympic experience began to descend on the athletes as distraction mounted. With so many watching on TV, apparel manufacturers tried to find ways to get the athletes to wear their clothes or shoes and often set up clandestine meetings to persuade them to don a particular track shoe or watch. There were enormous throngs of fans everywhere, pressing the athletes for pictures and autographs. The media swarmed, looking for exclusive interviews and stories as the athletes tried to focus and shed the mounting pressure.

The opening ceremonies had been a terrific success for the West German authorities. The dark and bitter days of Germany's past had been obscured, and a new spirit of international peace and brotherhood seemed to be emerging. "I deplore any instance where even the Olympic Games themselves are used as a lever in waging conflicts," Heinemann was moved to say, even though the nationalistic medal count would still be used by nations to prove that their social and economic systems were superior.[16] But the "levers of conflict" were being waged in many places. The world championship chess match in Reykjavik, Iceland, between American Bobby Fischer and Soviet Boris Spassky was so bitter that the Russians claimed the Americans were using hidden electronic devices and chemical substances to throw Spassky off his game. An investigation by chess officials found no evidence of such subterranean weapons. More direct conflict was waged in Vietnam. U.S. Air Force B-52 bombers dropped a million pounds of explosives on suspected Communist positions near Que Son as South Vietnamese forces captured five Soviet-made wire-guided missiles. The Games would soon directly experience levers of conflict that threatened both world peace and the end of the Olympic movement.

Chavoor worried that he'd brought an American women's team that was young and untested internationally. But his assistant coach was George Haines, who had coached in the Olympics since 1960 and mentored many female swimming stars; he was supremely confident and felt this was the strongest U.S. team ever. But there were nerves and fears to overcome. On the night of the 100-meter breaststroke, Cathy Carr faced Galena Stepanova of Russia, the heavy favorite in the event. Carr had never set a world record but knew she would have to swim the race of her life to win. Debbie Meyer gave the U.S. team a fiery pep talk and told them it was no time for doubt or self-pity. They would have to show the world some guts and win. Inspired, Carr beat her best time by almost two seconds, set the world record, and won gold.

Australian Shane Gould was the overwhelming favorite in the 100 free, the race she really wanted to win, but in a major upset was beaten by Sandy Neilson. Shirley Babashoff came in second, leaving the favored Australian a disappointing bronze medal. Fears that Gould would take six gold medals dissolved.

Keena Rothhammer, a star from Santa Clara, pulled an even bigger upset when she beat Gould in the 800-meter freestyle race, winning by three seconds. After the race, Gould shrank back in the water, crying in shock as Rothhammer was pulled from the pool and happily pummeled by her teammates. Another surprise U.S. Olympics star was fifteen-year-old Melissa Belote from Springfield, Virginia. Unknown going into the Olympic trials, she peaked at the perfect time, winning the 100 and 200 backstroke. She took a third gold as a member of the 4 x 100-meter relay, but her grand achievement was almost lost in the avalanche of publicity around Spitz and Gould. Another Santa Clara star, Karen Moe, set the world record in the 200 butterfly as the U.S. women swept the event, with Arden Hills' Ellie Daniel taking bronze. The medal parade continued as Jo Harshbarger, rumored to be romantically linked to Spitz, won gold in the 400 free relay. Although the Americans blunted her drive for six gold medals, Gould rose to the challenge and almost single-handedly fought them off. Putting on an impressive one-woman show, she won three individual gold medals in the 200 free, the 400 free, and the 200 individual medley. But even great as she was, she could not lift Australia's relay teams, and the rested Americans shut them out of any relay medals. The depth and overall speed of the U.S. team overwhelmed the other nations, and they won the 4 x 100 free relay and the 4 x 100 medley.

The young American women, all the products of age group swimming, took one of the great medal hauls in history. While not as dominant as the 1968 team, the 1972 team won eight gold medals of a possible fourteen, five silver medals of a possible twelve, and four bronze medals of a possible twelve. Combining the 1968 and 1972 records, Chavoor's women won nineteen of twenty-eight possible gold medals, twelve of twenty-four silver medals, and twelve of a possible twenty-four bronze medals. It was the last Olympic team Chavoor coached, and he went out on top. He said U.S. coaching techniques were now being spread throughout the rest of the world, which was closing the gap. Future U.S. teams would face an array of challenges that not even Chavoor could envision. But his two Olympic swimming teams had dominated the world competition and helped establish the U.S. women's program as the finest on earth.

22

TACT IS OVERRATED

After spending almost his entire life in the pool, Mark Spitz's reputation and legacy came down to one week of competition. All the physical and mental abilities and disabilities he possessed were tested as never before. His habits and inclinations were deeply forged. His inability to push himself hard in practice annoyed his coaches and teammates, who said they knew how great a swimmer he was and how much greater he could be if he worked harder. But Spitz knew his body, and he swam beautifully with no wasted motion, compact and efficient. He had an inner mechanism that exploded just in time to send him hurtling past rivals in the final meters of close races. His father's personality and beliefs were deeply ingrained in him: "Tact is overrated, fortitude will save you, backing down from other people is not an option, nothing is stronger than the familial bond" was the creed that guided and sustained father and son.[1]

Anything other than victory was a humiliation. In his first race as a child, he had failed to take home the winner's blue ribbon, and he still found the colors red and white, rewarded to second- and third-place finishers, offensive. Fear would shadow him almost all his time out of the water and haunt his dreams while he slept. His absolute focus on himself manifested itself in bouts of hypochondria, where he was constantly obsessing about sniffles, aches, and pains, worried that they were dark warnings of severe health problems. He often left competitors and teammates feeling cool toward him as he failed to acknowledge or even recognize them. His teammates at Indiana University struggled to understand him and rationalized his behavior this way: "It was as if he was born without tact and common sense, in the same way other people are born without arms or legs. He was something of a social paraplegic, no more to be hated than, say, someone with a deforming birth defect."[2] These were the strengths and weaknesses of the world's best swimmer on the eve of his final, life-defining quest in Munich.

His first challenge came on Monday, August 28, in the 200-meter butterfly, and he was directly confronted with overcoming his past failure. From the age of sixteen, he had been one of the world's great butterflyers and was the overwhelming favorite in the 1968 games. He suffered tremendous humiliation, however, when he not only failed to win the butterfly but finished in last place. Realizing the scar the defeat imposed on Spitz's psyche, Chavoor had worked relentlessly to rebuild his confidence. Spitz had dominated the butterfly races in the 1971 national championships in Houston and the Olympic trials in Chicago just a month earlier. But the pressure of the Olympics was warping his mind and his confidence, despite the fact he held the world record. "It really astounded me that he was still worrying about this old bugaboo event" on the eve of the Games, Chavoor said.[3] It was essential to get past the first race with a convincing win, and the coaches felt his performance would set the tone for not only him but for the entire men's team for the rest of the week.

On the way into the *Schwimmhalle* before the race, Spitz agonized over facing his roommate, Gary Hall. Spitz brooded and told Chavoor that Hall had beaten him once and had held the world record two years earlier, a record Spitz had since bested three times. Hall knew Spitz was afraid of the 200 fly and was determined to use that psychological advantage to knock him off. No one knew Spitz's moods better than Chavoor, who knew when he needed coddling, but he also knew how to smash the hammer down when Spitz's insecurities threatened to bolt out of control. Flashing his famed temper and raising his voice, Chavoor yelled at him, "Spitz, I'm not even thinking about the 200 butterfly. It's a foregone conclusion. All I want you thinking about is breaking two minutes."[4] No one had ever broken two minutes in that race, but Chavoor's challenge snapped Spitz out of his gloom. His mind cleared, Spitz destroyed the field, winning and setting another world record, the seventh time he had set the record in that event, finishing in 2:00.70. His record lasted four years and marked him as one of the greatest butterflyers of all time. Chavoor's strategy had worked, and surely Spitz would be rewarded. After the race, Spitz hugged Chavoor, looking for his mentor's approval. "It was as if he were ten years old again," Chavoor remembered. "'I won, Sherm! I did great! Didn't I?'"[5] Instead of a grin and a hug, Chavoor reverted to a tactic he had used many times with his great swimmers. He operatically rebuked him for not finishing under two minutes and accused him of going easy on the third lap, stunning reporters who heard the exchange. Chavoor had an ulterior motive in verbally lashing his superstar. He later confessed he didn't know if Spitz had eased up or not, but he wanted him to believe he could have gone faster, a psychological ploy to motivate him in upcoming races.

His second gold medal, won later that same day, was a foregone conclusion without the drama of his first race. The U.S. 4 × 100 freestyle relay team was so strong that only the U.S. "B" team could threaten it. To add to Spitz's chances, he rested and did not swim in the preliminary race, with Arden Hills teammate Dave Fairbank swimming in his place. Fairbank helped his team set a world record but received no glory for the accomplishment.[6] He was replaced by Spitz in the final and watched as Spitz swam the anchor leg as the Americans set another world record. Fairbank would see his name mentioned mainly in the agate print of the news stories covering the preliminary relay. At that time, the rules stated that swimmers who swam only in the prelims were ineligible for a medal. The rule was changed later, but the International Olympic Committee has not awarded medals retroactively.

Spitz going two for two in the gold medal chase sparked the media into action. Newspapers adorned their front pages with photo montages and headlines about him. Once again, they tried to bait Spitz into claiming he would win seven gold medals. Yet during his few media appearances, all reporters could get out of him were modest and monotonous utterances like, "I will do my best." The media grumbled that Spitz was "dull with the press, abrupt with photographers, reluctant to sign autographs."[7] U.S. Olympic team officials closely controlled his media appearances, once shoving him into the back end of a news conference with the women's swimmers. "Mark Spitz is here, gentlemen, and his coach says unless you ask your questions in the next five minutes, he is leaving," an Olympic factotum ominously declared. The press devoted the rest of the scant time to Spitz, and the official cut the news conference off after a few questions. "That's all, we promised you five minutes; we have given you nine," he said snidely.[8] The limited media time curtailed opportunities for Spitz to create controversy, but it also limited any opportunity to build rapport with journalists. Frustrated reporters wouldn't have to wait long before Spitz made unforced errors that gave them opportunities to blast him.

Spitz was back in the pool the next day, August 29, seeking his third gold medal in the 200-meter free. The *Schwimmhalle* was packed with nine thousand fans, many of whom paid scalpers' prices to see Spitz continue his medal quest. Fans wondered what rival swimmer could derail him, but no one guessed it could be a swimmer who had walked out of the hospital the day before with a hole in his chest.

Spitz had two formidable opponents in the race, defending Olympic champion Michael Wenden of Australia, who had shocked the U.S. team by beating Don Schollander in 1968, and fan favorite Steve Genter, the six-foot-five, 185-pound bald bundle of energy from UCLA. Many thought of Genter as a big, lovable kid who pulled stunts like painting a bold "#1" on his hairless pate. He developed a ritual of writhing and wiggling in the starting blocks in the minutes leading up to a race; an admitted psych job to get the crowd laughing and hooting and on his side while annoying his opponents, who, struggling to maintain their focus, glared at him in disdain. Heading into Munich, Spitz had beaten Genter five out of six times, and of course Spitz feared that the one loss proved Genter was capable of beating him when it counted most: in the Olympic final.

But in the days before the race, it seemed Genter would not even be able to crawl into the pool and compete. He developed a hacking cough on the flight from the United States to Munich. Not wanting his rivals to discover he might not be at full strength, he snuck off to the Olympic medical clinic. The doctors told him that he had suffered a partially collapsed lung, which generally took several days to heal. Just four days before his race, doctors made an incision under his right armpit and inserted a tube to repair his lung. The incision took thirteen stitches to close, and there were concerns from coaches and doctors that swimming could permanently injure his lung and even threaten his life. After a dispute between American and German doctors over whether it was safe for him to swim or not, Genter was cleared to leave the hospital the day before the race.

Word got around that when he found out that Genter was ailing, Spitz said, "Well, that's one way of getting rid of my competition."[9] Spitz later said he'd said it in sympathy and was not intending to disrespect Genter, a remark Genter found disingenuous. "As soon as he found out that I still might swim, he went to see my coach and told him that if I tried to come back, it might endanger my life," Genter said.[10] Genter made a quip about Spitz thinking he was an expert in anatomy because he had been accepted to Indiana University's dental school. But Genter was struggling with his own fears about the injuries he could suffer if he swam. Genter said that the next morning, as Genter prepared to test his patched-up lung in the preliminary race, Spitz approached him and once again tried to talk him out of competing due to concern for his health. Genter told Spitz his suggestion was ridiculous and said he was going to swim. Not only did Genter enter the race, but he also won the preliminary heat, qualifying for the final that night. But his chest was hurting, and at the end of the race he said, "I thought I was gonna die." Spitz approached him again that evening before the final, and "he came along and told me he didn't think it would be wise for me to swim hard in the final."[11]

Genter thought Spitz was trying to psych him out, pulling a trick on Genter that others had pulled on Spitz in 1968. "He's been trying to get me mad and upset about him supposedly being the superior person. Mark came over to me and did me a favor when he said, 'you know it's not worth it to try to swim tonight.' I said, Mark, you and I are swimming in the same race. There's only one gold medal tonight, and I'm out to get it. Careful, watch your back; I'm coming."[12]

Spitz went out strong and took a half-second lead over Genter at 50 meters. Genter was relieved that he felt no pain during the first lap and powered up and surged past a shocked Spitz at 100 meters. But at the turn, some stitches popped open, blood seeped into the water, and he felt a sharp pain in his chest. He ignored the agony and stayed in first place until the turn for the final lap. He struggled down the last 50 meters, laboring to get as much oxygen into his lungs as possible, but he felt his strength ebbing away. Just 25 meters from the finish, Spitz finally shot past him as Genter began to feel like he was about to black out from pain and exhaustion. Spitz won by a second over Genter. Despite the loss, Genter's determined effort became legendary in the annals of sports and Olympic swimming.

The media took a dim view of Spitz's actions. "Spitz the Runaround, Idiot, Jerk,"[13] one headline read, while another proclaimed, "Mark Psyches His Pal."[14] When congratulated on his superhuman effort, Genter simply replied, "Nothing would have pleased me more than to beat him." Referring to the popular Gary Hall, who was struggling in the competition that week, Genter said, "I like people who are interested in other people and not themselves so much."[15] After the race, Spitz was conciliatory and said he was not trying to psych Genter out and that Genter's performance would go down as one of the most extraordinary feats in Olympic history.

At least publicly, the two reconciled, although reporters speculated the coaches had enforced the peace on them. Later that year, Genter said he was still upset about the incident: "I'll never forgive or forget that Mark tried to intimidate me."[16] Years later, Spitz again displayed his lack of tact. Some had speculated that Genter's strong performance indicated he would have won gold if he'd been healthy. Spitz noted they had been even at the third and final turn, but "when I was even with anybody with 50 meters to go, I was going to win. I had the ability to turn up the speed whenever I needed to." Spitz concluded that his statement was "perhaps a bit brash," but said he had the talent to back it up.[17]

The dramatic race over, Spitz walked to the medal stand for the gold medal presentation. In his version of what happened next, he recounted that he did not have time to put his shoes on before the medal ceremony. Shoes in hand, he rushed to the platform and put his shoes behind the platform out of the crowd's sight. After the ceremony, Spitz said Fédération Internationale de Natation (FINA) president Dr. Harold Henning led the swimmers around the pool to receive the crowd's adulation. Spitz said Henning told him to "acknowledge your fans," and "Mark raised his left hand, again holding the shoes he had yet to find time to put on and waved in appreciation."[18] A UPI Telephoto appears to support this story, showing him holding the shoes above his head in a haphazard fashion.[19] But another picture presents a different image. An Associated Press photo of the medal ceremony shows Spitz standing on the top riser of the medal platform with his left arm extended high above his head. The two shoes are displayed next to each other with the Adidas name and three distinctive stripes, an Adidas trademark, clearly visible.[20] A third photo shows Spitz carrying the shoes pointed down in his left hand while he waves with his right hand. The shoelaces are tied. If he had not had time to put them on, would they be tied?[21] "That simple act . . . unleashed a maelstrom that became Mark's most formidable opponent in the games," one biography stated.[22] At that time, there were strict rules about amateurs not commercially benefiting from their athletic exploits. Sponsors and athletes devised ingenuous ways to get around the rules to display products. Under-the-table payments were made to athletes for wearing specific attire or, it was suspected, for driving or riding in a particular car model. Athletes forfeited their medals and were banned from Olympic competition if officials discovered they had contracts or received gifts or payments.

The story about Spitz waving his shoes spread quickly. One Munich newspaper ran the headline "Skandal" over a story about the purported ethical breach.[23] The Russians, keenly aware of the medal count competition and wanting to pick off a gold medal, filed a complaint with the International Olympic Committee questioning Spitz's amateur status. While Olympic officials told the press there was no investigation into the matter, Spitz met with the Eligibility Committee of the IOC to explain why he had waved the Adidas shoes. Chavoor feared the committee would take his three gold medals away because of the incident. The officials wanted to know why Spitz didn't wear the red shoes the IOC had given him. His old superstition came to the rescue as he explained that he always wore blue, the color of champions, and never wore red, which he associated with second place. He showed them the shoes he wore, which he said were an old pair he had purchased in Sacramento.

The meeting ended with no action taken against Spitz. In a separate encounter with Spitz and Chavoor, IOC president Brundage asserted that Spitz's actions were serious and said Adidas "got a hundred thousand dollars' worth of free publicity." Spitz remained silent but later said that all he could think about was, "Wow! A hundred grand. That's a lot of money. Maybe I'll take a deal. They can have the medals."[24] After a few more questions, the meeting ended without incident, but his lack of tact surfaced once more. Spitz let it be known that he thought the Olympic officials just wanted to meet him. Many in the media took the flap less than seriously. One wondered how track shoes could help a swimmer, and the boys in the press box composed a little ditty:

> There was a young fellow named Spitz,
> Who gave the West Germans fits,
> He held up his shoes,
> And that was good news,
> For the twelve million American Jews.[25]

But was it all as harmless as Spitz and the media portrayed it? On June 1, 1979, Chavoor told the *Sacramento Bee*, "Spitz waved the Adidas shoe. I talked to the company's representatives, and we determined the amount. They gave me the money, and I passed it onto Spitz."[26] In 1988, Don Bloom, a Sacramento newspaper reporter who was close to Spitz and Chavoor, wrote a book about his exploits as a sportswriter. He wrote that Chavoor told him, "You probably saw him wave those Adidas warm-up shoes when he was on the victory platform. They paid him $6,000 for that."[27] Other Olympians privately said they heard Spitz received as much as $20,000 for the stunt.

Chavoor never had regrets about the incident. "That son-of-a-bitch Avery Brundage . . . with all the hypocrisy that bastard allows to go on with the Communist bloc countries paying athletes, he had the gall to reprimand Mark. . . . [A]ccording to Brundage, it's still okay for the Communists to pay their athletes, give them homes, jobs and cars, but Mark can't do anything out of the ordinary on the victory stand."[28] He didn't elaborate on what "out of the ordinary" meant.

After a day's rest, Spitz was back for his shot at a historic fourth gold medal in the 100-meter butterfly. If he got it, he would tie Don Schollander's 1964 record of four gold medals in one Olympics. Spitz was nearly unbeatable in that stroke and distance and had set five consecutive world records in the 100-meter fly, holding the record since October 1967. As predicted, Spitz took his fourth gold medal in four days, setting another world record. His swimming was now drawing rave reviews. Self-described "cynical old sportswriter Joe Falls" broke his sunglasses while pounding enthusiastically on his desk while watching the race from the pressroom. "Spitz does that to you," he explained, telling his readers that Spitz was now being called a *superschwimmer* by the adoring Bavarians. The crowd's roars were so loud and authentic that Spitz saw it as a sign that Germany had overcome much of the virulent anti-Semitism that existed just three decades earlier and was genuinely embracing him, a Jewish swimming champion.

The sense of Spitz's invincibility was steadily growing. While he was still plagued with fits of doubt, other swimmers were suffering from the thought of facing him. Their confidence ebbed as he set one record after another. Swimmers were now thrilled by taking a silver medal when up against Spitz. When Canadian swimmer Bruce Robertson finished second in the 100 butterfly, he was so excited he forgot to report for his mandatory drug test after the race; instead, he headed for the beer halls to quaff large steins of fine Bavarian beer in celebration. His fellow Canadian swimmer and lifelong friend Leslie Cliff, a silver medalist, realized Robertson hadn't taken the test. If he didn't return before the "peeorium"—the athletes' snarky name for the drug testing room—closed in an hour and a half, he would be disqualified and have to forfeit his medal. In the true spirit of the Olympic movement, she organized athletes from many nations in the Olympic Village and sent the international team on the search mission. They finally found him in a vast beer parlor, and he raced back just in time to take the test. "I think they might have found a little alcohol in that test," Robertson joked. But he did pass it, and he kept the silver medal.[29]

While it turned out to be a harmless and humorous escapade, the drug tests (or "dope" tests, as some called them) were deadly serious. The tests were instituted in 1968, and many coaches, athletes, and officials were confused about the protocols surrounding them and what substances were banned. This was a combination that would result in tragic and heartbreaking consequences for U.S. swimmers and coaches in the upcoming days.

Spitz's opportunity to set the record for the most gold medals by a swimmer in an Olympiad came in the 800-meter freestyle relay two days later, when he was almost assured of eclipsing Don Schollander, "the god of American swimming," who had won four gold medals in Tokyo in 1964. Once again, another Arden Hills swimmer aided Spitz, as Mike Burton swam in the preliminary while Spitz and the other "first string" U.S. swimmers rested for the final. Spitz joined Genter, John Kinsella, and Fred Taylor to set another world record in the final as the United States won easily. As Spitz brought the victory home, ABC Sports announcer Keith Jackson summed up the accomplishment: "Here is Mark Spitz, suave, sophisticated, and in the opinion of some outright arrogant, but supremely gifted as an athlete, confident as an athlete and a person." His color commentator Murray Rose, a great former Australian champion who had watched Spitz struggle in Mexico City, remarked on the changes he'd observed: "He is a confident man, but I don't think Mark has always been that way. It's only the last year or two that we've seen Mark Spitz confident as a swimmer."[30]

Schollander, now twenty-six years old, never fully embraced Spitz. Even though he was on the board of directors of the U.S. Olympic Committee, Schollander did not play the role of senior statesman very diplomatically. "He's a great swimmer, he's probably the greatest talent of all time, but I do not rate him the greatest swimmer of all time," he told the press. That honor, he said, belonged to Johnny Weissmuller, who had won five gold medals in the Paris and Amsterdam games in the 1920s. Schollander thought Weissmuller's victories were more "dominating" than Spitz's. He also thought the contemporary East German star Roland Matthes deserved consideration, since he had dominated the backstroke events in 1968 and 1972.[31]

Arguments comparing athletes from different eras are better left for barroom discussions. What was clear was that Spitz was now the top swimmer in the world, and he felt relief at fulfilling the expectations many had thrust upon him. He also knew his future was altered forever and that new financial opportunities awaited him. Schollander had never been able to cash in on his victories, but Weissmuller had parlayed his medals into lasting fame and fortune. His most famous movie role had been that of Tarzan, from which he had made millions of dollars, but people forgot that he had also portrayed the mythological Greek god Adonis. Soon Spitz would have to consider what role he wanted to play in life. But first, he had to confront the all-too-mortal question of whether he should attempt to win two more gold medals in Munich or get out of the pool without risking an embarrassing defeat that could overshadow his five gold medals. Spitz had one remaining individual event, the 100-meter freestyle, and would finish the Games on the medley relay team, an all-but-certain American victory.

The 100-meter freestyle is swimming's marquee event, similar to the 100-meter dash in track, but the race was Spitz's weakest event, and the blazing pace of the race, where even the most minor slip could be devastating, made it the most unpredictable. While Spitz had been a clear favorite in his other races, many saw the 100-free as a toss-up. Defending Olympic champion Michael Wenden of Australia and American Jerry Heidenreich posed the most serious challenges. But before the race began, Spitz almost quit. His proclivity to come down with an illness or injury as a big race approached, a condition he had experienced since childhood, manifested itself two days before the race, when he said he had suffered a slightly strained back fooling around on a mini-car amusement ride in the Olympic Village. Then, during workouts, he told teammate Gary Conelly he was seriously considering not entering the race.

Spitz told ABC's Donna de Varona, "I know I say I don't want to swim before every event, but this time I'm serious. If I swim six and win six, I'll be a hero. If I swim seven and win six, I'll be a failure."[32] Later he mentioned his doubts to men's head coach Pete Daland, who, knowing how Chavoor could influence Spitz's thoughts, ran and pleaded with him to talk Spitz into staying in the race. The two huddled alone for four hours. Emerging from the meeting, Chavoor warned Spitz that if he didn't swim in the 100, he would be scratched from the upcoming medley relay. He'd end up with five gold medals, not seven, and that record could be broken in the next Olympics. The coaches told him he could break the record for the most gold medals won in a single Games, breaking the record of five held by three different people, all set before 1925. Spitz demurred.

Realizing he was not getting anywhere, Chavoor shifted his argument. He confronted Spitz and accused him of being a coward who was afraid of competing against Jerry Heidenreich. When Spitz looked at Heidenreich, he saw a near mirror image of himself. They had been born just days apart in February 1950. They both had strong fathers and families who supported them fervently. They excelled in the butterfly and freestyle strokes. They had similar physiques. They had tangled in the NCAA championships as Heidenreich led his underdog Southern Methodist University Mustangs against the swimming machine that was Indiana University. The difference came in their personalities. Spitz was somber and aloof, often brooding with his insecurities. Heidenreich "was a charmer, a rogue, a practical joker, the kind of guy everybody liked to be around. He wore funny hats and concocted silly nicknames for his friends. Heidenreich never shut up and never shut down."[33] Heidenreich was also a noted hard partier. He had begun smoking and drinking in high school and continued those habits through college. Heidenreich demonstrated earlier in the week that he could beat Spitz when he swam his leg of the 400 freestyle relay faster than Spitz swam his leg. It added to his confidence and gave Spitz yet another excuse to not get in the pool for the 100. Finally, Chavoor got through to Spitz. "Do you want the whole world to think you're chicken?" Chavoor bellowed.[34] Spitz snapped out of his funk and finally decided to take the risk and compete.

Mentally and physically exhausted, Spitz had trouble preparing himself for the race. He swam listlessly in the heat and semifinal, losing a race for the first time. Concerned, Chavoor told him, "Stop fooling around; this is your last big race. For once, you go out hard all the way. He won't catch you." Spitz agreed to go out fast, feeling he did not have the energy for one of his trademark thrusts at the finish line. Spitz burst out fast, reaching the turn three-tenths of a second faster than the world record time he'd set at the trials. About 20 meters from the finish, Spitz's stroke slipped, and he broke rhythm as Heidenreich lunged forward. Chavoor remembered holding his breath. Spitz led by "the width of a backyard swimming pool" and struggled to hold on for the last few feet. Spitz touched out by inches for the victory, 51.22 to 51.65. Heidenreich pounded his fist on the edge of the pool in frustration at the narrow loss, then smiled and congratulated his rival.

The close victory had taken just about every drop of energy Spitz had left. He was exhausted and relieved when the race ended, with barely enough strength to make it through one final relay race. On the medal stand, Spitz put his arm around Heidenreich and offered a paternal warning: "Great race, Jerry. But for God's sake, don't go out and get drunk tonight. We have the medley relay tomorrow."[35]

Heidenreich had enjoyed a terrific Olympiad. He won gold in the medley and freestyle relays, silver in the 100-meter freestyle, and bronze in the 100-meter butterfly, breaking five Olympic and four world records that week. It was a tremendous achievement, but it was lost in the wake of the tsunami of media coverage Spitz received. "[Spitz] always gave me something to chase, and I always helped push him," Heidenreich said. The *London Independent* agreed: "Behind every genius is a mortal who pushes them on to superhuman deeds. And behind Mark Spitz was Jerry Heidenreich."[36] What if Heidenreich had beaten Spitz in the 100 instead of being touched out by an instant? Would their lives have been changed? They left Munich separated by .43 of a second, but their lives would diverge wildly from then on. Heidenreich went back home to Texas after the Olympics, where he faced his domineering father. "Dad would bring it up all the time," said Heidenreich's brother Max. "'Don't you ever get tired of coming in second to Spitz?' Dad just didn't know when to quit."[37]

Heidenreich struggled with addiction and had several careers and relationships. However, nothing seemed to fulfill him. Finally, in his late forties, his health began to fail, and he suffered a stroke. In 2002, at age fifty-one, he quietly took his own life by overdosing on prescription medications. He left his Olympic medals in a butter dish.

Spitz had to be shielded by police and coaches as he was shepherded out of the *schwimhalle* past legions of star-struck, shrieking teenage girls to a waiting Mercedes. His fan mail was swamping the coach's Olympic Village room and stood four feet high by the end of the swimming competition. Spitz was quickly becoming the most famous athlete and one of the most recognizable faces in the world. Hundreds of nations worldwide recognized and hailed Spitz as a hero, while they had little or no idea who American heroes like Jack Nicklaus or Joe Namath were. Perhaps the Brazilian soccer-star Pelé was the only comparable figure on the sports stage at that time. Just before his last race, Pulitzer Prize–winning author Lucinda L. Franks managed to corner Mark and his father, Arnold, and ask a few questions. Mark was beyond mental and physical exhaustion. "This has been the hardest six days of my life," he told her. He didn't think his medals would help him earn much money and said he would "hang them on the wall somewhere" when he got home. Asked if the toil was worth it, Arnold said, "We would do it all over again if we thought we had the same chance for success." But his son differed. "I probably wouldn't. I've done thirty-eight laps now. There are only two to go."[38]

Spitz's final task was to swim the butterfly leg in his last race, the 4 x 100 medley relay, a sure victory for the Americans. With the pressure off, he joked with the media that the American team had a "decent chance" at winning the relay. News reports that Spitz would make history and win his seventh gold medal spread around the world, and the famous flocked to watch the historic race. In attendance would be Adonis himself, sixty-eight-year-old Johnny Weissmuller, with his sixth wife, Maria. Spitz noted the air of faded Hollywood celebrity that enveloped Weissmuller and his wife and wondered how he would end up if he went to Hollywood. Movie great Kirk Douglas, known for athletic performances in films such as *Spartacus*, and his wife sat and watched the race with Spitz's parents. The actor told them to expect many film offers to come their handsome son's way.

Spitz was joined by teammates Mike Stamm, Tom Bruce, and Heidenreich for his last race. They faced a solid East German team led by Roland Matthes, who had won two gold medals in the backstroke. In the third lap, Spitz opened up a two-second lead for Heidenreich, who had taken Spitz's advice and stayed out of the beer halls the previous night. Heidenreich swam the anchor leg and brought victory home for the Americans, giving Spitz his seventh gold medal, a feat many thought would never be matched. Spitz had received thunderous ovations all week, but none as loud as the final tribute. The crowd roared in appreciation for twenty minutes as his teammates lifted him on their shoulders and paraded around the pool. Sportswriter Joe Falls summed up the feelings of many when he wrote, "No one should be that intense, that confident, that handsome, and that good."[39] His record stood for thirty-six years until the Beijing Summer Olympic Games, when Michael Phelps won eight gold medals.

Finally, the tribulations were over, and the challenges of the Games were forever behind him. His last official duty would be the obligatory final news conference the next morning. Then Spitz planned to relax and attend some of the other Olympic events for a few days before heading home.

While Spitz was dealing with fame and pondering how to leverage it into a fortune, two other Arden Hills swimmers were laboring in obscurity. Dave Fairbank, who had set a world record in the heats in the 4 x 100-meter freestyle earlier in the week, once again assisted Spitz by swimming in the preliminaries of the medley relay. The U.S. "B" team won easily but would not be awarded medals since they did not compete in the final, so Fairbank went home with nothing more than a pat on the back.

Mike Burton had also swum and won on a preliminary relay team without hope of reward. His only shot at a medal was in the 1,500 freestyle, but he faced long odds. Although Burton was a four-time world record holder and defending Olympic champion, he was given little chance of contending for any medal, let alone gold. He was twenty-five, and the consensus was that the old man was over the hill. Rick DeMont, the sixteen-year-old teenage swimming whiz, held the world record. He solidified his claim as the new top distance swimmer by winning the gold medal in the 400-meter free earlier in the week. He joined Australians Graham Windeatt and Brad Cooper as the top contenders for the 1,500 championship.[40]

The race was turned upside down just minutes before the starting gun. A bevy of Olympic officials descended on the American swimmers while they were warming up. The race was delayed for ten minutes with no explanation given to the press, swimmers, or the fans. Then the momentous announcement came across the loudspeakers: Rick DeMont was disqualified from the race. Olympic officials had just received the results of DeMont's drug test taken after his victory in the 400 free, and it showed he had twelve parts per million of ephedrine in his urine. DeMont had asthma and regularly used the drug to ward off shortness of breath, chest tightness, and wheezing. But the IOC had banned the drug. He was pulled from the 1,500, and his gold medal was taken away.

In one stroke, Olympic officials had taken away one American gold medal and disqualified the favorite for another, enraging the U.S. team. Assistant Coach Don Gambril grabbed Burton and the other American swimmer in the race, Doug Northway. The coach was red-faced in anger, so mad he was shaking. "Go out and show 'em what the U.S.A. has," he yelled, gesturing toward the pool. "Stick it to 'em."[41] The usually calm Burton felt confusion and anger flowing through him at the perceived injustice. But while the Americans were burning with rage, the Australians rejoiced in their newfound fortune. Australia had won several gold medals in the 1,500 over the years, and they considered it their national Olympic event. With DeMont disqualified, they thought they had the gold medal.

Burton went out in a white-hot flash, adrenaline pumping harder than he ever remembered, taking the early lead. Windeatt fought back, caught him after 500 meters, and stayed confidently ahead. In the stands, the Australian fans began to celebrate. Comebacks were rare in the mile race. The Americans hoped Burton could hang on for the silver medal. As he battled to stay in the race, he felt a dull pain rising from his abdomen and into his chest and shoulders. When his arms tightened, he moved them faster. He had always struggled to make smooth, effortless turns, and this became more challenging as he got older. Perhaps it was his anger at DeMont's disqualification or the way he had been overlooked, but he regained his form and started clicking smoothly through the turns. His legs flipped over faster, pushing off the walls more firmly, propelling him through the water. The years of hard work that astounded everyone kicked in. As he approached the last 400 meters, the pain throttled up from a dull throb to excruciating. The water felt colder, and goosebumps, a prehistoric reflex that kicks in during stress, rose on his back. With just 300 meters left in the race, he surged past the Australian. The sharp roar of the crowd spurred him on. Then the pain disappeared. His body went numb, and he knew he was swimming perfectly, beyond pain and emotion. He flashed through the final meters stronger than he had ever done. It was the race of his life, and he won it by six lengths, setting another world record. An earsplitting ovation rocked the hall, and DeMont, sitting out of view behind the stands, rushed out and hugged him. In the stadium, Americans tore paper into tiny squares and produced a small shower of confetti. In disbelief, Burton climbed out of the pool, fighting back tears. He and Chavoor embraced. For once, the "eccentric wit," the man who was never satisfied with his swimmers' accomplishments, had nothing snappy to tell Burton. "Go ahead and cry; you earned it," was all he could muster.[42]

Burton became the first swimmer in history to win back-to-back gold medals in the 1,500 in the Olympics. In swimming's most grueling race, he set his last world record seven years after his first. Burton's effort inspired millions of people watching on television. Back in Sacramento, a man named Kenneth Allard spoke for many when he wrote, "Watching the Olympics, I cheered for Spitz, but I could not make a sound for Mike Burton as tears came to my eyes. He, more than anyone I know or have read about, represents the true spirit of the Olympic Games."[43]

23

"OUR GREATEST HOPES AND OUR WORST FEARS"

Mark Spitz and Mike Burton headed out into Munich that night to celebrate their victories in different ways. Burton, his wife and parents, and a group of swimmers, friends, and coaches went out and closed two bars, raising a toast to every one of Mike's fifteen split times. Spitz went to a quiet dinner at the restaurant Käfer-Schänke with *Sports Illustrated* reporter Jerry Kirshenbaum, who had written many stories about him over the years and become a friend, and photographer Heinz Kluetmeier. Spitz was the toast of the evening as fellow diners applauded when he sat down to dinner and sent drinks his way, all politely declined by the abstemious Spitz.

After a festive night of celebration, Kirshenbaum and Kluetmeier drove Spitz back to the Olympic Village and dropped him off around 2 a.m. on September 5. He waved goodbye and said he would see them at his final Olympic news conference at 9 a.m. At about 4 a.m., eight Palestinians approached the six-foot-high fence near Gate 25a, dressed in sweat suits and carrying athletic bags. The few guards in the area that night were dressed in light-blue uniforms and armed only with walkie-talkies. If they noticed anything, they likely assumed the small group was athletes returning from a night at the bars, hopping the fence to return to their rooms. That was the ruse the Palestinians meant to use, and it worked perfectly when they encountered a group of athletes who, thinking they were Olympians, unwittingly helped them over the wall. Kirshenbaum would always wonder if the terrorists were milling around when he dropped Spitz off that early morning. He calculated Spitz was less than one hundred yards from where they breached the fence. "When we dropped Mark off there, we had no idea what was happening," Kluetmeier later said. "Can you imagine what it would have meant for those terrorists to have seized a Jewish-American who had won seven gold medals?"[1]

Spitz had one final noxious Olympian task, his last press conference. He and the media had grown weary of each other. "He'd been difficult, defiant, arrogant and elusive." Spitz was "a hero as lofty as Mount Olympus itself,"[2] a journalist wrote, not knowing that within a few hours, Mount Olympus would be calling on him for help.

Spitz awoke at 8 a.m., looking forward to reveling in his status as the new golden boy of swimming. His coaches, Pete Daland, George Haines, Sherm Chavoor, and Don Gambril, piled into a Volkswagen minibus with him for the short ride to the press center. Once again, fate decreed that his coaches would be with him when he needed them most. The small van nosed its way through the streets without any police escort. None of the passengers knew that the terrorists had seized members of the Israeli Olympic team and were holding them hostage.

They arrived at the press center and immediately knew something unusual was going on. There were an estimated six hundred people there. Even though Spitz had just finished the greatest Olympic performance in modern history, Chavoor realized there were far too many journalists on hand and something bigger must be brewing. Chavoor said the U.S. Olympic Committee officials were aware of the hostage situation but did not share any information with him. Kirshenbaum, the *Sports Illustrated* reporter, had heard the news about the terrorists. He recognized that something was off, since Spitz and his coaches smiled and seemed relaxed. Kirshenbaum cut through the mob of reporters and quickly shared the horrific, unbelievable news with them. Spitz was stunned by the information and became frightened and distraught at the prospect of facing a press corps in the throes of a feeding frenzy, desperate for any details on a breaking news story. He overheard someone wondering if a terrorist was in the room while he overheard Chavoor arguing with Olympic officials about getting a bodyguard for him.

Spitz scanned the crowd for signs of terrorists while wondering what would happen if he was attacked. The terrorists would not have any trouble picking out the face of the most famous man in the world. "I don't want to get up at that microphone. I'd be a perfect target for someone with a gun," he told the Olympic officials.[3] Only Kirshenbaum provided advice about what he should say to the media. He counseled him to express his sad feelings about the attack and, most of all, avoid saying "no comment."[4]

As he mounted the steps toward the microphones, Spitz saw West German guards with long rifles take up positions in the room. Taking seats in the auditorium, his coaches instinctively formed a protective ring around him. Spitz shrunk back from the microphones while his coaches sat so close to him they were identified as security guards in press photos. Spitz struggled to discern the questions shouted at him from all sides. The media surrounded him, all working on getting a view of him, and photographers got into shoving matches with each other as they jockeyed for position to take unobstructed pictures. Media mixed with uncredentialed bystanders wandering throughout the room.

Without any preparation, Spitz searched for the correct words to use when asked about the hostage situation. "I think it's very tragic. I don't have any other comment," he responded to the first barrage of questions. When a reporter shouted, "You are a Jew. Jews are being killed; what does that mean to you?" He answered, "I didn't come here as a Jew; I came to the Olympics as an American athlete to represent my country, my teammates, and myself." He immediately knew his answer sounded tone-deaf and wondered why he didn't express his true feelings and say something heartfelt about the tragedy and how he had felt the sting of anti-Semitism during his life.[5] The press was brutal. Journalists complained that they could not hear Spitz because he was not close enough to the microphones. "He was a puppet with Chavoor sitting there pulling the strings," railed the *Philadelphia Daily News*.[6] "The more he talked, giving unsatisfactory one-sentence answers to the most probing questions, the more the arrogance showed through," another journalist reported.[7]

The day continued to devolve into chaos and confusion. Olympic and German officials finally figured out that Spitz indeed could be a target for the terrorists. After about an hour of questions, he left the news conference escorted by German soldiers. An American soldier was dispatched to guard him for the day. He went to the ABC studio for an interview, then back to his apartment in the Olympic Village, arriving before noon. Finally, a heavy guard was put around his building. No one knew what was going on in the hostage drama. German authorities helicoptered Arnold Spitz in from Garmish, the town where he was staying, to Munich. The television was on in German, and Spitz struggled to digest the news reports that claimed he was in different places. One minute they said he was in Frankfurt, the next, that he was in Italy. The entire world was on edge, waiting for information on the fate of the hostages as seconds ticked away. Then Chavoor once again called upon his skills as a master media manipulator. He picked up the phone and called the Associated Press's Hubert Mizell, a reporter he had chatted with a few times during the week. Chavoor told the reporter that Spitz was scared, afraid the terrorists were after him: "We're going to get Mark out of Germany. Please do not write anything yet. I will call you and nobody else from the media when something is definite." About an hour later, Chavoor called again: "He's gone. We put Spitz on a plane for London. He's safe. You can put out the news." The AP quickly flashed a bulletin "about the Games' great Jewish hero being on his way home to Sacramento, Calif." But it was a ruse, or, as the reporter put it bluntly, "a lie." Chavoor was using him. "The swimming coach knew that my AP bulletin would go not only to the United States but to Europe. And specifically to German radio stations."[8] Chavoor had played it perfectly. Once the story aired, no one would be looking for Spitz in Munich.

At about 6 p.m., U.S. Olympic officials decided he should leave Germany. Under heavy security, he was escorted to an underground garage, where officials stuck him in the backseat of a Mercedes, put a blanket over his head, and drove him to the Munich airport to catch a commercial flight to London. The trip was supposed to be a secret, but they landed in England to a swarm of reporters and photographers who took his picture as he got off the plane and then followed him to his hotel, where he was photographed with an obliging doorman. Finally, he began to feel safe. But he got another scare that night. Security guards posted outside the hotel room left their post and took a break early in the morning. Suddenly there was a knock on the door and the sounds of men speaking in heavily accented English. Chavoor flew to the door, convinced terrorists had caught up with them. It turned out that a pair of enterprising Italian journalists had found them and wanted an interview, which was hastily and firmly declined. Once the confusion was sorted out, Spitz and Chavoor tried to go back to bed but couldn't sleep the rest of the night. "Boy, you're dangerous to be around," Chavoor quipped to his star.[9]

The next day in London, the newspapers told of the final tragic outcome of the Olympic hostage crisis. Negotiations had failed, and all eleven Israeli hostages were murdered. Germany's efforts to embrace peace and downplay the role of police at the games had ended in tragedy. Manfred Schreiber, Munich's police chief, said, "We were trained for everyday offenses, to be close to the people, unarmed, not for an action against paramilitary trained terrorists."[10] The world had watched in agony as the suspense of the tragedy played out on ABC. Broadcaster Jim McKay announced the end in words that resonated throughout the world: "When I was a kid, my father used to say our greatest hopes and our worst fears are seldom realized. Our worst fears have been realized tonight. They have now said there were eleven hostages; two were killed in their rooms yesterday morning, nine were killed at the airport tonight. They're all gone."[11]

While in London, Spitz posed for what became the photo on his iconic poster, clothed only in his swimsuit with the seven gold medals draped around his neck. Chavoor, now acting as an agent, sold the rights for $7,500 but initially did not negotiate for a royalty on every poster sold. (That situation was remedied a few months later when Spitz's new Hollywood agents negotiated a deal that paid him fifteen cents a copy.) The poster sold 2 million copies, the most in the world until movie star Farrah Fawcett's poster eclipsed it four years later.

Spitz and Chavoor headed for the airport and a nonstop flight to Los Angeles. Spitz carried his medals onto the plane in a carry-on bag and stowed them in the cockpit with the pilots. Another media horde greeted them in Los Angeles. They had to battle through the crowd to reach their connecting flight to Sacramento. When Spitz complained about the press and the crush of humanity, Chavoor replied, "Don't win so many medals next time."

Don Bloom of the *Sacramento Bee* was able to call in his chits for doing so many favors for Chavoor over the years: Chavoor gave him the seat next to Spitz on the flight from Los Angeles to Sacramento. Bloom asked him about the Olympic Committee's decision to resume the Games after a brief halt to memorialize the Israeli victims. Spitz told Bloom he agreed with that sentiment: "The games are for men and women to get together regardless of color, religion or political beliefs. Outsiders came to the [Olympic] Village. They could do the same thing at other events. If [the Games] are stopped, it would prove the Games are moving toward the political realm. It is an $800 million theatrical stage for athletes, not radicals."[12] Chavoor agreed: "They didn't stop the Olympic Games for the Vietnam War, did they? That's even more tragic."[13]

While many remember IOC president Avery Brundage's speech declaring "the Games must go on," few recall that it came after Olympic Israeli delegation leader Shmuel Lakin told the vast crowd at the memorial that "Israel came together with other countries in a spirit of Olympic peace. We deeply mourn the rape of the Olympic Spirit in which 11 members of our team were murdered. We will leave this place deeply shocked, but Israel will compete in the future again in the true spirit of brotherhood."[14]

Another throng of five hundred fans met Spitz at Sacramento Metro Airport. "Heroes Return, Hundreds of Girls Shriek Welcome to Spitz," read the headline.[15] Spitz, who had not slept since he left Munich, held his first news conference since he left Germany and just wanted to go home and rest. No one noticed the lumpy white travel bag by his feet that held his gold medals. "I'm retiring, not quitting," he announced, telling the crowd that "the last two years of my career, I swam 20 times, and I broke a world record 19 of those times." Spitz looked on with "amiable tolerance" as girls fought to touch him. "Nobody compares to Mark, not even my boyfriends," one girl said. A woman asked his permission, then kissed him on the cheek.[16]

Chavoor said Arden Hills had received five thousand pieces of mail, all asking for a picture or autograph from Spitz. Hollywood agents, talk show bookers, advertising firms, and marketing representatives bombarded the club with phone calls and telegrams trying to sign Spitz up. Chavoor handled the calls, in effect operating as Spitz's agent. He loudly declared he needed a vacation and wanted to get away from the furor, but *Bee* reporter Bloom knew Chavoor relished every second of being the ringmaster of a global media circus. Speculation rose as to how much money Spitz could make. Sacramento sportscaster Creighton Sanders proclaimed that Spitz would quickly become a millionaire, while Chavoor upped the ante and said he'd soon be worth $5 million.[17]

Finally, Spitz could get out of the crush and go home to relax and watch the Olympics on TV like everyone else. The only difference was guards parked outside his house for a few weeks. The tragedy of Munich did not hit him until a few days later, when he was in temple for a Rosh Hashanah service, sitting next to Governor Ronald Reagan as the slain Israeli athletes were memorialized.

After a few days, he signed with the William Morris Agency, the same firm that had helped land swimming star Johnny Weissmuller his role as Tarzan. Spitz moved to Los Angeles and quickly signed endorsement and appearance deals worth an estimated $7 million. While he didn't land a big movie deal, he scored lucrative guest appearances fees on the *Bob Hope Show* and other prime-time programs.[18] Thoughts of attending dental school at Indiana vanished. "Two-and-a-half weeks after the last event in 1972, I was supposed to be on a plane to Indianapolis for the Indiana University dental school. The tragedy sidelined my plans. I elected to go home to Sacramento and ask the dean for a one-year leave of absence. I had the intention to go back but never made it," Spitz said.[19]

Even with Spitz gone, Chavoor was basking in glory with the media. Overall, the Soviets had given the United States a thrashing, taking home fifty gold medals to the U.S. team's thirty-three, and they won the overall medal count ninety-nine to ninety-four. Chavoor reminded everyone that almost half of the U.S. gold medals came from swimmers he coached, eight from the women swimmers, and eight from Spitz and Burton.

The Games struggled to a conclusion. The controversial decision to resume was widely castigated in the media, and many believed the Games had been so severely damaged they would never be held again. Moreover, if the Olympics were to continue, it would be without the stern hand of Avery Brundage, the man who fought to preserve amateurism in the Olympics, who was retiring. Lord Killanin of Ireland replaced him.

Because of the tragedy, many athletes left Munich before the closing ceremonies, held on the raw and cold night of September 11, as the world continued to grieve the loss of the Israeli athletes. The nations' flags snapped in the breeze, with Israel's at half-mast. The gloomy weather heightened the contrast between the closing ceremonies and the perfect warm day of the opening ceremonies held just two weeks earlier. The joyous celebration in Mexico City four years earlier was forgotten. Instead of festive dancing, soldiers with submachine guns lined the route to the stadium as fighter jets roared above the crowd, providing a protective blanket. Mike Burton stayed for the ceremonies, and his inspirational victory in the 1,500 earned him the honor of carrying the American flag. But once again, the recognition he deserved was muted; television announcers mistakenly said on air that discus thrower Olga Connolly was carrying the flag. After the games, Burton met with a few agents. But the greatest distance swimmer of his era, renowned for his modesty and work ethic, did not attract interest from Hollywood or land any sponsorships. The media sympathized with the swimmer they admired but recognized reality: "Unlike Mark Spitz, there is fame but no fortune for fellow Olympics champion swimmer Mike Burton."[20] He returned to Arden Hills and cast about for a job. Finally, he accepted the coaching position at the Multnomah Athletic Club in Portland, Oregon. His Olympic performance resulted in his third nomination for the Sullivan Award, but he was again passed over on the final vote.

After the success, drama, excitement, and tragedy he'd experienced during the 1972 Olympics, many thought Chavoor would wind down and still his competitive instincts. Instead, Chavoor wrote that he was looking forward to developing "a new generation of kids" and named eleven of his swimmers, most less than sixteen years old, as the future nucleus of the 1976 U.S. Olympic team. He had almost twenty male swimmers, many on college scholarships, competing at major universities across the United States. In 1976, the Olympic Trials were held in Long Beach. Once again, a strong contingent of eight Arden Hills swimmers descended on the magnificent Belmont Plaza Olympic Pool, the site of the club's fantastic performance during the 1968 Olympic Trials. The 1976 team was led by Dave Fairbank, who had been an alternate on the 1972 Olympic team; Rex Favero, who had set a world record in the 800-meter freestyle relay the year before; and Jeff Float, a fast-rising sixteen-year-old high school student who, Chavoor said, had more promise than Burton or Spitz. But this time, none of the swimmers found magic in the Long Beach water, and there were no Sacramento swimming Olympians for the first time in eight years.

In April 1977, Mark Spitz, Debbie Meyer, Mike Burton, and Sherm Chavoor were inducted into the International Swimming Hall of Fame in Fort Lauderdale, Florida. Sue Pedersen was again left out and would not be inducted into the Hall until May 1995. It was a first-class gala event, and many of swimming's glitterati were in attendance. Most flocked to see Spitz, the now twenty-seven-year-old former champion who remained the face of swimming. But now, five years after his glorious 1972 run, some journalists saw him as a fading star who had never reached his potential. "Ignored by show business, shunned by Schick's pulling out of a $500,000 deal, dumped by CBS as a sportscaster, Mark Spitz's $5 million dream has turned into something of a nightmare." The article noted that Spitz was a millionaire but said he had bombed as a guest on the Johnny Carson and Bob Hope shows and that a CBS sports executive called him "a dunce." Spitz blamed Hollywood: "Everybody in that industry has terminal cancer. They are only interested in flaunting themselves. I'd rather be a has-been than a never was."[21] Instead of making movies, "he represent[ed] a water goggles company, a mask and fin company, and he [was] president of his own toy company."[22] Spitz's hall of fame induction speech was panned by another reporter: "Spitz comes across as a terribly shy, inarticulate man, egocentric, but lacking in confidence at the same time. What I find unfortunate is that his personality seems destined to obscure forever his achievement, which must rank as one of the greatest exhibitions in the Olympics ever seen."[23]

Mike Burton had never been the guy with the catchy quote and had never been a media darling. But finally, the spotlight found him. "I've got to say that, with all the effort it took on the part of everybody, were it not for Mike Burton and all that he did to revolutionize middle distance swimming, his inspiration, well none of us would be here, and that includes Mark Spitz," Chavoor said.[24]

Fighting back tears, Meyer struggled to introduce him. "My biggest honor tonight isn't my own induction, it's introducing Mike Burton. You've always taken a backseat. But not tonight. This is your night, yours more than mine or any of the other honorees. He's been everything to us, everything. And he always stayed in the background. I dedicate this night to Mike Burton."

"An athlete's sacrifice is nothing compared to the sacrifices his parents make. It's nothing compared to what a brother or sister or a wife goes through," Burton said in his speech. Meyer hugged her parents as emotions reached an emotional crescendo. "The tears followed. The place sort of fell apart."[25]

Chavoor's hall of fame induction may have stirred some jealousy in Sacramento. The man whose coaching accomplishments put Sacramento on the world sports map and who had coached two of the greatest Olympic swim teams in history was put upon by his rivals. People who had butted heads with Chavoor or were envious of his success quickly spread rumors that the old coach's best days were behind him. He was described as losing his touch and loving real estate, Italian marble, German cars, and Swiss watches while losing interest in coaching. Rival swim clubs that had lost to Arden Hills for decades and had to read about its Olympic success were finally getting some revenge. When swimmers from nearby Foothill Farms beat Arden Hills in a meet, "hoots of elation" were heard throughout the area. In a *Sacramento Bee* story headlined, "Arden Hills Dives but Chavoor Basks in Past Success,"[26] a young sports reporter named R. E. Graswich gave unnamed coaches, swimmers, and parents a platform to blast Chavoor. Graswich visited the club, where he found the lion-in-winter basking in opulence, a $1,000 Rolex Oyster watch on his wrist, ruminating about the old days of Debbie Meyer, Mike Burton, and Mark Spitz. As evidence of his decline, Graswich reported that after the 1972 Olympics, "world-class swimmers seemed to stop emerging from the pool,"[27] and that the team had not won any Olympic medals in 1976.

"Young coaches" were anonymously quoted as saying he was not adapting to new training techniques like weightlifting. They said he had lost his enthusiasm, had seen it all and done it all, and was enamored of his wealth and past success. Perhaps never knowing that Chavoor had started his career befriending poor kids at the YMCA and driving them to meets in his own car, rivals said, "He simply doesn't care anymore."[28] His temper and blunt approach to handling parents was blamed for chasing promising swimmers away. "The days of Arden Hills as an AAU swimming powerhouse are over," they confidently asserted. "He was no. 1 for a long time, the most influential swimming coach in the world, but time has passed him by," said a source. When confronted with the quotes, Chavoor "got a bit defensive," the reporter wrote. Finally, Chavoor asked him, "Who have you been talking to?"[29]

Of course, reporters don't reveal their sources, and the coaches were reluctant to be identified because Chavoor was "an important and powerful person in Sacramento." Chavoor aptly summed up his critics when he said, "There are a lot of young swimming coaches in this area, and they might be something someday, but right now they're too young, and they're in no position to criticize me."[30] None of the criticizing coaches who "might be something someday" ever approached his accomplishments. Mocking his own newspaper, Graswich wrote that in the past, "as far as the beguiling [Sacramento] media was concerned, there was only one swim team and one coach in Sacramento."[31] History confirms the "beguiling" media's assessment: There *was* only one team and one coach. And there would never be another one remotely like them.

24

"I LOVE YOU"

While many thought he was done producing Olympic champions, Chavoor had another great homegrown swimmer in the pool, the perfectly named Jeff Float. But Float faced a special challenge: He had contracted viral meningitis when he was thirteen months old. Inflammation attacked his cochlea, a part of the inner ear that is responsible for sending sound waves to the brain, and Float lost his hearing. He became 90 percent deaf in his right ear and 65 percent deaf in his left. Despite the condition, he was full of energy, and when his parents got tired of him chasing the dog around the house, they sought another outlet for his energy and enrolled him at Arden Hills. Chavoor wasn't used to coddling young swimmers and made no exception for young Float: "Hey, you deaf-and-dumb kid. Let's get moving. Ya got a banana in your ear?"[1]

In 1970, Chavoor said ten-year-old Float would be on the 1976 Olympic team. He dominated an AAU meet, setting age group records in the 100-yard backstroke, the 200 free and individual medleys, and the 100-yard butterfly. He became a dominant age group swimmer, but he seldom responded to the congratulations of his fellow swimmers, who, not realizing he could not hear, branded him as "arrogant" and teased him because he spoke with a lisp. But he stood up to the roughhousing and the bullying, answering his tormenters with success in the pool. Like Sue Pedersen and Debbie Meyer before him, he was inspired by Mike Burton, his "big brother," who took time to work with him while preparing for the Olympics.[2] Float grew to a muscular six-foot-two and became one of the top high school swimmers in the nation. As a sixteen-year-old, he had a shot at making the Olympic team but came up short in the trials. The following year he won ten gold medals at the World Games for the Deaf and went on to win gold in the 400-meter freestyle at the 1978 U.S.

National Championships. He earned a scholarship to the University of Southern California, where he was named All-American six times and developed a loyal throng of enthusiastic Trojan fans who would chant, "Floater, floater" during races, a tribute Float could not hear.[3]

In his prime as a twenty-year-old, Float realized his lifelong goal and qualified in three individual events on the 1980 Olympic team. But politics intervened again, this time with devastating consequences. President Jimmy Carter decided to boycott the Games scheduled for Moscow that summer. Float and other Olympic hopefuls saw their years of dedication and endless toil come to naught as their dreams of Olympic glory were snuffed out. All they could do was watch as the Soviets and East Germans earned thirty gold medals. Vladimir Salnikov emerged as a new world star, becoming the first person to swim 1,500 under fifteen minutes and winning three gold medals. His intimidating wins earned him the nicknames "Tsar of the Pool" and "Monster of the Waves."

The next Olympics were four long years away, but fortunately for Float, they would be held in Los Angeles. Although he would be considered old for a swimmer by the time they began, he was determined to stay in swimming and make a gold medal run. In 1981, he and the U.S. swimmers reasserted their supremacy when they traveled to Kyiv and demolished the Russians in a head-to-head meet. Float silenced the home crowd by upsetting the Tsar by a second in the 400 free, surprising even himself. "I didn't think I'd go that fast; in fact, I looked up and thought the clock was wrong," he said.[4] Float continued swimming at USC and won a world championship in the 4 x 200 relay in 1982. But once again international politics threatened to derail the Games when the Soviets said they would sit them out in retribution for the 1980 U.S. boycott. Float wondered if the effort required to compete in the Games was worth it without Russian participation, and many said the Games would be diminished with the Soviets' absence. But Chavoor encouraged Float to compete, telling him the Olympic experience was worth it even if the Russians didn't compete.

Float had accomplished almost everything a swimmer could hope for: a world championship gold medal, a spot on the Pan American team. He had competed in every national championship since he was fifteen years old. At age twenty-four, it seemed like his Olympic hopes had ended. But Chavoor convinced him to put in a hard season of training under his rigid direction, and Float ran up close to twenty thousand yards a day working out. Having put up with the animated coach for years, Float had learned to deal with him. When the coach yelled at him too loudly, Float merely switched off his hearing aid. Even though he was not the fastest qualifier during the trials in the 200 free, Chavoor felt sure he would win gold in that event and on the freestyle relay team. All it would take, Chavoor said, was a few weeks of hard training for Float to bring home the gold.

To win it, he would have to defeat one of the most intimidating swimmers in history, West Germany's Michael Gross, the world record holder who was two seconds faster than Float. At six-foot-seven and with a seven-foot, five-inch arm span, Gross looked like a giant creature surging through the water; he was nicknamed "the Albatross." While some thought Float should pull back and aim for a silver medal in his race against the "unbeatable" Albatross, Float was determined to hold nothing back and went all out for the gold. Using his typical negative motivational method, Chavoor's last words of advice to Float as he entered the pool were "don't embarrass me."[5]

Float went out as strong as he could and stayed close to the lead through the first three laps, only to falter at the last turn as the Albatross proved too strong, winning in world record time. Float barely missed taking bronze and finished fourth. "Time May Have Passed Float By,"[6] the headline in the *Sacramento Bee* read after his loss. But Float had one more chance for a medal in the 800-meter free relay. Gross and his West German team were the favorites, but the Americans had a noisy, jubilant home crowd behind them. The U.S. team had carved out a slim lead when Float dove into the pool to swim the third leg. He swam his fastest 200 ever and increased the lead almost half a second, time his teammate Bruce Hayes desperately needed to hold off Gross in the final leg.

Float got out of the pool and saw the excited fist pumps of the American fans, feeling the noise vibrations from the crowd when he stood on the pool deck. And then, for the first time in his life, he heard it—the excited yelling and staccato applause. The wild cheering had penetrated his deafness. His effort gave Hayes the tiniest lead over the Albatross, who relentlessly closed the margin. The American held on just enough to out-touch Gross by four-hundredths of a second in a race ranked as one of the most exciting in Olympic history. The jubilant American team, dubbed "the Gross Busters" by the media, mounted the stand to accept their medals and sing the national anthem. The television cameras focused on Float, capturing the tears of joy that flowed down his cheeks as he sang loudly and enthusiastically. He created an indelible image for millions worldwide when he instinctively flashed "I love you" to the crowd in sign language.

Float's moment of glory ended, but not his efforts for Team USA. Instead, he wore his gold medal to the daily competition to cheer on the American divers. He was "smiling, signing autographs cheering for whoever else was in the pool or on the diving board." He came "to visit with people, pose for pictures, wave to the television cameras." He stayed for the last medal presentation, and then the games ended. A reporter asked him if he would ever take off his medal. "Tonight," he said. "After the Olympic flame goes out. Maybe."[7]

25

DOGFIGHT

In June 1985, Chavoor announced he'd sold Arden Hills to a corporation headed by a local dentist whose kids had been in Chavoor's swimming program for many years. The new owners had plans to remodel the clubhouse and upgrade the club into "a really neat" place. "I felt 30 years of running a very successful business was enough," Chavoor said. He would, however, continue to train swimmers at the Rancho Arroyo Racquet Club, a renovated club in a suburban industrial area. He had no plans of quitting. "Twenty years from now, I'll probably retire," he said.[1] In January 1990, Chavoor finally retired, but the competitive flame continued to roar inside of him. He tried playing softball in an old-timers' league but found it not challenging enough. So instead, he found a greater challenge in racquetball, having "dogfights" with younger players. He often added a half dozen years to his age so his rivals would underestimate him, then he would unleash on "the kids." "I beat their tails," he said. "Boom, boom, boom!"[2]

In 1992, word got around that Chavoor was sick with "a spot of cancer on his liver." He shrugged it off, saying he would beat it. In July, the *Sacramento Bee* sent Dixie Reid, a lifestyle reporter, to do a feature story on him. She found him tan and fit, "very Californian." She was surprised there was no swimming pool in his yard, and Chavoor, reemploying the yarn that had served him for a lifetime, told her it was no big deal since he couldn't swim anyway. Chavoor took her into a den he called his trophy room, stuffed with pictures and mementos from the glory days. Talking about the keys to his success, he said he'd been a stern disciplinarian who gave no second chances and told the kids, "You don't drink, you don't smoke, you don't do drugs." Violators were shown the door. "That's the goal I set—to win everything," he said. But "it was fun, watching those kids develop, little squirts to men." So what was his secret to success? "If

I knew, I'd bottle it and sell it," he said, leaving the reporter wondering if he was telling the truth or just being modest. In the end, he said, it was all about his swimmers: "There were a million swimmers in the sea, but only a few had the heart to succeed."[3]

Sherm Chavoor died at home on September 3, 1992, from the "spot" of cancer. The *Bee* noted his passing in a front-page story.[4] He was the "irascible" coach who had made legends of his students and became a legend himself. The news about the death of the swimming coach who couldn't swim was reported around the world. In a brief item, the *New York Times*, apparently bereft of adjectives, headlined its story "Sherm Chavoor, 73, A swimming coach."[5]

While medal and record counts differ, Chavoor's swimmers are generally credited with winning 31 Olympic medals, 20 of them gold, and setting 83 world and 131 U.S. records. He was the only swim coach to produce two Sullivan Award winners.

His former star swimmers –his "nuts"—had stayed in touch with him and were saddened by his death. "I loved him, and he loved me," Mike Burton said, adding that Chavoor was the best thing that ever happened to him and had molded him into a man. Jeff Float was overcome with grief and struggled to control his emotions and talk to the media about his mentor. Chavoor, he said, was a strong man who thought "everything could be overcome with guts and determination." Debbie Meyer, who had continued to visit regularly with the man she regarded as her second father, was devastated by the news. She and Burton looked back on their relationship with him and struggled to understand the Chavoor enigma. "We couldn't put our finger on it," she said. "There was just something that made us want to succeed for him, something other than the fact that we loved him, and he loved us. But that's what carried us through." Mark Spitz was sad and gave Chavoor credit for his greatest achievements: "He was the one directly responsible for the cornerstone of my swimming career and for my encouragement and development."[6]

Chavoor had decreed that there would be only a private family ceremony to mark his passing. The memory of him and what he had accomplished passed quickly. When a new television sportscaster in town reported on his death, he mispronounced his name and called him "Sherm Sheerer." An old hand on the *Bee* sports desk heard it and wailed, "It doesn't get any worse than that."[7]

Sacramento metamorphosed into a new place. In the 1970s, at the height of Chavoor's renown, the metro area population was around 630,000. By early 2020, more than 2 million people lived in the area. Most of the new arrivals had never heard of Chavoor or his swim team. He had once hinted it might be fitting if a swimming pool or recreation facility was named for him, but nothing was ever done. Many area residents have no idea that one of the most remarkable medal runs in any sport in Olympic history came out of one Sacramento swimming pool.

Chavoor should be unforgettable. His was the prototypical American success story, the man who pulled himself up by his bootstraps. Born into poverty, he could have settled into a life of middle-class respectability if he had remained an educator. But he seized on every opportunity that presented itself. From his first days at the Sacramento YMCA, he produced swimmers and teams that didn't just win, they dominated. When people and conditions stood in his way and tried to prevent him from accomplishing something, he determinedly went around or over them to get his way. Prevented from coaching the way he wanted, he created his own swim club. He could have just followed the convention of the day: cut out a hole in the ground, filled it with water, built a concrete apron around it, planted a few trees, and called it a club. Instead, he created one of the finest swimming and tennis clubs in the country, one visitors marveled at. Within a decade of starting the club, he was wealthy beyond anything he or his family could have imagined when he was a child. He could have run a traditional swimming program, hired a recreational director and reaped the profits. But he kept charging, landing national events, getting sponsors to support the meets, working the media, and spreading the Arden Hills name throughout the world swimming community, ranked with Santa Clara and other top clubs. His renown grew as the tough coach who piled on the work despite the "fact" that he could not swim. It did not surprise him when Debbie Meyer, Sue Pedersen, Johnny Ferris, and Mike Burton won national championships and then Olympic medals. He expected it. He had somehow reached into their souls and pulled out performances even they had not thought possible.

Chavoor seemed to possess a magic key when it came to unlocking that puzzling economic, cultural, political, and athletic event called the Olympics. Mark Spitz said Chavoor had the ability to handle the Olympic atmosphere. The rhythms of living in the Olympic Village, the massive global media presence, and the pressure of international competition humbled even the most robust constitutions. But Chavoor had the talent "to make sure that everybody in the pool" took in his every word and deployed his instructions at precisely the right instant to win.[8]

When Debbie Meyer and Mike Burton were preparing for the 1968 Olympic Games, the great Indiana University coach Doc Counsilman stopped by Arden Hills and came away in awe of what Chavoor was doing. "I can't recall any other coach having two such swimmers as Debbie and Mike Burton, who's the world's greatest male distance swimmer," he said. "The remarkable thing is they're strictly Sherm's, developed right here, not kids who came fairly well established from elsewhere. It's a unique situation, believe me, and it didn't just happen, Chavoor saw that it happened."[9] When Spitz stumbled and fell after his disastrous performance in the 1968 Olympics, Chavoor pulled him out of the abyss and kept him on track for his record-shattering performance four years later in Munich.

Who, really, was Sherm Chavoor, or Izikiel Correa? He claimed he was a college football player, boxer, track star, psychologist, World War II combat bomber pilot, the only millionaire swim coach, the swim coach who couldn't swim. He was pugnacious, combative, a storyteller, a fable maker, a promoter, a teacher, a Svengali. But, most important to him and the world of top competitive swimming, he was a winner. Was winning all there was? Years before Chavoor died, he had talked about the role of teachers and coaches. He said they did everything possible for their students, only to be unceremoniously forgotten. "Did you ever have a teacher who really influenced you?" he asked a reporter. "And did you ever go back and thank that teacher for what she did? No, I didn't either. Boy, I wish now that I'd gone back and thanked her for everything she did for me."[10]

NOTES

CHAPTER 1

1. Certificate of Hawaiian Birth. The name "Izikiel" is listed on the certificate. On a Passenger and Crew List dated December 4, 1919, his name was listed as "Ezikel Correa." There would be many variations on spellings of his name in future years. I have used his birth name throughout the chapter.

2. "Honolulu Hawaii, U.S. Arriving and Departing Passenger and Crew Lists, 1900–1959," Ancestry.com, https://www.ancestry.com/search/collections/1502/. The name listed is Ezikel Correa, but the United States Federal Census of 1930 spelled his name Ezikiel Correa.

3. John Malos, "Swimming Coach Sherm Chavoor," KCRA-TV, Center for Sacramento History Archives, February 1, 1981, https://archive.org/details /kcrasp051chavoorspitzmeyerinterviewsfeb1981.

4. Dixie Reid, "Legacy in Water," *Sacramento Bee*, July 16, 1992.

5. Kevin Starr, *Endangered Dreams: The Great Depression in California* (New York: Oxford University Press, 1996), 85–86.

6. Sherman Chavoor, with Bill Davidson, *The 50-Meter Jungle: How Olympic Gold Medal Swimmers Are Made* (New York: Coward, McCann, Geoghegan, 1973), 29.

7. Malos, "Swimming Coach Sherm Chavoor."

8. Name change petition, Judgment Book 1481, p. 88, Los Angeles County Court, November 30, 1944.

9. Chavoor, with Davidson, *The 50-Meter Jungle*, 29.

10. Army of the United States, Certificate of Service, November 14, 1945.

11. Bosley Crowther, "The Screen in Review: 'Battleground,' Metro Film on Heroic American Soldiers at Bastogne, Opens at Astor," *New York Times*, November 12, 1949, https://www.nytimes.com/1949/11/12/archives/the -screen-in-review-battleground-metro-film-on-heroic-american.html.

12. Tak Iseri, telephone interview with the author, Sacramento, October 28, 2020.

13. Iseri, telephone interview with the author.

14. Ned Wirth, "Chavoor Deserves Induction," *Sacramento Bee*, June 1, 1979.

15. Iseri, telephone interview with the author.

16. Iseri, telephone interview with the author.

17. Marco Smolich, "Write or Wrong," *Sacramento Bee*, April 24, 1977.

18. "Winners All," *Sacramento Bee*, July 5, 1949.

19. "A Future Champ?" *San Francisco Examiner*, April 11, 1948.

20. Wilbur Adams, "Breaststroke Twins," *Sacramento Bee*, June 10, 1948.

21. Murray Olderman, "Sports Vignettes," *Sacramento Bee*, July 9, 1948

22. Iseri, telephone interview with the author.

23. Chavoor, with Davidson, *The 50-Meter Jungle*, 23.

24. Marco Smolich, "Between the Sport Lines," *Sacramento Bee*, August 25, 1955.

25. "What about a Loan?" *Los Angeles Times*, April 8, 1956.

26. William Manchester, *The Glory and the Dream: A Narrative History of America, 1932–1972* (New York: Bantam, 1975), 428.

CHAPTER 2

1. Larine O'Brien, "Crippled Children's Society Readies Easter Seal Fund Campaign," *Daily Independent Journal* (San Rafael, CA), February 28, 1950.

2. "Carl Bauer," International Swimming Hall of Fame, https://www.ishof.org/honoree/honoree-carl-bauer/.

3. Sherman Chavoor, with Bill Davidson, *The 50-Meter Jungle: How Olympic Gold Medal Swimmers Are Made* (New York: Coward, McCann, Geoghegan, 1973), 96.

4. Cecil M. Colwin, *Breakthough Swimming* (Champaign, IL: Human Kinetics, 2002), 202–203.

5. Arthur Daley, "The Youth Wave," *New York Times*, April 20, 1967.

6. Chuck Thomas, "Along Marin's Sports Trail," *Daily Independent Journal*, October 16, 1951.

CHAPTER 3

1. Lance Armstrong, "Arden Hills Founder's Success as a Swimming Coach Began in the 1940s," *Arden-Carmichael News*, January 8, 2015.

2. Sherman Chavoor, with Bill Davidson, *The 50-Meter Jungle: How Olympic Gold Medal Swimmers Are Made* (New York: Coward, McCann, Geoghegan, 1973), 30.

3. Ralph Mohr, email to author, November 17, 2019.

4. Lance Armstrong, "Arden Hills Owner Speaks about History, Legacy of Local Wellness Resort," *Valley Community Newspapers,* January 28, 2015.

5. Mohr, email to author.

6. "5 Junior Olympic Swimmers Win National Championships," *Sacramento Bee,* November 26, 1955.

7. Wayne Harbert, "Sacramento Prep Swimmers Are Splashing Way to Fame," *Sacramento Bee,* April 17, 1956.

8. Dixie Reid, "Legacy in Water," *Sacramento Bee,* July 16, 1992.

9. Jimmy Babcock, "Junior Swimmers Will Vie in Meet during Weekend," *Sacramento Bee,* June 5, 1959.

10. Ann Bragdon, "Swimming Ferris Sisters Are High Among AAU Contenders," *Sacramento Bee,* April 19, 1962.

CHAPTER 4

1. Mike Burton, telephone interview with the author, May 28, 2021.

2. Burton, telephone interview with the author.

3. Sherman Chavoor, with Bill Davidson, *The 50-Meter Jungle: How Olympic Gold Medal Swimmers Are Made* (New York: Coward, McCann, Geoghegan, 1973), 50–51.

4. Chavoor, with Davidson, *The 50-Meter Jungle,* 50–51.

5. Burton, telephone interview with the author.

6. Chavoor, with Davidson, *The 50-Meter Jungle,* 52.

7. Burton, telephone interview with the author.

8. Ben Swesey, "Swimmer, 16, Faced, Beat Challenge of Handicap," *Sacramento Bee,* July 28, 1963.

9. Burton, telephone interview with the author.

CHAPTER 5

1. Richard J. Foster, *Mark Spitz: The Extraordinary Life of an Olympic Swimmer* (Santa Monica, CA: Santa Monica Press, 2008), 16.

2. Foster, *Mark Spitz,* 18.

3. Renee Ghert-Zand, "How Eichlers Brought Design to Suburbia," *Forward,* March 2, 2012.

4. Foster, *Mark Spitz,* 20.

5. "Paul M. Herron," *Sacramento Bee,* September 13, 2005.

6. Foster, *Mark Spitz,* 11–12.

7. Sherman Chavoor, with Bill Davidson, *The 50-Meter Jungle: How Olympic Gold Medal Swimmers Are Made* (New York: Coward, McCann, Geoghegan, 1973), 28.

8. "Capital Swimmer Equals Record," *Sacramento Bee*, February 14, 1960.

9. Butler, a fine youth swimmer, should not be confused with Mike Burton.

10. Chavoor, with Davidson, *The 50-Meter Jungle*, 31.

11. Chavoor, with Davidson, *The 50-Meter Jungle*, 27.

12. Chavoor, with Davidson, *The 50-Meter Jungle*, 38.

13. Chavoor, with Davidson, *The 50-Meter Jungle*, 38.

14. "Temple Sisterhood Sets Dinner Event," *Sacramento Bee*, February 8, 1960.

15. Chavoor, with Davidson, *The 50-Meter Jungle*, 37.

16. Chavoor, with Davidson, *The 50-Meter Jungle*, 37.

17. Marco Smolich, "Arden Hills Juniors Top North State Swim Groups," *Sacramento Bee*, November 26, 1960.

18. Chavoor, with Davidson, *The 50-Meter Jungle*, 38.

19. William F. Reed, "Swimming Isn't Everything, Winning Is," *Sports Illustrated*, March 9, 1970, https://vault.si.com/vault/1970/03/09/swimming-isnt-everything-winning-is.

20. Foster, *Mark Spitz*, 29–30.

21. Foster, *Mark Spitz*, 17.

22. Reed, "Swimming Isn't Everything."

23. Chavoor, with Davidson, *The 50-Meter Jungle*, 49.

CHAPTER 6

1. Susan Pedersen, interview with the author, October 20, 2020.

2. "Happy Birthday, Sue Pedersen," International Swimming Hall of Fame, October 16, 2020, https://www.ishof.org/honoree/honoree-sue-pedersen/.

3. "Only 10, But Susan Is Swim Star Already," *Sacramento Bee*, June 7, 1964.

4. "Only 10, But Susan Is Swim Star Already."

5. Marco Smolich, "Between the Lines," *Sacramento Bee*, June 7, 1965.

6. Arthur Daley, "Sue Pedersen Typifies Modern Swimmer," *New York Times*, April 20, 1965.

7. Debbie Meyer, telephone interview with the author, May 2, 2020.

8. Joe Davidson, "Thrills in Swim Official's Saga," *Sacramento Bee*, May 29, 2014.

9. Meyer, telephone interview with the author.

10. John McDermott, "Three Who Reached for Olympic Gold," *Life*, November 1, 1968, 54.

11. Sherman Chavoor, with Bill Davidson, *The 50-Meter Jungle: How Olympic Gold Medal Swimmers Are Made* (New York: Coward, McCann, Geoghegan, 1973), 52.

12. Meyer, telephone interview with the author.

13. Meyer, telephone interview with the author.

14. Chavoor, with Davidson, *The 50-Meter Jungle,* 54.

15. Marco Smolich, "11 Meet Marks Fall as Junior Olympians Dazzle Audience," *Sacramento Bee,* June 6, 1965; Marco Smolich, "18 Marks Are Rewritten in Junior Olympics Swim Test," *Sacramento Bee,* June 7, 1965; Meyer and Pedersen, telephone interviews with the author.

16. Don Bloom, "On Peanut Butter, Jelly Diet," *Sacramento Bee,* January 29, 1967.

17. Chavoor, with Davidson, *The 50-Meter Jungle,* 57.

CHAPTER 7

1. "Junior Olympic Summaries," *Sacramento Bee,* June 7, 1964.

2. Richard J. Foster, *Mark Spitz: The Extraordinary Life of an Olympic Swimmer* (Santa Monica, CA: Santa Monica Press, 2008), 31.

3. Foster, *Mark Spitz,* 31.

4. William F. Reed, "Swimming Isn't Everything, Winning Is," *Sports Illustrated,* March 9, 1970. https://vault.si.com/vault/1970/03/09/swimming-isnt-everything-winning-is.

5. John R. McDermott, "Here Comes the Next Bubbling Generation," *Life,* August 16, 1968, 55.

6. McDermott, "Here Comes the Next Bubbling Generation," 56.

7. Reed, "Swimming Isn't Everything."

8. McDermott, "Here Comes the Next Bubbling Generation," 55.

9. Kim Chapin, "The Times Came for Two Teens," *Sports Illustrated,* April 17, 1967, https://vault.si.com/vault/1967/04/17/the-times-came-for-two-teens.

10. Ben Swesey, "12-Year-Old Susan Beats Best," *Sacramento Bee,* March 15, 1966.

11. Debbie Meyer, telephone interview with the author, May 2, 2020.

12. Mike Burton, telephone interview with the author, May 28, 2021.

13. Sherman Chavoor, *The 50-Meter Jungle: How Olympic Gold Medal Swimmers Are Made* (New York: Coward, McCann, Geoghegan, 1973), 73; Foster, *Mark Spitz,* 41, 42.

14. Foster, *Mark Spitz,* 19.

15. Chavoor, with Davidson, *The 50-Meter Jungle,* 73.

16. Chavoor, with Davidson, *The 50-Meter Jungle,* 74.

17. Foster, *Mark Spitz,* 37.

18. John Lohn, "Remembering John Ferris, Olympic Medalist and Man of the World," *Swimming World,* September 17, 2020, https://www.swimmingworldmagazine.com/news/remembering-john-ferris-olympic.

19. Ralph Mohr, "How I Came to Appreciate Mark Spitz Part 2," July 18, 2019, Oregon Masters Swimming, https://swimoregon.org/swim-bits-how-i-came-to-appreciate-mark-spitz-part-2/.

20. Marco Smolich, "Spotlight on Disqualification," *Sacramento Bee*, June 13, 1966; Mohr, "How I Came to Appreciate Mark Spitz Part 2."

21. Ralph Mohr, "How I Came to Appreciate Mark Spitz—Part 3: Spitz, Burton and a Cute Redhead," Oregon Masters Swimming, August 19, 2019, https://swimoregon.org/how-i-came-to-appreciate-mark-spitz-part-3-spitz-burton-and-a-cute-redhead/.

22. Chuck Woodling, "Schollander Proves Human," *Lincoln* (Nebraska) *Journal Star*, August 22, 1966.

23. Burton, telephone interview with the author.

24. Jerry Kirshenbaum, "Now Look Who's an Old Lady," *Sports Illustrated*, August 31, 1970. https://vault.si.com/vault/1970/08/31/now-look-whos-an-old-lady.

25. Chavoor, with Davidson, *The 50-Meter Jungle*, 57.

26. Chavoor, with Davidson, *The 50-Meter Jungle*, 60.

27. Wilbur Adams, "Between the Sport Lines," *Sacramento Bee*, September 19, 1967.

28. Adams, "Between the Sport Lines."

29. Observances on club operations were gathered by the author with former club members and the coach's daughters, Shelly and Sheron Chavoor.

30. Chavoor, with Davidson, *The 50-Meter Jungle*, 44.

31. Chavoor, with Davidson, *The 50-Meter Jungle*, 44–48.

32. Don Bloom, "Five in NCAA Track," *Sacramento Bee*, June 3, 1975.

33. "Chavoor to pay $20,000 for Name Calling," *Sacramento Bee*, November 13, 1985.

CHAPTER 8

1. "Swimming Formula: Hurt, Pain, Agony," *Time*, August 23, 1963, https://content.time.com/time/subscriber/article/0,33009,875110,00.html.

2. Sherman Chavoor, with Bill Davidson, *The 50-Meter Jungle: How Olympic Gold Medal Swimmers Are Made* (New York: Coward, McCann, Geoghegan, 1973), 19–20.

3. Chavoor, with Davidson, *The 50-Meter Jungle*, 18.

4. Debbie Meyer, telephone interview with the author, May 2, 2020.

5. Shelly Chavoor, interview with author, June 18, 2021.

6. Chavoor, with Davidson, *The 50-Meter Jungle*, 19–20.

7. John Malos, "Sherm Chavoor at Home," KCRA-TV, 1979, https://archive.org/details/kcrasp052shermchavoorathome.

8. Chavoor, with Davidson, *The 50-Meter Jungle*, 64–67.

9. "Furuhashi Tips 400 Mark," *Pasadena Independent*, August 19, 1949.

10. Dick Hyland, "Records Fall in AAU Meet," *Los Angeles Times*, August 20, 1949.

11. Maxwell Stiles, "Japan Early Favorite," *Mirror-News* (Los Angeles), August 20, 1949.

12. Chavoor, with Davidson, *The 50-Meter Jungle*, 67.

13. Chavoor, with Davidson, *The 50-Meter Jungle*, 64.

14. Susan Pedersen, telephone interview with the author, October 20, 2020.

15. Tim Cahill, "Mark and the Seven Wisemen," *Rolling Stone*, April 26, 1973, 38.

16. Mike Burton, telephone interview with the author, May 28, 2021.

CHAPTER 9

1. Richard J. Foster, *Mark Spitz: The Extraordinary Life of an Olympic Swimmer* (Santa Monica, CA: Santa Monica Press, 2008).

2. "World Record at Chabot Pool," *Argus* (Fremont, CA), June 26, 1967.

3. Don Schollander and Duke Savage, *Deep Water* (New York: Crown, 1971), 184.

4. William Manchester, *The Glory and the Dream: A Narrative History of America, 1932–1972* (New York: Bantam, 1975), 1114.

5. "Tune In Turn On & Drop Out 1967," YouTube, uploaded March 25, 2016, https://www.youtube.com/watch?v=UQWyC9Z5X-8.

6. Don Bloom, "Is Debbie Meyer Best? Just Ask Swim Coach Chavoor," *Sacramento Bee*, January 29, 1967.

7. R. L. Shaffer, "Miss Meyer Wins AAU Freestyle," *Sacramento Bee,* April 16, 1967.

8. R. L. Shaffer, "Pedersen Sets Medley Record," *Sacramento Bee*, April 15, 1967.

9. "Television Listings," *Sacramento Bee*, April 21, 1967.

10. "Pride in Champions," *Sacramento Bee*, April 18, 1967.

11. "Spitz Sets Second World Mark in Berlin Swim Event," *Sacramento Bee*, October 9, 1967.

12. "25,000 to See Prince Philip Open Pan American Games Today at Winnipeg," *New York Times*, July 23, 1967.

13. "Debbie Sets Second World Record," *Sacramento Bee*, July 30, 1967.

14. Will Grimsley, "Hottest Pan-Am Rivalry Between U.S. Swimmers Spitz, Schollander," *Waukesha* (Wisconsin) *Daily Freeman*, August 1, 1967.

15. Kim Chapin, "Old and New Pool Their Talent," *Sports Illustrated*, August 21, 1967, https://vault.si.com/vault/1967/08/21/old-and-new-pool-their-talent.

16. Foster, *Mark Spitz*, 59–60.

17. John Dell, "Debbie Smashes 1500 Meter Record," *Philadelphia Inquirer*, August 21, 1967.

18. "Hobby Puts Principal in Swim," *New York Daily News*, August 21, 1967.

19. "Coach Hails Selection," *Sacramento Bee*, December 20, 1967.

20. "Other Men's Views," *Manitowoc* (Wisconsin) *Herald-Times*, January 4, 1968.

21. Manchester, *The Glory and the Dream*, 1123–50.

22. "Arden Hills Benefit Is Scheduled," *Sacramento Bee*, February 21, 1968.

23. Sherman Chavoor, with Bill Davidson, *The 50-Meter Jungle: How Olympic Gold Medal Swimmers Are Made* (New York: Coward, McCann, Geoghegan, 1973), 75.

24. Schollander and Savage, *Deep Water*, 237.

25. Chavoor, with Davidson, *The 50-Meter Jungle*, 170.

26. Chavoor, with Davidson, *The 50-Meter Jungle*, 173.

CHAPTER 10

1. Sherman Chavoor, with Bill Davidson, *The 50-Meter Jungle: How Olympic Gold Medal Swimmers Are Made* (New York: Coward, McCann, Geoghegan, 1973), 79–80.

2. Chavoor, with Davidson, *The 50-Meter Jungle*, 79–80.

3. Debbie Meyer, telephone interview with author, May 2, 2020.

4. Chavoor, with Davidson, *The 50-Meter Jungle*, 79–80.

5. Harvey Shapiro, "Record Time Is Too Slow for Fish-Like Debbie," *Pittsburgh Press*, April 21, 1968.

6. Shapiro, "Record Time Is Too Slow."

7. Chuck Woodling, "Change of Pace," *Lincoln Journal*, August 2, 1968.

8. "Coach Predicts U.S Swim Team Will Be Best Ever," *Sacramento Bee*, July 8, 1968.

9. Spence Conley, "Santa Clara Stars Set World Marks," *Oakland Tribune*, July 7, 1968.

10. "World Record in Santa Clara Swim," *Oakland Tribune*, July 6, 1968.

11. "Sue Pedersen Gets 2 Marks—Or Does She?" *Sacramento Bee*, July 6, 1968.

12. *Swimming World and Junior Swimmer*, August 1968.

13. Brent C. Wagner, "Woods Pool Once Was a Center of Swimming World," *Lincoln Star Journal*, July 21, 2008, https://journalstar.com/sports/woods-pool-once-was-at-center-of-swimming-world/article_58ed6c85-644e-56fe-aa5b-3b2ce5d812ed.html.

14. Vicky King, telephone interview with author, March 15, 2022.

15. Don Bloom, "Chavoor's Arden Hills Girls Go for Olympic Team Spots," *Sacramento Bee*, August 24, 1967.

16. Richard Rollins, "The Only Year of Their Lives," *Sports Illustrated*, August 12, 1968, https://vault.si.com/vault/1968/08/12/the-only-year-of-their-lives.

17. Sue Pedersen, telephone interview with the author, October 20, 2020.

18. Rollins, "The Only Year of Their Lives."

19. Chuck Woodling, "Teen Age Girls Steal Show at Women's National L.C. Championships," *Lincoln Journal Star*, August 4, 1968.

20. Marco Smolich, "Is Chavoor Getting Soft?" *Sacramento Bee*, August 6, 1968.

21. Kent Savery, "Kinsella Presses Burton," *Lincoln Star*, August 5, 1968.

22. United Press International Telephoto, *Ogden* (Utah) *Standard-Examiner*, August 1, 1968.

23. Rollins, "The Only Year of Their Lives."

24. Milton Richman, "Retiring Early," *Martinsville* (Indiana) *Times Reporter*, September 10, 1968.

25. Chuck Woodling, "World Record Sweet Topping for Eadie's Pancakes," *Lincoln Journal Star*, August 3, 1968.

26. "Schollander Toppled," *Sacramento Bee*, August 5, 1968.

27. Richard J. Foster, *Mark Spitz: The Extraordinary Life of an Olympic Champion* (Santa Monica, CA: Santa Monica Press, 2008), 43.

28. *Argus* (Fremont, CA), August 3, 1968.

29. *Tucson* (Arizona) *Citizen*, August 3, 1968.

30. "Spitz Tops Schollander," *San Francisco Examiner*, August 2, 1968.

31. "Schollander, Spitz Rivalry Expanding," *Tyler* (Texas) *Courier-Times*, August 4, 1968.

32. "Arden Hills Stars Stole AAU Laurels," *Sacramento Bee*, August 5, 1968.

33. Smolich, "Is Chavoor Getting Soft?"

34. "Gophers Get in Swim," *Sacramento Bee*, August 9, 1968.

35. Rollins, "The Only Year of Their Lives."

36. Don Bloom, "Sue Pedersen Stars in L.A., Sacramento Girl Establishes New U.S. Record in 100," *Sacramento Bee*, August 29, 1968.

37. Don Schollander and Duke Savage, *Deep Water* (New York: Crown, 1971), 41.

38. Schollander and Savage, *Deep Water*, 236.

CHAPTER 11

1. Ross Andrews, "Altitude Had Major Impact on Performances at Mexico City Olympic Games," *Global Sports Matters*, October 11, 2018, https://globalsportmatters.com/1968-mexico-city-olympics/2018/10/11/altitude-major-impact-performances-mexico-city-olympic-games/.

2. Mike Burton, telephone interview with the author, May 28, 2021.

3. Doug Russell interview, 1968 U.S. Olympic Team Oral History Project, H. J. Lutcher Starke Center for Physical Culture and Sports, https://archives.starkcenter.org/1968ohp/.

4. Don Bloom, "Chavoor's Arden Hills Girls Go for Olympic Team Spots," *Sacramento Bee*, August 12, 1968.

5. Craig Lord, "Helene Madison, 90th Anniversary of the Advent of the Queen of the Waves," *Swimming World*, July 20, 2020, https://www.swimmingworldmagazine.com/news/helene-madison-90th-anniversary-of-the-advent-of-the-queen-of-waves/.

6. Don Bloom, "Sacramento Has 17 Swim Candidates," *Sacramento Bee*, August 23, 1968.

7. Don Bloom, "Chavoor's A.H. Girls for Olympic Team Spots," *Sacramento Bee*, August 24, 1968.

8. John Bushman, "Making the Team, That's the Name of the Game," *Swimming World and Junior Swimmer*, September 1968, 5.

9. Vicky King, telephone interview with the author, March 15, 2022; Sherman Chavoor, with Bill Davidson, *The 50-Meter Jungle: How Olympic Gold Medal Swimmers Are Made* (New York: Coward, McCann, Geoghegan, 1973), 173–75.

10. Bushman, "Making the Team," 5.

11. Don Bloom, "Breathing Helped Debbie to New World Record," *Sacramento Bee*, August 25, 1968.

12. Bloom, "Breathing Helped Debbie."

13. Bushman, "Making the Team," 18.

14. Don Bloom, "Sue Pedersen Stars in L.A. Sacramento Girl Establishes New U.S. Record in 100," *Sacramento Bee*, August 29, 1968.

15. Don Bloom, "Sue Pedersen Is Major U.S. Olympic Hope," *Sacramento Bee*, August 28, 1968.

16. *Swimming World*, August 1968, 25.

CHAPTER 12

1. Doug Russell interview, 1968 U.S. Olympic Team Oral History Project, H. J. Lutcher Starke Center for Physical Culture and Sports, https://archives.starkcenter.org/1968ohp/.

2. John Bushman, "All You Need Is a Record," *Swimming World and Junior Swimmer*, September 1968, 6.

3. Bushman, "All You Need Is a Record," 6.

4. "Mike Burton's Win Is a Tribute to His Refusal to Quit," *Sacramento Bee*, September 1, 1968.

5. Don Bloom, "Ferris Takes Second in Olympic Test," *Sacramento Bee*, September 2, 1968.

6. "Spitz, Ferris Note Training in Bee Junior Olympics," *Sacramento Bee*, September 2, 1968.

7. Bushman, "All You Need Is a Record," 6.

8. Don Schollander and Duke Savage, *Deep Water* (New York: Crown, 1971), 240.

9. Bushman, "All You Need Is a Record," 7.

10. Schollander and Savage, *Deep Water*, 243–44.

11. Mike Burton, telephone interview with the author, May 28, 2021.

12. Bob Ottum, "The Encore Will Be in Mexico," *Sports Illustrated*, September 16, 1968, https://vault.si.com/vault/1968/09/16/the-encore-will-be-in-mexico.

13. Don Bloom, "Chavoor Calls Burton's Win Greatest in Swim History," *Sacramento Bee*, September 4, 1968.

14. Bushman, "All You Need Is a Record," 34.

15. Bushman, "All You Need Is a Record," 34.

16. Bloom, "Chavoor Calls Burton's Win Greatest in Swim History."

17. Burton, telephone interview with the author.

18. Don Bloom, "Burton Shatters 1500 Meter Mark," *Sacramento Bee*, September 4, 1968.

CHAPTER 13

1. William A. Lippman Jr., "Olympic Report," *Swimming World and Junior Swimmer*, September 1968, 3.

2. Doug Russell interview, 1968 U.S. Olympic Team Oral History Project, H. J. Lutcher Starke Center for Physical Culture and Sports, https://archives.starkcenter.org/1968ohp/.

3. Richard J. Foster, *Mark Spitz: The Extraordinary Life of an Olympic Champion* (Santa Monica, CA: Santa Monica Press, 2008), 59–60.

4. Doug Russell interview.

5. Sherman Chavoor, with Bill Davidson, *The 50-Meter Jungle: How Olympic Gold Medal Swimmers Are Made* (New York: Coward, McCann, Geoghegan, 1973), 89–90.

6. Foster, *Mark Spitz*, 62.

7. Don Schollander and Duke Savage, *Deep Water* (New York: Crown, 1971), 245.

8. Chavoor, with Davidson, *The 50-Meter Jungle*, 74.

9. Susan Shields, telephone interview with the author, July 19, 2022.

10. Doug Russell interview.

11. Foster, *Mark Spitz*, 62.

12. Foster, *Mark Spitz*, 75.

13. Schollander and Savage, *Deep Water*, 245.

14. Debbie Meyer, telephone interview with the author, May 2, 2020.

15. John R. McDermott, "Three Who Reached for Olympic Gold," *Life*, November 1, 1968, 52.

CHAPTER 14

1. Eric Zolov, "Showcasing the 'Land of Tomorrow': Mexico and the 1968 Olympics," *The Americas* 61, no. 2 (October 2004): 164.

2. Emmet Byrne, "Radiant Discord: Lance Wyman on the '68 Olympic Design and the Tlatelolco Massacre," *The Gradient*, March 20, 2014, https://walkerart.org/magazine/lance-wyman-mexico-68-olympics-tlatelolco-massacre.

3. Claire Mullen and Avery Trufelman, "Mexico 68," *99% Invisible Newsletter*, episode 264, June 27, 2017, https://99percentinvisible.org/episode/mexico-68/.

4. Zolov, "Showcasing the 'Land of Tomorrow,'" 164.

5. George B. Leonard, "A Different Journey on the Eve of the Olympics," *Look*, September 3, 1968, 44.

6. Bob Green, "U.S. Athletes Snub Newsmen from Mexico City Papers," *Sacramento Bee*, October 10, 1968.

7. John Underwood, "Games in Trouble," *Sports Illustrated*, September 30, 1968, https://vault.si.com/vault/1968/09/30/games-in-trouble.

8. Steve Cady, "Brundage Declares Olympics Will Be Held Despite Riots," *New York Times*, October 4, 1968.

9. Sherman Chavoor, with Bill Davidson, *The 50-Meter Jungle: How Olympic Gold Medal Swimmers Are Made* (New York: Coward, McCann, Geoghegan, 1973), 76.

10. "Olympians Put Avery Brundage on the Spot," *Sports Illustrated*, August 27, 1956, https://vault.si.com/vault/1956/08/27/olympians-put-avery-brundage-on-the-spot.

11. George Strickler, "Pigeons, Balloons, and Pageantry," *Chicago Tribune*, October 13, 1968.

12. Don Bloom, "For Debbie It Started Like Any Day: Get up, Go, Swim," *Sacramento Bee*, January 24, 1969.

13. "Pattern of Ailments Puzzle for Doctors," *Province* (Vancouver, BC), October 25, 1968.

14. "Victories and Trauma at Mexico 68," *Swimming World*, November 1968, 4.

15. "Sue Pedersen Wants Medal for Birthday," *Journal News* (White Plains, NY), October 15, 1968.

16. Bob Green, "Racial Unrest Overshadows Record-Breaking Performances," *Durham* (North Carolina) *Sun*, October 15, 1968.

CHAPTER 15

1. "Swimmers Collect First Gold Medals of Olympics," *Sacramento Bee*, October 18, 1968.

2. Sue Pedersen, telephone interview with the author, October 20, 2020.

3. "Victories and Trauma at Mexico 68," *Swimming World-Junior Swimmer*, November 1968, 8.

4. Pedersen, telephone interview with author.

5. John R. McDermott, "Three Who Reached for Olympic Gold," *Life*, November 1, 1968, 54.

6. Sherman Chavoor, with Bill Davidson, *The 50-Meter Jungle: How Olympic Gold Medal Swimmers Are Made* (New York: Coward, McCann, Geoghegan, 1973), 97.

7. McDermott, "Three Who Reached for Olympic Gold," 54.

8. Ned Wirth, "Chavoor Deserves Induction," *Sacramento Bee,* June 1, 1979.

9. Chavoor, with Davidson, *The 50-Meter Jungle*, 179.

10. McDermott, "Three Who Reached for Olympic Gold," 54.

11. McDermott, "Three Who Reached for Olympic Gold," 55.

12. McDermott, "Three Who Reached for Olympic Gold," 55.

13. "Victories and Trauma at Mexico 68," 12.

14. McDermott, "Three Who Reached for Olympic Gold," 54–55.

15. "Victories and Trauma at Mexico 68," 14; Debbie Meyer, telephone interview with the author, May 2, 2020.

16. McDermott, "Three Who Reached for Olympic Gold," 55.

17. "Victories and Trauma at Mexico 68," 14.

18. "Victories and Trauma at Mexico 68," 17.

19. "Victories and Trauma at Mexico 68," 16.

20. "Debbie Plans Own Olympics Medals Award Ceremony," *Sacramento Bee*, October 25, 1968.

21. Karen Crouse, "1500 Meters Seems out of Reach for Women in Olympics," *New York Times*, August 10, 2014.

CHAPTER 16

1. Richard J. Foster, *Mark Spitz: The Extraordinary Life of an Olympic Champion* (Santa Monica, CA: Santa Monica Press, 2008), 77.

2. "Victories and Trauma at Mexico 68," *Swimming World and Junior Swimmer*, November 1968, 8.

3. Marie Doezema, "The Murky History of the Butterfly Stroke," *New Yorker*, August 11, 2016, https://www.newyorker.com/sports/sporting-scene/the-murky-history-of-the-butterfly-stroke.

4. Doezema, "The Murky History of the Butterfly Stroke."

5. "Men's 100m Butterfly Final—Swimming | Mexico 1968 Replays," International Olympic Committee, https://olympics.com/en/video/mark-spitz-100m-butterfly-swimming.

6. Christopher Hadron, "Russell Recalls Golden Moment from Olympics 50 Years Ago," *Midland Reporter-Telegram,* October 20, 2018.

7. Foster, *Mark Spitz*, 82.

8. "U.S. Medal Winner Collapses on Stand," *Park City Daily News* (Bowling Green, KY), October 21, 1968.

9. "Victories and Trauma at Mexico 68," 18.

10. Jim Murray, "Mark Spitz: Alive and Well and Living in California," *Los Angeles Times*, September 15, 1979.

11. Foster, *Mark Spitz*, 75.

12. Don Schollander and Duke Savage, *Deep Water* (New York: Crown, 1971), 266.

13. John Burton, telephone interview with the author, May 28, 2021.

14. Burton, telephone interview with the author.

15. "Victories and Trauma at Mexico 68," 51.

16. "The Death of a Swimmer," *Swimming World and Junior Swimmer*, November 1968, 3.

17. "Debbie All-Time Olympic Great," *Sacramento Bee*, October 26, 1968.

18. Ron Speer, "Athletes Rap Olympic Unit for New Closing Ceremony," *Des Moines Register*, October 26, 1968.

19. "Mexico 1968—Closing Ceremony," International Olympic Committee, https://olympics.com/en/video/mexico-1968-closing-ceremony-x5334.

20. Don Bloom, "Cheering Crowd, Motorcade Pay Honor to Sacramento Olympians," *Sacramento Bee*, October 29, 1968.

21. Larry Levelle, "Burton, Ferris Seek New Swim Laurels," *Sacramento Bee*, October 29, 1968.

CHAPTER 17

1. Sherman Chavoor, with Bill Davidson, *The 50-Meter Jungle: How Olympic Gold Medal Swimmers Are Made* (New York: Coward, McCann, Geoghegan, 1973), 142.

2. Marco Smolich, "Same Ol' Sherm," *Sacramento Bee*, August 20, 1969.

3. Don Bloom, "For Debbie It Starts Like Any Day: Get up, Go Swim," *Sacramento Bee*, January 24, 1969.

4. Don Bloom, "Debbie Meyer Becomes Youngest Recipient of Sullivan Award," *Sacramento Bee*, March 9, 1969.

5. Smolich, "Same Ol' Sherm."

6. Bloom, "Debbie Meyer Becomes Youngest Recipient."

7. "Burton Breaks Own Freestyle Mark; Debbie Meyer Matches Her Record," *Sacramento Bee*, April 14, 1969.

CHAPTER 18

1. Richard J. Foster, *Mark Spitz: The Extraordinary Life of an Olympic Champion* (Santa Monica, CA: Santa Monica Press, 2008), 90.

2. "Top H.S. Swimmer Will Attend I.U.," *Indianapolis News*, January 15, 1969.

3. "Perkowski Enjoys a New Role as BSC Coach," *Bloomington-Bedford Sunday Herald-Times*, July 20, 1969.

4. Bob Williams, "Hickcox, Spitz Anchor I.U. Sweep," *Indianapolis Star*, March 31, 1969.

5. *Alexandria* (Louisiana) *Daily Town Talk*, July 14, 1969.

6. *Times Record* (Troy, NY), July 14, 1969.

7. "Debbie Meyer Tires of Freestyle, Looks to I.M.," *Sacramento Bee*, July 14, 1969.

8. Murray Olderman, "Mark Spitz Plans to Ignore U.S. Meet," *Napa Valley Register*, August 8, 1969.

9. Richard J. Foster, *Mark Spitz: The Extraordinary Life of an Olympic Champion* (Santa Monica, CA: Santa Monica Press, 2008), 120.

10. "Spitz Will Miss AAU Swim Meet," *San Francisco Examiner*, August 13, 1969.

11. John Flynn, "While Spitz Marks Time, Teammates Watch Win Streak Sink at Plantation," *Louisville Courier-Journal*, August 17, 1969.

12. Sherman Chavoor, with Bill Davidson, *The 50-Meter Jungle: How Olympic Gold Medal Swimmers Are Made* (New York: Coward, McCann, Geoghegan, 1973), 93.

13. William F. Reed, "Swimming Isn't Everything, Winning Is," *Sports Illustrated*, March 9, 1970, https://vault.si.com/vault/1970/03/09/swimming-isnt-everything-winning-is.

14. Frank Litsky, "George Haines, Coach of Elite Swimmers, Dies at 82," *New York Times*, May 3, 2006.

15. Cecil Colwin, "Coach George Haines, Swim Maestro: A Remembrance," *Swimming World*, May 1, 2006, https://www.swimmingworldmagazine.com/news/coach-george-haines-swim-maestro-a-remembrance/.

16. "World Record for Debbie, Burton Also Breaks Mark in AAU Swim," *San Francisco Examiner*, August 18, 1969.

17. John Flynn, "Wins Elate Miss Meyer, Disappoint Burton," *Louisville Courier-Journal*, August 18, 1969.

18. Marco Smolich, "Same Ol' Sherm," *Sacramento Bee*, August 20, 1969.

19. "Sue Pedersen (USA)," International Swimming Hall of Fame, https://www.ishof.org/honoree/honoree-sue-pedersen/.

CHAPTER 19

1. Sherman Chavoor, with Bill Davidson, *The 50-Meter Jungle: How Olympic Gold Medal Swimmers Are Made* (New York: Coward, McCann, Geoghegan, 1973), 106.

2. Chavoor, with Davidson, *The 50-Meter Jungle*, 107.

3. Don Bloom, "Nahan Plus a Bunch of Notes," *Sacramento Bee*, September 14, 1969.

4. Don Bloom, "Sullivan Award for Mike Burton," *Sacramento Bee*, November 9, 1969.

5. Mike Burton, telephone interview with the author, May 28, 2021.

6. Joseph M. Sheehan, "Rare Decision Makes Toomey Nominee for Sullivan Award; Decathlon Champion Added to List of 9 Finalists after Poll of Committee," *New York Times*, December 31, 1969.

7. Don Bloom, "Size 19 'Tennies' for Bob Lanier," *Sacramento Bee*, January 27, 1970.

8. "Munich Construction Right on Schedule," *Times Mail* (Bedford, IN), December 27, 1970.

9. Peter Gyallay-Pap, "Munich Gears for Olympics," *Record* (Hackensack, NJ), August 30, 1970.

10. Marco Smolich, "Between the Sports Line," *Sacramento Bee*, July 23, 1970.

11. "Debbie Meyer Shatters Own 400-Meter Record," *Sacramento Bee*, August 21, 1970.

12. Jerry Kirshenbaum, "Now Look Who's an Old Lady," *Sports Illustrated*, August 31, 1970.

13. "Debbie Has Praise for Chavoor," *Sacramento Bee*, January 24, 1972.

14. "19-Year-Old Debbie Meyer Calls It Quits as Swimmer," *New York Times*, January 25, 1972.

15. "Greatest Deserves the Best," *Sacramento Bee*, January 25, 1972.

16. Debbie Meyer, telephone interview with the author, May 2, 2020.

17. "Debbie Breaks Leg Skiing," *Sacramento Bee*, February 2, 1972.

18. "New Swim Star Is Built for Football," *Courier-Post* (Camden, NJ), August 26, 1970.

19. Jim Murray, "Thar' She Blows, Mates!" *Los Angeles Times*, August 21, 1970.

20. Chavoor, with Davidson, *The 50-Meter Jungle*, 95.

21. Chavoor, with Davidson, *The 50-Meter Jungle*, 135.

22. Richard J. Foster, *Mark Spitz: The Extraordinary Life of an Olympic Champion* (Santa Monica, CA: Santa Monica Press, 2008), 150.

23. Neil Amdur, "Spitz's Sixth Gold Medal Sets an Olympic Record," *Louisville Courier-Journal*, September 4, 1972.

24. Chavoor, with Davidson, *The 50-Meter Jungle*, 132.

25. Joe Falls, "Mark of Excellence," *Akron Beacon Journal*, September 3, 1972.

26. Foster, *Mark Spitz*, 123.

27. Don Bloom, "500 See Spitz Get Sullivan Prize," *Sacramento Bee*, April 1, 1972.

CHAPTER 20

1. William F. Reed, "Redemption after a False Start," *Sports Illustrated*, April 6, 1970, https://vault.si.com/vault/1970/04/06/redemption-after-a-false-start.

2. Tim Cahill, "Mark and the Seven Wisemen: Everybody Needs Milking," *Rolling Stone*, April 26, 1973, 40.

3. Julia Keller, "The Descent of an Olympic Champion," *Chicago Tribune*, May 17, 2002.

4. Sherman Chavoor, with Bill Davidson, *The 50-Meter Jungle: How Olympic Gold Medal Swimmers Are Made* (New York: Coward, McCann, Geoghegan, 1973), 155.

5. Chavoor, with Davidson, *The 50-Meter Jungle*, 159–60.

6. "Heat Causes Losses in Tomato, Peach Crops," *Sacramento Bee*, July 9, 1972.

7. Richard J. Foster, *Mark Spitz: The Extraordinary Life of an Olympic Swimmer* (Santa Monica, CA: Santa Monica Press, 2008), 151–52.

8. Mike Burton, telephone interview with the author, May 28, 2021.

9. Don Bloom, "Schollander Is a U.S.A. Ombudsman," *Sacramento Bee*, July 14, 1972.

10. Don Bloom, "Chavoor: 'Arden Hills Will Win 10 Gold Medals,'" *Sacramento Bee*, July 9, 1972.

11. "Spitz Does It Again—Record in Freestyle," *Sacramento Bee*, August 6, 1972.

12. "Goal of 7 Gold Medals Puts Heat on Mark Spitz," *Fort Meyers News*, August 23, 1972.

13. David Russell, "Swimming Squad Example of Our Own Nation in '72," *Daily Herald* (Elk Grove Village, IL), August 14, 1972.

14. Chavoor, with Davidson, *The 50-Meter Jungle*, 164.

15. Jerry Kirshenbaum, "Mark of Excellence," *Sports Illustrated*, August 14, 1972, https://vault.si.com/vault/1972/08/14/mark-of-excellence.

16. Mike Burton, telephone interview with the author, May 28, 2021.

17. Debbie Meyer, telephone interview with the author, May 2, 2020.

18. Leo Zainea, "Kinsella Falters in Trials," *Chicago Tribune*, August 7, 1972.

19. Don Riseborough, "Greatest U.S. Swim Week," *Sydney Morning Herald*, August 13, 1972.

20. "Chavoor: 'U.S. Team Better Than in '68,'" *Sacramento Bee*, August 9, 1972.

21. "U.S. Girls Swim Team Best Ever?" *Paducah* (Kentucky) *Sun*, August 9, 1972.

22. Foster, *Mark Spitz*, 146.

CHAPTER 21

1. Cooper Rollow, "What Do Olympics Mean?" *Chicago Tribune*, September 3, 1972.

2. "Wide Choice of Munich Souvenirs," *San Francisco Examiner*, August 27, 1972.

3. Will Grimsley, "Singing Hippies Gulp Beer as Munich Greets Olympians," *Philadelphia Inquirer*, August 20, 1972.

4. Sherman Chavoor, with Bill Davidson, *The 50-Meter Jungle: How Olympic Gold Medal Swimmers Are Made* (New York: Coward, McCann, Geoghegan, 1973), 179.

5. Grimsley, "Singing Hippies Gulp Beer."

6. "Mark Spitz, An Olympian Wave of Records," *Time*, September 11, 1972.

7. "Olympic Track Coach Says It's a Lousy Job," *Miami News*, August 29, 1972.

8. "Olympic Pressure on His Back Again," *Palm Beach Post*, August 23, 1972.

9. "Olympic Pressure on His Back Again."

10. "Schollander Claims Spitz Can Win 7 Gold Medals," *News-Press* (Fort Myers, FL), August 22, 1972.

11. Chavoor, with Davidson, *The 50-Meter Jungle*, 193.

12. Jerry Kirshenbaum, "Mexico to Munich: Mark Spitz and the Quest for Gold," *Sports Illustrated*, September 4, 1972.

13. Karen Harris, "Olympian Mark Spitz: True Stories of Munich's Gold Medalist," Groovy History, https://groovyhistory.com/the-mark-spitz-you-dont-know.

14. "West German Leader Asks Games Unity," *Arizona Republic*, August 20, 1972.

15. "Ceremonies Open XX Olympic Games," *Bradenton* (Florida) *Herald*, August 26, 1972.

16. "U.S. Blacks Boycott Track Meet," *Indianapolis News*, August 19, 1972.

CHAPTER 22

1. Richard J. Foster, *Mark Spitz: The Extraordinary Life of an Olympic Swimmer* (Santa Monica, CA: Santa Monica Press, 2008), 21.

2. Tim Cahill, "Mark and the Seven Wisemen: Everybody Needs Milking," *Rolling Stone*, April 26, 1973, 39.

3. Sherman Chavoor, with Bill Davidson, *The 50-Meter Jungle: How Olympic Gold Medal Swimmers Are Made* (New York: Coward, McCann, Geoghegan, 1973), 197.

4. Chavoor, with Davidson, *The 50-Meter Jungle*, 197.

5. Chavoor, with Davidson, *The 50-Meter Jungle*, 196.

6. "Freestyle Relay," *Hartford Courant*, August 29, 1972.

7. "Pressure on Spitz," *Times Recorder* (Zanesville, OH), September 2, 1972.

8. Joe Falls, "Mark of Excellence" *Akron Beacon Journal*, September 3, 1972.

9. Chavoor, with Davidson, *The 50-Meter Jungle*, 195.

10. "Teammate Accuses Swimming Champ," *Signal* (Santa Clarita, CA), September 1, 1972.

11. "Teammate Accuses Swimming Champ."

12. Matthew De George, "Filmmaker John L. McLeod Looking to Go 'Beyond' in Telling Olympic Stories," *Swimming World*, March 30, 2021, https://www.swimmingworldmagazine.com/news/filmmaker-john-l-mcleod-looking-to-go-beyond-in-telling-olympic-stories/.

13. *Philadelphia Daily News*, September 1, 1972.

14. *Evening Sun* (Baltimore, MD), September 1, 1972.

15. "Teammate Accuses Swimming Champ."

16. Mark Hollingworth, "Genter No Mark Spitz Fan," *Long Beach* (California) *Independent Press*, November 26, 1972.

17. Foster, *Mark Spitz*, 174.

18. Foster, *Mark Spitz*, 177.

19. "Olympic Hero Mark Spitz Carries His Shoes," *Dayton Daily News*, August 30, 1972.

20. "Spitz Waves His Shoes after Accepting Third Gold," *Calgary Albertan*, August 30, 1972.

21. "Elated Mark Spitz Waves to Crowd," *Miami Herald*, August 31, 1972.

22. Foster, *Mark Spitz*, 177.

23. Shirley Povich, "Two Shoemakers War in Munich," *Record* (Hackensack, NJ), September 3, 1972.

24. Foster, *Mark Spitz*, 179.

25. Joe Falls, "Munich Really Digs Track and Field," *Detroit Free Press*, September 1, 1972.

26. Ned Wirth, "Chavoor Deserves Induction," *Sacramento Bee*, June 1, 1979.

27. Don Bloom, *Confessions of a Sportswriter* (New York: Vantage, 1988), 222.

28. Bloom, *Confessions of a Sportswriter*, 222.

29. Jim Kearney, "Swimmers Pass Test," *Vancouver Sun*, September 1, 1972.

30. Quoted in Foster, *Mark Spitz*, 187.

31. "Mark Spitz—He's Through at 22," *Salinas Californian*, September 4, 1972.

32. Kenny Moore, "Bionic Man," *Sports Illustrated*, October 23, 1989.

33. Julia Keller, "The Descent of an Olympic Champion," *Chicago Tribune*, May 17, 2002.

34. Chavoor, with Davidson, *The 50-Meter Jungle*, 204.

35. Chavoor, with Davidson, *The 50-Meter Jungle*, 205.

36. Keller, "The Descent of an Olympic Champion."

37. Keller, "The Descent of an Olympic Champion."

38. Lucinda Franks, "2 Laps to Go and Things Look Rosy for Spitz' 7th," *Miami Herald*, September 4, 1972.

39. Joe Falls, "Mark of Excellence," *Akron Beacon Journal*, September 3, 1972.

40. Don Bloom, "Uncle Sam's Flag Bearer Burton Is off to Oregon," *Sacramento Bee*, September 17, 1972.

41. Mike Burton, telephone interview with the author, May 28, 2021.

42. Burton, telephone interview with the author.

43. Don Bloom, "Little Notes on Some Big People," *Sacramento Bee*, September 22, 1972.

CHAPTER 23

1. Lisa Furlong, "Photo Finish," *Dartmouth Alumni Magazine*, July–August 2016.

2. "Hubert Mizell," *Tampa Bay Times*, August 28, 1988.

3. Sherman Chavoor, with Bill Davidson, *The 50-Meter Jungle: How Olympic Gold Medal Swimmers Are Made* (New York: Coward, McCann, Geoghegan, 1973), 210.

4. "Letter from the Publisher," *Sports Illustrated*, May 14, 1973.

5. Richard J. Foster, *Mark Spitz: The Extraordinary Life of an Olympic Swimmer* (Santa Monica, CA: Santa Monica Press, 2008), 212.

6. Stan Hochman, "Spitz Scared Shiftless or Just a Puppet?" *Philadelphia Daily News*, September 6, 1972.

7. Frank Dolson, "Spitz Like Fish out of Water in Final Olympic Appearance," *Philadelphia Inquirer*, September 6, 1972.

8. "Hubert Mizell."

9. Foster, *Mark Spitz*, 214.

10. Matthias von Hein, "Munich 1972: A Preventable Massacre?" *DW*, September 7, 2017, https://www.dw.com/en/1972-munich-olympics-massacre-an-avoidable-catastrophe/a-40405813.

11. Jim McKay, "The End of Innocence," ABC Sports, December 13, 2002, https://www.espn.com/abcsports/columns/mckay_jim/2002/0904/1427112.html.

12. Don Bloom, *Confessions of a Sportswriter* (New York: Vantage, 1988), 220.

13. Don Bloom, "Spitz Swims into Gold Rush," *Sacramento Bee*, September 7, 1972.

14. Alvin Shuster, "'Despicable Act' Decried at Arena Rites," *New York Times*, September 7, 1972.

15. Art McGinn, "Hero's Return," *Sacramento Bee*, September 7, 1972.

16. McGinn, "Hero's Return."

17. Bloom, "Spitz Swims into Gold Rush."

18. Susan Lydon, "All That Gold Waiting to Glitter," *New York Times*, March 11, 1973.

19. Howard Blas, "Swimming with the Tide: Athlete, Actor, Volunteer and Israeli Supporter Mark Spitz," *Cleveland Jewish News*, March 18, 2022.

20. Jim Jenkins, "Spitz's Cohort-Fame No Fortune," *Tracy* (California) *Press*, December 15, 1972.

21. Bernie Lincicome, "Spitz: Jenner's Gold Worth That Much?" *Fort Lauderdale News*, April 19, 1977.

22. Pete Jeff, "Spitz Warms to Fans, Press for Hall of Fame Induction," *Miami Herald*, April 19, 1977.

23. Dale Dempsey, "Hall of Famers Honored," *Daily Advocate* (Greenville, OH), April 23, 1977.

24. "Mike Burton Inspiration Says Chavoor," *Sacramento Bee*, April 19, 1977.

25. John Wolin, "Swimming Hall Introduction: Not an Eye Was Dry," *Fort Lauderdale News*, April 19, 1977.

26. R. E. Graswich, "Arden Hills Dives but Chavoor Basks in Past Success," *Sacramento Bee*, November 8, 1977.

27. Graswich, "Arden Hills Dives."

28. Graswich, "Arden Hills Dives."

29. Graswich, "Arden Hills Dives."

30. Graswich, "Arden Hills Dives."

31. Graswich, "Arden Hills Dives."

CHAPTER 24

1. Tim Leber, "Float—Jeff's Journey Will End in L.A.," *Sacramento Bee*, July 1, 1984.

2. Jeff Float, telephone interview with the author, February 18, 2021.

3. Leber, "Jeff's Journey Will End in L.A."

4. Float, telephone interview with the author.

5. Float, telephone interview with the author.

6. Joe Hamelin, "Time May Have Passed Float By," *Sacramento Bee*, July 30, 1984.

7. Tracy Dodds, "Floating through the Never-Ending Olympic Valley," *Los Angeles Times*, August 14, 1984.

CHAPTER 25

1. Bob Burns, "Arden Hills Swimmers Move after 30 Years," *Sacramento Bee*, July 11, 1985.

2. Dixie Reid, "Legacy in Water," *Sacramento Bee*, July 16, 1992.

3. Reid, "Legacy in Water."

4. Dixie Reid, "Swim Coach of Legends, Sherm Chavoor Is Dead," *Sacramento Bee*, September 4, 1992.

5. "Sherm Chavoor, 73, A Swimming Coach," *New York Times*, September 5, 1992.

6. Reid, "Swim Coach of Legends."

7. Jim Van Vliet, "Around the Dial," *Sacramento Bee*, September 15, 1992.

8. KCRA-TV, "Sacramento Olympic Swimmers," Center for Sacramento History, February 1, 1981, https://archive.org/details/kcrasp051chavoorspitz meyerinterviewsfeb1981.

9. Marco Smolich, "Comments by Counsilman," *Sacramento Bee*, May 20, 1968.

10. R. E. Graswich, "Arden Hill Dives but Chavoor Basks in Past Success," *Sacramento Bee*, November 8, 1977.

REFERENCES

BOOKS

Bloom, Don. *Confessions of a Sportswriter*. New York: Vantage, 1988.

Chavoor, Sherman, with Bill Davidson. *The 50-Meter Jungle: How Olympic Gold Medal Swimmers Are Made*. New York: Coward, McCann, Geoghegan, 1973.

Checkoway, Julie. *The Three-Year Swim Club: The Untold Story of Maui's Sugar Ditch Kids and Their Quest for Olympic Glory*. New York: Grand Central, 2015.

Colwin, Cecil M. *Breakthrough Swimming*. Champaign, IL: Human Kinetics, 2002.

Foster, Richard J. *Mark Spitz: The Extraordinary Life of an Olympic Champion*. Santa Monica, CA: Santa Monica Press, 2008.

Jahn, Cornelia, and Katharina Wohlfart. *Olympia 72 in Bildern*. Munich: Bayerische StaatsBibliothek, 2022.

Klein, Maury. *A Call to Arms, Mobilizing America for World War II*. New York: Bloomsbury, 2013.

Llewellyn, Matthew P., and John Gleaves. *The Rise and Fall of Olympic Amateurism*. Urbana: University of Illinois Press, 2016.

Lohn, John. *Below the Surface: The History of Competitive Swimming*. Lanham, MD: Rowman and Littlefield, 2021.

Manchester, William. *The Glory and the Dream: A Narrative History of America, 1932–1972*. New York: Bantam, 1975.

Mullen, P. H. *Gold in the Water: The True Story of Ordinary Men and Their Extraordinary Dream of Olympic Glory*. New York: Thomas Dunne Books, 2001.

Olympics '68: The Exclusive ABC Sports Guidebook. New York: Routledge, 2009.

Schollander, Don, and Duke Savage. *Deep Water*. New York: Crown, 1971.

Shulevitz. Judith. "Pool Shark: Mark Spitz (1950–)." In *Jewish Jocks: An Unorthodox Hall of Fame*, edited by Franklin Foer and Marc Tracy, 165–72. New York: Hachette, 2012.

Starr, Kevin. *California: A History*. New York: Modern Library, 2005.

————. *Endangered Dreams: The Great Depression in California*. New York: Oxford University Press, 1996.

ORAL HISTORY

1968 U.S. Olympic Team Oral History Project. H. J. Luther Stark Center for Physical Culture and Sports at the University of Texas Arlington. https://archives.starkcenter.org/1968ohp/about/about.html.

INDEX

ABC's Wide World of Sports, 61, 74, 83
Adidas shoe controversy, 172–73
age group swimming, 14–15, 36
Allard, Kenneth, 180
altitude concerns, 71–72, 81, 117, 119
Amateur Athletic Union (AAU): age
    group swimming, 14–15; early
    years, 13–14; Far Western meet,
    26, 43; Float's domination, 193;
    Japanese participation in 1949,
    55–56; Junior Olympics, 14–15, 20,
    21, 38–39, 43, 44–46; Long Course
    National Championship, 73–78;
    National Outdoor Championships,
    46–47, 144; National Women's
    Championships, 61, 63; Northern
    California Invitational, 69; Short
    Course Championships, 20, 149;
    Spitz's criticism of, 152; Spitz's
    participation in, 29, 44. *See also*
    Sullivan Award
amateur status, 102, 127
American Swimming Coaches
    Association, 127
anti-Semitism, 27, 44, 95–96, 174, 185
Arden Hills Swimming and Tennis
    Club: about, 18–20; accolades for,
    85; brimming with "material,"
    54; Olé Olympics luncheon, 65;

popularity in 1960s, 49; practice
    sessions, 19–20; preparing for 1968
    Olympics, 78–80; preparing for 1972
    Olympics, 150–52; publicity, 19,
    20–21; sale of, 197. *See also* Burton,
    Mike; Chavoor, Sherman; Ferris,
    John; Meyer, Debbie; Pedersen,
    Susan; Spitz, Mark; Spitz, Nancy
Atwood, Susie, 157
Australian competition at Olympics,
    105–6, 156, 157, 165. *See also*
    Wenden, Michael

B-24 Liberator Bombers, 2–3
Babashoff, Shirley, 157
Baker, John, 56
Ball, Catie, 105
Bannister, Roger, 55
Bauer, Carl, 13–14
Belote, Melissa, 157, 165
Berkeley City Club, 41
Bloom, Don: on Arden Hills news,
    137; on Burton, 93, 138–39; on
    Echevarria, 93–94; on Meyer,
    39–40, 47, 61, 107, 127–28; on
    Spitz, 187
Bookstover, Laurabelle, 41
Bowerman, Bill, 161
"breaststroke twins," 8–9

ABOUT THE AUTHOR

Bill George has worked in journalism, public relations, and marketing. He began his career as a television journalist in Iowa and Sacramento, California. He transitioned to public relations and was appointed by Governor Pete Wilson as assistant secretary of the California Trade and Commerce Agency. He later served as western states public affairs manager and global marketing communications manager for Ford Motor Company. George then formed a documentary film production company and has produced several award-winning films on California history. This is his second book.

www.ingramcontent.com/pod-product-compliance
Lightning Source LLC
Chambersburg PA
CBHW030302100426
42812CB00002B/537